Communication and Conflict: Studies in International Relations

Communication and Conflict: Studies in International Relations

S.K. Desai

CYBER TECH PUBLICATIONS
4264/3, Ansari Road, Daryaganj, New Delhi-110002 (India)
Ph.: 011-23244078, 011-43559448 Fax: 011-23280028
E-Mail: cyberpublicationsdelhi@yahoo.com
Website: www.cybertechpublications.com

COMMUNICATION AND CONFLICT: STUDIES IN INTERNATIONAL RELATIONS

S.K. Desai

First Edition 2011

Published by :

G.S. Rawat for Cyber Tech Publications
4264/3, Ansari Road, Daryaganj, New Delhi-110002 (India)
Ph.: 011-23244078, 011-43559448 Fax: 011-23280028
E-Mail: cyberpublicationsdelhi@yahoo.com
Website: www.cybertechpublications.com

CONTENTS

PREFACE

Political history is the narrative and analysis of political events, ideas, movements, and leaders. It is usually structured around the nation state. The first "scientific" political history was written by Leopold von Ranke in Germany in the 19th century. His methodologies profoundly affected the way historians critically examine sources; see historiography for a more complete analysis of the methodology of various approaches to history. However, the discipline has a clear set of antecedents such as moral philosophy, political philosophy, political economy, history, and other fields concerned with normative determinations of what ought to be and with deducing the characteristics and functions of the ideal state. In each historic period and in almost every geographic area, we can find someone studying politics and increasing political understanding.

According to Hegel, Political History "is a concept of the state with a moral and spiritual force beyond the marerial interests of its subjects: it followed that the state was the main agent of historical change."

Sometimes referred to as "Rankian History", diplomatic history focuses on politics, politicians and other high rulers and views them as being the driving force of continuity and change in history. It is the study of the conduct of international relations between states or across state boundaries. This is the most common form of history and is often the classical and popular belief of what history should be.

Although history which might be classified as diplomatic history has been written for as long as history has been in existence -Thucydides, certainly, is among other things, highly concerned with the relations among states -the modern form of diplomatic history was codified in the 19th century by Leopold von Ranke, a German historian. Ranke wrote largely on the history of Early

Modern Europe, using the diplomatic archives of the European powers (particularly the Venetians) to construct a detailed understanding of the history of Europe wie es eigentlich gewesen ("as it actually happened.") Ranke saw diplomatic history as the most important kind of history to write because of his idea of the "Primary of Foreign Affairs" (Primat der Aussenpolitik), arguing that the concerns of international relations drive the internal development of the state. Ranke's understanding of diplomatic history relied on the large number of official documents produced by modern western governments as sources.

—Author

1

INTRODUCTION

While the study of politics is first found in ancient Greece and ancient India, political science is a late arrival in terms of social sciences.

However, the discipline has a clear set of antecedents such as moral philosophy, political philosophy, political economy, history, and other fields concerned with normative determinations of what ought to be and with deducing the characteristics and functions of the ideal state. In each historic period and in almost every geographic area, we can find someone studying politics and increasing political understanding.

ANCIENT INDIA

In ancient India, the study of politics can be traced back to several Vedic Sanskrit texts: Rig-Veda (c. 1500-1200 BC), the Samhitas (c. 1200-900 BC), and the Brahmanas (c. 1200-900 BC). The study of politics is also found in the Buddhist Pali Canon (c. 6th century BC). Chanakya (c. 350-275 BC) was a professor of political science at Takshashila University, and later the Prime Minister of Mauryan emperor Chandragupta Maurya.

Chanakya is regarded as one of the earliest known political thinkers, economists and king-makers, and is also known as the Indian Machiavelli.

He wrote the Arthashastra, which was one of the earliest treatises on political thought, economics and social order, and can be considered a precursor to Machiavelli's The Prince. It discusses monetary and fiscal policies, welfare, international relations, and war strategies in detail, among other topics on political science.

ANCIENT GREECE

The antecedents of western politics trace their roots back even earlier than Plato and Aristotle, particularly in the works of Homer, Hesiod, Thucydides, Plato, Xenophon, and Euripides. Later, Plato analyzed political systems and abstracted their analysis from more literary-and history-oriented studies and applied an approach we would understand as closer to philosophy. Similarly, Aristotle built upon Plato's analysis to include historical empirical evidence in his analysis.

ROMAN EMPIRE

During the rule of Rome, famous historians such as Polybius, Livy and Plutarch documented the rise of the Roman Republic, and the organization and histories of other nations, while statesman like Julius Caesar, Cicero and others provided us with examples of the politics of the republic and Rome's empire and wars. The study of politics during this age was oriented toward understanding history, understanding methods of governing, and describing the operation of governments.

MEDIEVAL EUROPE

With the fall of the Roman Empire, there arose a more diffuse arena for political studies. The rise of monotheism and particularly for the Western tradition, Christianity, brought to light a new space for politics and political action. During the Middle Ages, the study of politics was widespread in the churches and courts. Works such as Augustine of Hippo's The City of God synthesized current philosophies and political traditions with those of Christianity, redefining the borders between what was religious and what was political. Most of the political questions surrounding the relationship between church and state were clarified and contested in this period.

ISLAMIC WORLD

In the Middle East and later other Islamic areas, works such as the Rubaiyat of Omar Khayyam and Epic of Kings by Ferdowsi provided evidence of political analysis, while the Islamic Aristotelians such as Avicenna and later Maimonides and Averroes, continued Aristotle's tradition of analysis and empiricism, writing commentaries on Aristotle's works.

EUROPEAN RENAISSANCE

During the Italian Renaissance, Niccolò Machiavelli established the emphasis of modern political science on direct empirical observation of political institutions and actors in The Prince. Later, the expansion of the scientific paradigm during the Enlightenment further pushed the study of politics beyond normative determinations.

POLITICAL HISTORY

Political history is the narrative and analysis of political events, ideas, movements, and leaders. It is usually structured around the nation state. The first "scientific" political history was written by Leopold von Ranke in Germany in the 19th century. His methodologies profoundly affected the way historians critically examine sources; see historiography for a more complete analysis of the methodology of various approaches to history.

According to Hegel, Political History "is a concept of the state with a moral and spiritual force beyond the marerial interests of its subjects: it followed that the state was the main agent of historical change."

DIPLOMATIC HISTORY

Sometimes referred to as "Rankian History", diplomatic history focuses on politics, politicians and other high rulers and views them as being the driving force of continuity and change in history. It is the study of the conduct of international relations between states or across state boundaries. This is the most common form of history and is often the classical and popular belief of what history should be.

Although history which might be classified as diplomatic history has been written for as long as history has been in existence -Thucydides, certainly, is among other things, highly concerned with the relations among states -the modern form of diplomatic history was codified in the 19th century by Leopold von Ranke, a German historian. Ranke wrote largely on the history of Early Modern Europe, using the diplomatic archives of the European powers (particularly the Venetians) to construct a detailed understanding of the history of Europe wie es eigentlich gewesen ("as it actually happened.") Ranke saw diplomatic history as the most important kind of history to write because of his idea of the "Primary of Foreign Affairs" (Primat der Aussenpolitik), arguing that the concerns of international relations drive the internal development of the state. Ranke's understanding of diplomatic history relied on the large number of official documents produced by modern western governments as sources.

Ranke's understanding of the dominance of foreign policy, and hence an emphasis on diplomatic history, remained the dominant paradigm in historical writing through the first half of the twentieth century. This emphasis, combined with the effects of the War Guilt Clause in the Treaty of Versailles (1919) which ended the First World War, led to a huge amount of historical writing on the subject of the origins of the war in 1914, with the involved governments printing huge, carefully edited, collections of documents and numerous historians writing multi-volume histories of the origins of the war. In general, the early works in this vein, including Fritz Fischer's controversial (at the time) 1961 thesis that German goals of "world power" were the principal cause of the war, fit fairly comfortably into Ranke's emphasis on Aussenpolitik.In the course of the 1960s, however, some German historians (notably Hans-Ulrich Wehler and his cohort) began to rebel against this idea, instead suggesting a "Primacy of Domestic Politics" (Primat der Innenpolitik), in which the insecurities of (in this case German) domestic policy drove the creation of foreign policy. This led to a considerably body of work interpreting the domestic policies of various states and the ways this influenced their conduct of foreign policy.

At the same time, the middle of the twentieth century began to see a general de-emphasis on diplomatic history. The French Annales school had already put an emphasis on the role of geography and economics on history, and of the importance of broad, slow cycles rather than the constant apparent movement of the "history of events" of high politics. The most important work of the Annales school, Fernand Braudel's The Mediterranean and the Mediterranean World in the Age of Philip II, contains a traditional Rankean diplomatic history of Philip II's Mediterranean policy, but only as the third and shortest section of a work largely focusing on the broad cycles of history in the longue durée ("long term"). The Annales were broadly influential, leading to a turning away from diplomatic and other forms of political history towards an emphasis on broader trends of economic and environmental change. In the 1960s and 1970s, an increasing emphasis on giving a voice to the voiceless and writing the history of the underclasses, whether by using the quantitative statistical methods of social history or the more qualitative assessments of cultural history, also undermined the centrality of diplomatic history to the historical discipline. Nevertheless, diplomatic history has always remained a historical field with a great interest to the general public, and considerable amounts of work are still done in the field, often in much the same way that Ranke pioneered in the middle years of the 19th century.

HISTORIOGRAPHY

Historiography is the study of the practice of history. This can take many forms, including the study of historical method and the historical development of history as an academic discipline. The term can also be used to refer a specific body of historical writing. For instance, "medieval historiography during the 1960s" can be taken to mean the methodological approaches and ideas about medieval history present in written history during that decade. As a meta-analysis of descriptions of the past, this third conception can relate to the first two in that the analysis usually focuses on the narratives, interpretations, worldview, use of evidence, or method of presentation of other historians.

DEFINING HISTORIOGRAPHY

Conal Furay and Michael J. Salevouris define "historiography" as "the study of the way history has been and is written -the history of historical writing... When you study 'historiography' you do not study the events of the past directly, but the changing interpretations of those events in the works of individual historians." (The Methods and Skills of History: A Practical Guide, 1988, p. 223. Although questions of method have concerned historians since Thucydides, many trace the modern study of historiography to E. H. Carr's 1961 work What is History?. Carr challenged the traditional belief that the study of the methods of historical research and writing were unimportant. His work remains in print to this day, and is used in many postgraduate programs of study in the English-speaking world. Historiography is often political in nature. For example, the Dunning school of historiography, which was sympathetic to former slave owners and leaders of the Confederacy, contended that black people, particularly former slaves, should neither be permitted to vote nor bear arms.

In the 1960s, historiography corrected the racism of the Dunning School viewpoint, and history that included the viewpoint of African Americans who had been disenfranchised by the Jim Crow political and economic system that grew up alongside the powerful Dunning School and its way of telling history from the viewpoint of former slave owners. Mid-twentieth century historians also focused on primary sources to reveal previously excluded roles of women, minorities, and labor from earlier histories of the United States. According to these historiographers, historians in the 1930s and 1940s had a bias toward wealthy and well-connected white males. Some historians from that point onward devoted themselves to what they saw as more accurate representations of the past, casting a light on those who had been previously disregarded as non-noteworthy.

The study of historiography demands a critical approach that goes beyond the mere examination of historical fact. Historiographical studies consider the source, often by researching the author, his or her position in society, and the type of history being written at the time.

BASIC ISSUES STUDIED IN HISTORIOGRAPHY

Some of the common questions of historiography are:

- Who wrote the source (primary or secondary)?
- For primary sources, we look at the person in his or her society, for secondary sources, we consider the theoretical orientation of the approach for example, Marxist or Annales School, ("total history"), political history, etc.
- What is the authenticity, authority, bias/interest, and intelligibility of the source?
- What was the view of history when the source was written?
- Was history supposed to provide moral lessons?
- What or who was the intended audience?
- What sources were privileged or ignored in the narrative?
- By what method was the evidence compiled?

- In what historical context was the work of history itself written?

Issues engaged in so-called critical historiography includes topics such as:

- What constitutes an historical "event"?
- In what modes does a historian write and produce statements of "truth" and "fact"?
- How does the medium (novel, textbook, film, theatre, comic) through which historical information is conveyed influence its meaning?
- What inherent epistemological problems does archive-based history contain?
- How does the historian establish their own objectivity or come to terms with their own subjectivity?
- What is the relation of historical theory to historical practice?
- What is the "goal" of history?
- What is history?

THE HISTORY OF WRITTEN HISTORY

Understanding the past appears to be a universal human need and the telling of history has emerged independently in civilisations around the world. What constitutes history is a philosophical question. For the purposes of this survey it is written history recorded in a narrative format for the purpose of informing future generations about events. The earliest critical historical thought emerged in Greece, a development which would be an important influence on the writing of history elsewhere in the world.

EARLY WESTERN HISTORIOGRAPHY

Written history appeared first with the ancient Greeks, whose historians greatly contributed to the development of historical methodology. The very first historical work were The Histories composed by Herodotus of Halicarnassus (484 BC-ca.425 BC), who became later known as the 'father of history' (Cicero). Herodotus personally conducted research into the history of various Mediterranean cultures, and attempted to distinguish between more and less reliable accounts. His research confirmed for him the belief that divinity plays a crucial role in the determination of historical events. Thucydides, on the other hand, largely eliminated divine causality from his account of the war between Athens and Sparta, and the same holds true for his successors, such as Xenophon and Polybius.

Reports exist of other near-eastern histories, such as that composed by the Phoenician historian Sanchuniathon; but his very existence is considered semi-fabled and writings attributed to him are fragmentary, known only through the later historians Philo of Byblos and Eusebius, who asserted that he wrote before even the Trojan war.

Concerning the Bible, there is considerable debate about its historiographical character. To some scholars the use of a divinity to provide historical explanations contradicts the basic aim of any truly historical work, namely to provide rational explanations for events. Others argue that the Biblical search for an underlying cause of historical events is itself a characteristic of historiographical research, and point moreover to the Bible's frequent recourse to double-causation, whereby events are attributed to both human and divine causation. Controversy over this issue is complicated by the fact that the Bible is seen as an inspired text by many members of Western society today.

Writing history was popular among Christian monks in the Middle Ages. They wrote about the history of the Church and of their patrons, the dynastic history of the local rulers. History was written about states or nations during the Renaissance. The study of history changed during the Enlightenment and Romanticism. Voltaire described the history of certain ages that were important according to him, instead of describing events in a chronological order. History became an independent discipline. It was not called philosophia historiae anymore, but merely history (historiae).

CHINESE HISTORIOGRAPHY

The writing of history in China began with the work of Sima Qian around 100 BC. Its scope extends as far back as the 16th century BC. Traditionalist Chinese historiography describes history in terms of dynastic cycles. In this view, each new dynasty is founded by a morally righteous founder. Over time, the dynasty becomes morally corrupt and dissolute. Eventually, the dynasty becomes so weak as to allow its replacement by a new dynasty.

ISLAMIC HISTORIOGRAPHY

Islamic historiography began developing with the reconstruction of Muhammad's life in the centuries following his death. Due to numerous conflicting narratives regarding Muhammad and his companions from various sources, it was necessary to verify which sources were more reliable. In order to evaluate these sources, various methodologies were developed, such as the "science of biography", "science of Hadith" and "Isnad" (chain of transmission). These methodologies were later applied to other historical figures in the Islamic World. Famous Muslim historians included Urwah (d. 712), Ibn Ishaq (d. 768), Al-Waqidi (745 -822), Ibn Hisham (d. 834), Al-Tabari (838 -923), Ibn Khaldun (1332 -1406) and Ibn Hajar (1372 -1449) among others.

Ilm ar-Rijal (Arabic) is the "science of biography" especially as practiced in Islam, where it was first applied to the sira, the life of the prophet of Islam, Muhammad, and then the lives of the four Rightly Guided Caliphs who expanded Islamic dominance rapidly. Since validating the sayings of Muhammad is a major study ("Isnad"), accurate biography has always been of great interest to Muslim biographers, who accordingly became experts at sorting out facts from accusations, bias from evidence, etc., and were renowned throughout the known world for their honesty in recording history. Modern practices of scientific citation and historical method owe a great deal to the rigor of the Isnad tradition of early Muslims. The earliest surviving Islamic biography is Ibn Ishaq's Sirat Rasul Allah, written in the 8th century.

The "science of Hadith" is the process that Muslim scholars use to evaluate Hadith. The classification of Hadith into Sahih (sound), Hasan (good) and Da'if (weak) was firmly established by Ali ibn al-Madini (161 AH -234 AH). Later, al-Madini's student Muhammad al-Bukhari (810 -870) authored a collection that he believed contained only Sahih Hadith, which is now known as the Sahih Bukhari.

MODERN HISTORIOGRAPHY

Modern historiography began with Ranke in the 19th century, who was very critical on the sources used in history. He was opposed to analyses and rationalizations. His adagium was writing history the way it was. He wanted eyewitness accounts and wanted an emphasis on the point of view of the eyewitness. Hegel and Marx introduced the change of society in history. Former historians had focused on cyclical events of the rise and decline of rulers and nations. A new discipline emerged in the late nineteenth century that analyzed and compared these perspectives on a larger scale and that discipline was sociology.

The French Annales School radically changed history during the 20th century. Fernand Braudel wanted history to become more scientific by demanding more mathematical evidence in history, in order to make the history discipline less subjective. Furthermore, he added a social-economic and geographic framework to answer historical questions. Other French historians, like Philippe Ariès and Michel Foucault described history of daily life topics as death and sexuality. They wanted history to be written about all topics and that all questions should be asked.

In the 1970s, some historians began to focus on case-studies. Case studies describe particular aspects of history in a thorough fashion, to describe history as it was or to measure it precisely. Several well chosen case studies can enhance or change the major picture and can bring more truth to the answers of the questions that the Annales School likes to ask. However, because case studies focus so narrowly on particular pieces of place and time, i.e., the living conditions of female agricultural workers in 15th century Sussex, their findings cannot always be applied to broader sets of data i.e., using the data from the Sussex study to postulate about conditions in Kent, or France, or in seventeenth century Sussex. Case studies are best used in addition to raw data and primary sources.

In the 1980s, American historians compared the differences and similarities between different world regions and to come to new concepts to describe them in the study of World History.

DIPLOMACY

Diplomacy is the art and practice of conducting negotiations between representatives of groups or states. It usually refers to international diplomacy, the conduct of international relations through the intercession of professional diplomats with regard to issues of peace-making, culture, economics, trade, and war. International treaties are usually negotiated by diplomats prior to endorsement by national politicians. The word stems from the Greek word "diploma", which literally means 'folded in two'. In ancient Greece, a diploma was a certificate certifying completion of a course of study, typically folded in two. In the days of the Roman Empire, the word diploma was used to describe official travel documents, such as passports and passes for imperial roads, that were stamped on double metal plates. Later, the meaning was extended to cover other official documents such as treaties with foreign tribes. In the 1700s the French called their body of officials attached to foreign legations the corps "diplomatique". The word "diplomacy" was first introduced into the English language by Edmund Burke in 1796, based on the French word "diplomatie".

In an informal or social sense, diplomacy is the employment of tact to gain strategic advantage, one set of tools being the phrasing of statements in a non-confrontational, or polite manner.

DIPLOMATS AND DIPLOMATIC MISSIONS

A diplomat is someone involved in diplomacy; the collective term for a group of diplomats from a single country who are resident in another country is a diplomatic mission. Ambassador is the most senior diplomatic rank; a diplomatic mission headed by an ambassador is known as an embassy. The collective body of all diplomats of particular country is called that country's diplomatic corps.

HISTORY

The ability to practice diplomacy is one of the defining elements of a state, and diplomacy has been practiced since the first city-states were formed millennia ago. For most of human history diplomats were sent only for specific negotiations, and would return immediately after their mission concluded. Diplomats were usually relatives of the ruling family or of very high rank in order to give them legitimacy when they sought to negotiate with the other state. One notable exception involved the relationship between the Pope and the Byzantine Emperor; papal agents, called apocrisiarii, were permanently resident in Constantinople. After the 8th century, however, conflicts between the Pope and Emperor (such as the Iconoclastic controversy) led to the breaking of close ties. Modern diplomacy's origins are often traced to the states of Northern Italy in the early Renaissance, with the first embassies being established in the thirteenth century. Milan played a leading role, especially under Francesco Sforza who established permanent embassies to the other city states of Northern Italy. It was in Italy that many of the traditions of modern diplomacy began, such as the presentation of an ambassadors credentials to the head of state. From Italy the practice was spread to the other European powers. Milan was the first to send a representative to the court of France in 1455. However, Milan refused to host French representatives fearing espionage and that the French representatives would intervene in its internal affairs. As foreign powers such as France and Spain became increasingly involved in Italian politics the need to accept emissaries was recognized. Soon the major European powers were exchanging representatives. Spain was the first to send a permanent representative; it appointed an ambassador to the Court of England in 1487. By the late 16th century, permanent missions became customary. The Holy Roman Emperor, however, did not regularly send permanent legates, as they could not represent the interests of all the German princes (who were in theory subordinate to the Emperor, but in practice independent).

During that period the rules of modern diplomacy were further developed. The top rank of representatives was an ambassador. At that time an ambassador was a nobleman, the rank of the noble assigned varying with the prestige of the country he was delegated to. Strict standards developed for ambassadors, requiring they have large residences, host lavish parties, and play an important role in the court life of their host nation. In Rome, the most prized posting for a Catholic ambassador, the French and Spanish representatives would have a retinue of up to a hundred. Even in smaller posts, ambassadors were very expensive. Smaller states would send and receive envoys, who were a rung below ambassador. Somewhere between the two was the position of minister plenipotentiary.

Diplomacy was a complex affair, even more so than now. The ambassadors from each state were ranked by complex levels of precedence that were much disputed. States were normally ranked by the title of the sovereign; for Catholic nations the emissary from the Vatican was paramount, then those from the kingdoms, then those from duchies and principalities. Representatives from republics were considered the lowest of the low. Determining precedence between two kingdoms depended on a number of factors that often fluctuated, leading to near constant squabbling.

Ambassadors, nobles with little foreign experience and no expectation of a career in diplomacy, needed to be supported by large embassy staff. These professionals would be sent on longer assignments and would be far more knowledgeable than the higher-ranking officials about the host country. Embassy staff would include a wide range of employees, including some dedicated to espionage. The need for skilled individuals to staff embassies was met by the graduates of universities, and this led to a great increase in the study of international law, modern languages, and history at universities throughout Europe.

At the same time, permanent foreign ministries began to be established in almost all European states to coordinate embassies and their staffs. These ministries were still far from their modern form, and many of them had extraneous internal responsibilities. Britain had two departments with frequently overlapping powers until 1782. They were also far smaller; France, which boasted the largest foreign affairs department, had only some 70 full-time employees in the 1780s.

The elements of modern diplomacy slowly spread to Eastern Europe and Russia, arriving by the early eighteenth century. The entire edifice would be greatly disrupted by the French Revolution and the subsequent years of warfare. The revolution would see commoners take over the diplomacy of the French state, and of those conquered by revolutionary armies. Ranks of precedence were abolished. Napoleon also refused to acknowledge diplomatic immunity, imprisoning several British diplomats accused of scheming against France.

After the fall of Napoleon, the Congress of Vienna of 1815 established an international system of diplomatic rank. Disputes on precedence among nations (and therefore the appropriate diplomatic ranks used) persisted for over a century until after World War II, when the rank of ambassador became the norm. Diplomatic traditions outside of Europe were very different. A feature necessary for diplomacy is the existence of a number of states of somewhat equal power, as existed in Italy during the

Renaissance, and in Europe for much of the modern period. By contrast, in Asia and the Middle East, China and the Ottoman Empire were reluctant to practice bilateral diplomacy as they viewed themselves to be unquestionably superior to all their neighbours. The Ottomans, for instance, would not send missions to other states, expecting representatives to come to Constantinople. It would not be until the nineteenth century that the Empire established permanent embassies in other capitals. As European power spread around the world in the eighteenth and nineteenth century so too did its diplomatic system.

DIPLOMATIC STRATEGY

Real world diplomatic negotiations are very different from intellectual debates in a university where an issue is decided on the merit of the arguments and negotiators make a deal by splitting the difference. Though diplomatic agreements can sometimes be reached among liberal democratic nations by appealing to higher principles, most real world diplomacy is heavily influenced by raw power.

The interaction of strength and diplomacy can be illustrated by a comparison to labor negotiations. If a labor union isn't willing to strike, then the union isn't going anywhere because management has absolutely no incentive to agree to union demands. On the other hand, if management isn't willing to take a strike, then the company will be walked all over by the labor union, and management will be forced to agree to any demand the union makes. The same concept applies to diplomatic negotiations. Good diplomacy and strength go together.

DIPLOMATIC IMMUNITY

The sanctity of diplomats has long been observed. This sanctity has come to be known as diplomatic immunity. While there have been a number of cases where diplomats have been killed, this is normally viewed as a great breach of honour. Genghis Khan and the Mongols were well known for strongly insisting on the rights of diplomats, and they would often wreak horrific vengeance against any state that violated these rights.

This was shown when, having sent an ambassador to Persia, Genghis Khan received his ambassador's head sent by the Persians. Because of this act the Mongols invaded the whole of Persia, leading to even larger invasions by Khan in the future. Diplomatic rights were established in the mid-seventeenth century in Europe and have spread throughout the world. These rights were formalized by the 1961 Vienna Convention on Diplomatic Relations, which protects diplomats from being persecuted or prosecuted while on a diplomatic mission.

If a diplomat does commit a serious crime while in a host country s/he may be declared as persona non grata (unwanted person). Such diplomats are then often tried for the crime in their homeland.

Diplomatic communications are also viewed as sacrosanct, and diplomats have long been allowed to carry documents across borders without being searched. The mechanism for this is the so-called "diplomatic bag" (or, in some countries, the "diplomatic pouch"). In recent years, however, signals intelligence has led to this use of diplomatic bags being largely discarded.

In times of hostility, diplomats are often withdrawn for reasons of personal safety, as well as in some cases when the host country is friendly but there is a perceived threat from internal dissidents. Ambassadors and other diplomats are sometimes recalled temporarily by their home countries as a way to express displeasure with the host country. In both cases, lower-level employees still remain to actually do the business of diplomacy.

DIPLOMATS AS A GUARANTEE

The Middle East and other parts of the world had a very different tradition. In the Ottoman Empire, the diplomats of Persia and other states were seen as a guarantee of good behaviour. If a nation broke a treaty or if their nationals misbehaved the diplomats would be punished.

Diplomats were thus used as an enforcement mechanism on treaties and international law. To ensure that punishing a diplomat mattered rulers insisted on high-ranking figures. This tradition is seen by supporters of Iran as a legal basis of the 1979 Iranian hostage crisis. In imitation of alleged previous practices supporters of the Iranian Revolution attempted to punish the United States for its alleged misdeeds by holding their diplomats hostage. Diplomats as a guarantee were also employed sometimes in pre-modern Europe and other parts of Asia.

DIPLOMACY AND ESPIONAGE

Diplomacy is closely linked to espionage or gathering of intelligence. Embassies are bases for both diplomats and spies, and some diplomats are essentially openly-acknowledged spies. For instance, the job of military attachés includes learning as much as possible about the military of the nation to which they are assigned. They do not try to hide this role and, as such, are only invited to events allowed by their hosts, such as military parades or air shows. There are also deep-cover spies operating in many embassies. These individuals are given fake positions at the embassy, but their main task is to illegally gather intelligence, usually by coordinating spy rings of locals or other spies. For the most part, spies operating out of embassies gather little intelligence themselves and their identities tend to be known by the opposition. If discovered, these diplomats can be expelled from an embassy, but for the most part counter-intelligence agencies prefer to keep these agents in situ and under close monitoring.

The information gathered by spies plays an increasingly important role in diplomacy. Arms-control treaties would be impossible without the power of reconnaissance satellites and agents to monitor compliance. Information gleaned from espionage is useful in almost all forms of diplomacy, everything from trade agreements to border disputes.

DIPLOMATIC RECOGNITION

Diplomatic recognition is an important factor in determining whether a nation is an independent state. Receiving recognition is often difficult, even for countries which are fully sovereign. For many decades after becoming independent, even many of the closest allies of the Dutch Republic refused to grant it full recognition. Today there are a number of independent entities without widespread diplomatic recognition, most notably the Republic of China, or Taiwan. Since the 1970s, most nations have stopped officially recognizing the ROC's existence on Taiwan, at the insistence of the People's Republic of China. Currently, the United States and other nations maintain informal relations through de facto embassies, with names such as the American Institute in Taiwan. Similarly, Taiwan's de facto embassies abroad are known by names such as the Taipei Economic and Cultural Representative Office. This was not always the case, with the US maintaining official diplomatic ties with Taiwan until 1979, when these relations were broken off as a condition for establishing official relations with China.

The Palestinian Authority has its own diplomatic service, however Palestinian representatives in most Western countries are not accorded diplomatic immunity, and their missions are referred to as Delegations General. Other unrecognized countries include Abkhazia, Transnistria, Somaliland, Nagorno Karabakh, and the Turkish Republic of Northern Cyprus. Nagorno Karabakh is the part of Azerbaijan Republic. Lacking the economic and political importance of Taiwan, these nations tend to be much more diplomatically isolated. Though used as a factor in judging sovereignty, Article 3 of the Montevideo Convention states, "The political existence of the state is independent of recognition by other states."

INFORMAL DIPLOMACY

Informal diplomacy (sometimes called Track II diplomacy) has been used for centuries to communicate between powers. Most diplomats work to recruit figures in other nations who might be able to give informal access to a country's leadership. In some situations, such as between the United States and the People's Republic of China a large amount of diplomacy is done through semi-formal channels using interlocutors such as academic members of thinktanks. This occurs in situations where governments wish to express intentions or to suggest methods of resolving a diplomatic situation, but do not wish to express a formal position.

Track II diplomacy is a specific kind of informal diplomacy, in which non-officials (academic scholars, retired civil and military officials, public figures, social activists) engage in dialogue, with the aim of conflict resolution, or confidence-building. Sometimes governments may fund such Track II exchanges. Sometimes the exchanges may have no connection at all with governments, or may even act in defiance of governments; such exchanges are called Track III.

POLITICAL FREEDOM

Political freedom is the right, or the capacity, of self-determination as an expression of the individual will.

TYPES

The concept of political freedom is closely allied with the concepts of civil liberties and human rights. Most democratic societies are characterized by various freedoms which are afforded the legal protection of the state. Some of these freedoms include (in alphabetical order):

- Freedom of assembly
- Freedom of association
- Freedom from government sanctioned discrimination
- Freedom of education
- Freedom of movement (or travel)
- Freedom of the press
- Freedom of religion (or belief)
- Freedom of speech
- Freedom of thought.

VIEWS

Various groups along the political spectrum naturally differ on what they believe constitutes "true" political freedom. Friedrich Hayek famously noted that "liberty" and "freedom" have probably been the most abused words in recent history.

In libertarianism, freedom is defined in terms of interference with the individual pursuit of happiness either by government or other persons, where interference is defined as unreasonably preventing others from realising their will in their chosen course of action or in their use of things. Contrary to popular belief, libertarians are not pro-business. Rather, they simply oppose interference in any consenting acts between adults, including capitalist acts.

Generally businesses favour regulations that protect them from competition, which requires many restrictions on consenting capitalist acts between adults. Libertarians call for freedom from coercion, governmental and civilian, in social, political, and economic matters. On the other hand, those on the political left place more emphasis on freedom as the ability of the individual to realize one's own potential and pursuit of happiness. Freedom in this sense may include freedom from want, poverty, deprivation, or oppression.

Many anarchists with the exception of individualist anarchists, anarcho-capitalists, and particularly anarchists that don't qualify their type of anarchism see negative and positive liberty as complementary concepts of freedom. Anarchists that recognize the concepts of negative and positive liberty tend to be left-leaning anarchists such as communist anarchists.

Some treat freedom as if it were almost synonymous with democracy, while others see conflicts or even opposition between the two concepts. E.g. some argue that Iraq was free under Paul Bremer, because it was a rational, humanist, non-subjugating government, long before elections were held. While some thought that Iraq was free under Saddam because Iraq was not a colony.

Environmentalists often argue that political freedoms should include some social constraint on use of ecosystems. They maintain there is no such thing, for instance, as "freedom to pollute" or "freedom to deforest" given the downstream consequences. The popularity of SUVs, golf, and urban sprawl has been used as evidence that some ideas of freedom and ecological conservation can clash. This leads at times to serious confrontations and clashes of values reflected in advertising campaigns, e.g. that of PETA regarding fur. There have been numerous philosophical debates over the nature of freedom, the claimed differences between various types of freedom, and the extent to which freedom is desirable. Determinists argue that all human actions are pre-determined and thus freedom is an illusion. Isaiah Berlin saw a distinction between negative liberty and positive liberty..

In jurisprudence, freedom is the right to autonomously determine one's own actions; generally it is granted in those fields in which the subject has no obligations to fulfil or laws to obey, according to the interpretation that the hypothetical natural unlimited freedom is limited by the law for some matters.

RECENT TRENDS

In modern times the expansion of "freedom" around the world is considered by some to be synonymous with increased participation in democratic political systems. In the 20th Century, the world observed a great reverse in terms of political situation, since the revolutionary struggles in areas of the world suddenly succeeded in establishing freedom from foreign colonialists and domination, at least in places like Africa, even though others may argue that the Cold War caused most of these new states to become puppet states for various regimes such as in Latin America, Africa, and Asia.

FREEDOM OF ASSEMBLY

Freedom of assembly is the freedom to associate with, or organize any groups, gatherings, clubs, or organizations that one wishes. It is held to be a key right in liberal democracies, whereby citizens may form or join any political party, special interest group, or union without government restrictions. In legal systems without freedom of assembly, certain political parties or groups can be banned with harsh penalties for any members. Public protests against the government are usually banned as well.

TIERED RIGHTS

In legal or political systems where rights tend to be ranked in a hierarchy, or "tiered", such that some rights are considered more worthy of protection by the state than others, freedom of assembly is generally located on the top tier. However, the very concept of assigning relative value to rights by way of tiers tends to be controversial.

Those who consider the right of assembly to exist on the "top" tier will sometimes concede that the state may legitimately ban groups which support terrorism or violence. This makes freedom of assembly closely linked with notions of freedom of speech. Thus, while one can be allowed to advocate the murder of the President, one is not necessarily allowed to be a member of a group that seeks to achieve this goal.

The freedom of assembly in order to protest sometimes conflicts with laws intended to protect public safety, even in democratic countries: in many cities, the police are authorized by law to disperse any crowd (including a crowd of political protesters) which threatens public safety, or which the police cannot control.

The idea is to prevent rioting. Often local law requires that a permit must be obtained in advance by protest organizers if a protest march is anticipated; the permit application can be denied. Sometimes this bureaucratic power is abused by lawmakers if the protest is not a popular one in the community or with the local government, with the permit process in some cities taking a great deal of time, organization, and even money required before a permit is issued —and then, when issued, time and location restrictions are sometimes added.

From time to time, local permit laws collide in court with the freedoms of assembly and of speech, such as in February 2003 when protests were anticipated over the exclusion of women from membership at the Augusta National Golf Club where golf's Masters Tournament is played every year.

The Richmond County, Georgia county commission implemented a new rule requiring 20 days of advance notice before a protest, and giving the county sheriff the power to approve or deny permits, and to dictate the location of demonstrations. The sheriff turned down a permit to protest in front of the golf club but approved a protest half a mile away. Two courts upheld the ordinance granting the sheriff this power.

FREEDOM OF ASSOCIATION

Freedom of association is a Constitutional (legal) concept based on the premise that it is the right of free adults to mutually choose their associates for whatever purpose they see fit. This concept has been included in several national constitutions, including the United States Constitution, the European Convention on Human Rights, and Canada's Charter of Rights.

UNITED STATES

While the United States Constitution's First Amendment identifies the rights to assemble and to petition the government, the text of the First Amendment itself does not make specific mention of a right to association. Nevertheless, the United States Supreme Court has held that the freedom of association is an essential part of the Freedom of Speech because, in many cases, people can only engage in effective speech when they join together with others. The Supreme Court has found the Constitution to protect the freedom of association in two cases:

1. *Intimate Associations:* A fundamental element of personal liberty is the right to choose to enter into and maintain certain intimate human relationships. These intimate human relationships are known as "intimate associations."

The paradigmatic "intimate association" is the family.

2. *Expressive Associations:* Expressive associations are groups that engage in activities protected by the First Amendment-speech, assembly, petitioning government for a redress of grievances, and the free exercise of religion. Because the role of these relationships is central to safeguarding individual freedoms, they may receive protection from undue intrusion by the State. Thus, there is a constitutional freedom to associate as a means of preserving other individual liberties.

LIMITATION

However, the implicit First Amendment right of association is not a general right of association. For example, it is illegal in the United States to consider race in the making and enforcement of private contracts other than marriage or taking affirmative action. This limitation of freedom of association results from Section 1981 of Title 42 of the Civil Rights Act, as weighed against the First Amendment according to the court decision Runyon v. McCrary, 427 U.S. 160 (1976).

The holding of Runyon is that the defendant private schools were free to express and teach their views, such as white separatism, but could not discriminate on the basis of race in the provision of services to the general public. So if the plaintiff African-American children wished to attend such private schools, and were clearly qualified in all respects (but race) and were able to pay the fees, and were willing to attend despite the fact that the schools strongly disliked them, then the schools were required by Section 1981 to admit them.

The general rule to be drawn from this is that the First Amendment protects the right to express, including expression of racial discrimination, but people may not practice such ideas even within private associations.

This doctrine rests on the interpretation of a private contract as a "badge" of slavery when either party considers race in choosing the other. The phrase "badges... of slavery" is from the Circuit Court decision 109 U.S. 3 (1883) upholding the power of Congress to pass laws under the Thirteenth Amendment to the United States Constitution compensating for the legacy of slavery.

LIBERTARIAN

Freedom of association is a term popular in libertarian literature. It is used to describe the concept of absolute freedom to live in a community or be part of an organization whose values or culture are closely related to what one wants; or on a more basic level, to associate with any individual one chooses. The right-libertarian (or "free market capitalist," "minarchist") concept of freedom of association is often rebuked from a moral/ethical context. Under laws in such a system, businessowners could refuse custom to anyone for whatever reason. Opponents argue that such practices are regressive and would lead to greater prejudice within society. Those right-libertarians sympathetic to freedom of association, such as Richard Epstein, in a case of refusing service, a case of the freedom of contract, respond that unjustified discrimination incurs a cost and therefore a competitive disadvantage.

WORKERS' FREEDOM OF ASSOCIATION

To most of the world, the freedom of association is a right identified under international labor standards as the right of workers' to organize and collectively bargain. The freedom of association is recognized as a fundamental human right by a number of human rights documents, including the Universal Declaration of Human Rights and International Labor Organization Convention C87 and Convention C98 —two of the eight fundamental, core international labor standards.

2

POLITICAL PHILOSOPHY

Political philosophy is the study of fundamental questions about the state, government, politics, liberty, justice, property, rights, law and the enforcement of a legal code by authority: what they are, why (or even if) they are needed, what makes a government legitimate, what rights and freedoms it should protect and why, what form it should take and why, what the law is, and what duties citizens owe to a legitimate government, if any, and when it may be legitimately overthrown-if ever. In a vernacular sense, the term "political philosophy" often refers to a general view, or specific ethic, belief or attitude, about politics that does not necessarily belong to the technical discipline of philosophy.

Three central concerns of political philosophy have been the political economy by which property rights are defined and access to capital is regulated, the demands of justice in distribution and punishment, and the rules of truth and evidence that determine judgments in the law.

HISTORY OF POLITICAL PHILOSOPHY

Ancient Period

As an academic discipline, Western political philosophy has its origins in ancient Greek society, when city-states were experimenting with various forms of political organization including monarchy, tyranny, aristocracy, oligarchy, and democracy. The first classic work of political philosophy is Plato's The Republic, which was followed by Aristotle's Politics. Roman political philosophy was influenced by the Stoics, and the Roman statesman Cicero wrote on political philosophy. Independently, Confucius, Mencius, Mozi and the Legalist school in China, and the Laws of Manu and Chanakya and in India, all sought to find means of restoring political unity and stability; in the case of the former three through the cultivation of virtue, in the last by imposition of discipline. In India, Kautilya, in his Arthashastra, developed a viewpoint which recalls both the Legalists and Machiavelli. Ancient Chinese and Indian civilization resembled Greek in that there was a unified culture divided into rival states. In the case of China, philosophers found themselves obliged to confront social and political breakdown, and seek solutions to the crisis that confronted their entire civilization.

The early Christian philosophy of Augustine of Hippo was by and large a rewrite of Plato in a Christian context. The main change that Christian thought brought was to moderate the Stoicism and theory of justice of the Roman world, and emphasize the role of the state in applying mercy as a moral example. Augustine also preached that one was not a member of his or her city, but was a citizen of the City of God. Augustine's The City of God is an influential work of this period that refuted the thesis, after the First Sack of Rome, that the Christian view could be realized on Earth at all -a view many Christian Romans held.

Islamic Period

The rise of Islam, based on both the Qur'an and Muhammad strongly altered the power balances and perceptions of origin of power in the Mediterranean region. Early Muslim philosophy emphasized an inexorable link between science and religion, and the process of ijtihad to find truth -in effect all philosophy was "political" as it had real implications for governance. This view was challenged by the Mutazilite philosophers, who held a more Greek view and were supported by secular aristocracy who sought freedom of action independent of the mosque. By the medieval period, however, the Asharite view of Islam had in general triumphed.

Islam was widely exposed to the writings of both Plato and Aristotle, however the main political writing from the Greeks that Islam encountered was Plato's Republic. The West and Christianity were exposed to both the Republic and Aristotle's Politics. Many credit this as to why the Middle East and the West developed differently "politically speaking". Islamic "political philosophy", was, indeed, rooted in the very sources of Islam i.e. the Qur'an and the Sunna, the words and practices of the Prophet. However, in the Western thought, it is generally known that it was a specific area peculiar merely to the great philosophers of Islam: Kindi, Farabi, Ibni Sina, Ibn-i Bacce and Ibni Rusd.

So, the political conceptions of Islam such as kudrah, sultan, ummah, cemaa -and even the "core" terms of the Qur'an, i.e. ibada, din, rab and ilah-should be taken as the very basis of an analysis. Hence, not only the ideas of the "Muslim political philosophers" but also many other "jurists" and "ulama" posed "political" ideas and even "theories." For example, the ideas of Hawarij in the very early years of Islamic history on Hilafa and Ummah, or that of Shia on the concept of Imamah deserve to be named as the proofs of "political" thought. In fact, the clashes between the Ehl-i Sunna and Shia in VII. and VIII. centuries had a genuine political character.

Muslim "political philosophy" did not ceased in the classical period. Despite the fluctuations in its original character during the medieval period, it has lasted even in the modern era. Especially with the emergence of "Islamic radicalism" as a "political" movement, political thought has revived in Muslim world. The political ideas of Abduh, Afgani, Kutub, Mawdudi, Shariati and Khomeini has caught on an ethusiasm in especially Muslim youth in 20th century.

Medieval Period

Medieval political philosophy in Europe was heavily influenced by Christian thinking. It had much in common with the Islamic thinking in that the Roman Catholics also subordinated philosophy to theology. Perhaps the most influential political philosopher of the medieval period was St. Thomas Aquinas who helped reintroduce Aristotle's works, which had been preserved in the interim only by the Muslims.

Aquinas's use of them set the agenda for scholastic political philosophy, and dominated European thought for centuries. The most influential work, however, was that which ended this period, that being Niccolò Machiavelli's The Prince, 1532. It is that work, and The Discourses, a rigorous analysis of the classical period, from which modern political philosophy is largely derived. Machiavelli was a republican, although he is falsely identified as the founder of a much harsher view of politics.

Enlightenment Period

During the Enlightenment period, new theories about what the human is and reality, along with the discovery of other societies in the Americas, and the changing needs of political societies (especially in the wake of the English Civil War, the American Revolution and the French Revolution) led to new questions and insights by such thinkers as Jean-Jacques Rousseau, Thomas Hobbes, Montesquieu and John Locke -known by most for his influential theory of the social contract.

These theorists were driven by two basic questions: by what right or need do people form "states," and what is the best form for a "state." These large questions involved a conceptual distinction between "state" and "government." Basically, "state" refers to a set of enduring institutions through which power is distributed and its use justified.

"Government" refers to a specific group of people who occupy these institutions, and exercise particular policies. This conceptual distinction continues to operate in political science, although some political scientists, philosophers, historians and cultural anthropologists have argued that most political action in any given society occurs outside of its state, and that there are societies that are not organized into states which nevertheless must be considered politically.

Political and economic relations were drastically changed by these views as the guild was subordinated to free trade, and Roman Catholic dominance of theology was increasingly challenged by Protestant churches subordinate to each nation-state and which preached in the "vulgar" or native language of each region.

In the Ottoman Empire, these reforms did not take place and these views did not spread until much later. Also, there was no contact with the New World and the advanced civilizations of the Aztec, Maya, Inca, Mohican, Delaware, Huron and especially the Iroquois, who gave a great boost to Christian thought and in many cases actually inspired some of the institutions adopted in the United States: for example, Benjamin Franklin was a great admirer of some of the methods of the Iroquois Confederacy, and much of early American literature emphasized the political philosophy of the natives.

Industrialization and the Early Modern Age

The industrial revolution produced a parallel revolution in political thought. Urbanization and capitalism greatly reshaped society. During this same period, the socialist movement began to form. In the mid-19th century, Marxism was developed, and socialism in general gained increasing popular support, mostly from the urban working class. By the late 19th century, socialism and trade unions were established members of the political landscape. In addition, the various branches of anarchism and syndicalism also gained some prominence. In the Anglo-American world, anti-imperialism and pluralism began gaining currency at the turn of the century. World War I was a watershed event in human.history. The Russian Revolution of 1917 (and similar, albeit less successful, revolutions in many other European countries) brought communism -and in particular the political theory of Leninism, but also on a smaller level Luxembourgism (gradually) -on the world stage. At the same time, social democratic parties won elections and formed governments for the first time, often as a result of the introduction of universal suffrage. In response to the sweeping social changes that occurred in the years after the war, ultra-reactionary ideologies such as fascism began to take shape. In particular, the rise of the Nazis in Germany would later lead to the Second World War.

All political thought was deeply affected by the Great Depression, which led many theorists to reconsider the ideas they had previously held as axiomatic. In the United States, President Franklin D. Roosevelt introduced the New Deal. In Europe, both the extreme left and the extreme right gained increasing popularity.

Contemporary Political Philosophy

After World War II political philosophy moved into a temporary eclipse in the Anglo-American academic world, as analytic philosophers expressed skepticism about the possibility that normative judgments had cognitive content, and political science turned toward statistical methods and behavioralism. The 1950s saw pronouncements of the 'death' of the discipline, followed by debates about that thesis. A handful of continental European emigres to Britain and the United States-including Hannah Arendt, Karl Popper, Friedrich Hayek, Leo Strauss, Isaiah Berlin, Eric Voegelin and Judith Shklar-encouraged continued study in the field, but in the 1950s and 60s they and their students remained somewhat marginal in their disciplines.

Communism remained an important focus especially during the 1950s and 60s. Zionism, racism and colonialism were important issues that arose. In general, there was a marked trend towards a pragmatic approach to political issues, rather than a philosophical one. Much academic debate regarded one or both of two pragmatic topics: how (or whether) to apply utilitarianism to problems of political policy, or how (or whether) to apply economic models (such as rational choice theory) to political issues. The rise of feminism and the end of colonial rule and of the political exclusion of such minorities as African Americans in the developed world has led to feminist, postcolonial, and multicultural thought becoming significant.

In Anglo-American academic political philosophy the publication of John Rawls's A Theory of Justice in 1971 is considered a milestone. Rawls used a thought experiment, the original position, in which representative parties choose principles of justice for the basic structure of society from behind a veil of ignorance. Rawls also offered a criticism of utilitarian approaches to questions of political justice. Robert Nozick's book Anarchy, State, and Utopia (1974) responded to Rawls from a libertarian perspective.

Contemporary with analytic ethics-oriented work in Anglo-American thought, within Europe several new lines of philosophy directed at critique of existing societies arose between the 1950s and 1980s. Many of these took elements of Marxist economic analysis, but combined them with a more cultural or ideological emphasis. Out of the Frankfurt School, thinkers like Herbert Marcuse, Theodor W. Adorno, Max Horkheimer, and Jürgen Habermas combined Marxian and Freudian perspectives. Along somewhat different lines, a number of other continental thinkers-still largely influenced by Marxism-put new emphases on structuralism and on a "return to Hegel". Within the (post-) structuralist line (though mostly not taking that label) are thinkers such as Gilles Deleuze, Michel Foucault, Claude Lefort, and Jean Baudrillard. The Situationists were more influenced by Hegel; Guy Debord, in particular, moved a Marxist analysis of commodity fetishism to the realm of consumption, and looked at the relation between consumerism and dominant ideology formation.

Another debate developed around the (distinct) criticisms of liberal political theory made by Bernard Williams and Charles Taylor. The liberalism-communitarianism debate is often considered valuable for generating a new set of philosophical problems, rather than a profound and illuminating clash of perspectives. Today some debates regarding punishment and law center on the question of natural law and the degree to which human constraints on action are determined by nature, as revealed by science in particular. Other debates focus on questions of cultural and gender identity as central to politics.

Influential Political Philosophers

A larger list of political philosophers is intended to be closer to exhaustive. Listed below are a few of the most canonical or important thinkers, and especially philosophers whose central focus was in political philosophy and/or who are good representatives of a particular school of thought.

- *Confucius:* The first thinker to relate ethics to the political order.
- *Chanakya:* Founder of an independent political thought in India, laid down rules and guidelines for social, law and political order in society.
- *Mozi:* Eponymous founder of the Mohist school, advocated a strict utilitarianism.
- *Socrates/Plato:* Named their practice of inquiry "philosophy", and thereby stand at the head of a prominent (often called "Western") tradition of systematic intellectual analysis. Set as a partial basis to that tradition the relation between knowledge on the one hand, and a just and good society on the other. Socrates is widely considered founder of Western political philosophy, via his spoken influence on Athenian contemporaries; since Socrates never wrote anything, much of what we know about him and his teachings comes through his most famous student, Plato.
- *Aristotle:* Wrote his Politics as an extension of his Nicomachean Ethics. Notable for the theories that humans are social animals, and that the polis (Ancient Greek city state) existed to bring about the good life appropriate to such animals. His political theory is based upon an ethics of perfectionism (as is Marx's, on some readings).

- *Mencius:* One of the most important thinkers in the Confucian school, he is the first theorist to make a coherent argument for an obligation of rulers to the ruled.
- *Han Feizi:* The major figure of the Chinese Fajia (Legalist) school, advocated government that adhered to laws and a strict method of administration.
- *Niccolò Machiavelli:* First systematic analyses of: (1) how consent of a populace is negotiated between and among rulers rather than simply a naturalistic (or theological) given of the structure of society; (2) precursor to the concept of ideology in articulating the epistemological structure of commands and law.
- *Thomas Hobbes:* Generally considered to have first articulated how the concept of a social contract that justifies the actions of rulers (even where contrary to the individual desires of governed citizens), can be reconciled with a conception of sovereignty.
- *Baruch Spinoza:* Set forth the first analysis of "rational egoism" in which the rational interest of self is conformance with pure reason. To Spinoza's thinking, in a society in which each individual is guided of reason, political authority would be superfluous.
- *John Locke:* Like Hobbes, described a social contract theory based on citizens' fundamental rights in the state of nature. He departed from Hobbes in that, based on the assumption of a society in which moral values are independent of governmental authority and widely shared, he argued for a government with power limited to the protection of personal property. His arguments may have been deeply influential to the formation of the United States Constitution.
- *Baron de Montesquieu:* Analyzed protection of liberty by a "balance of powers" in the divisions of a state.
- *David Hume:* Hume criticized the social contract theory of John Locke and others as resting on a myth of some actual agreement. Hume was a realist in recognizing the role of force to forge the existence of states and that consent of the governed was merely hypothetical.
- *Jean-Jacques Rousseau:* Analyzed the social contract as an

expression of the general will, and controversially argued in favor of absolute democracy where the people at large would act as sovereign.

- *Immanuel Kant:* Argued that participation in civil society is undertaken not for self-preservation, as per Thomas Hobbes, but as a moral duty. First modern thinker who fully analyzed structure and meaning of obligation. Argued that an international organization was needed to preserve world peace.
- *Adam Smith:* Often said to have founded modern economics; explained emergence of economic benefits from the self-interested behavior ("the hidden hand") of artisans and traders. While praising its efficiency, Smith also expressed concern about the effects of industrial labor (e.g. repetitive activity) on workers. His work on moral sentiments sought to explain social bonds outside the economic sphere.
- *Edmund Burke:* Irish member of the British parliament, Burke is credited with the creation of conservative thought. Burke's Reflections on the Revolution in France is the most popular of his writings where he denounced the French revolution. Burke was one of the biggest supporters of the American Revolution.
- *John Adams:* Enlightenment writer who defended the American cause for independence. Adams was a Lockean thinker, who was appalled by the French revolution. Adams is known for his outspoken commentary in favor of the American revolution. He defended the American form of republicanism over the French liberal democracy. Adams is considered the founder of American conservative thought.
- *Thomas Paine:* Enlightenment writer who defended liberal democracy, the American Revolution, and French Revolution in Common Sense and The Rights of Man.
- *Jeremy Bentham:* The first thinker to analyze social justice in terms of maximization of aggregate individual benefits. Founded the philosophical/ethical school of thought known as utilitarianism.
- *John Stuart Mill:* A utilitarian, and the person who named

the system; he goes further than Bentham by laying the foundation for liberal democratic thought in general and modern, as opposed to classical, liberalism in particular. Articulated the place of invididual liberty in an otherwise utilitarian framework.

- *Karl Marx:* In large part, added the historical dimension to an understanding of society, culture and economics. Created the concept of ideology in the sense of (true or false) beliefs that shape and control social actions. Analyzed the fundamental nature of class as a mechanism of governance and social interaction.
- *John Dewey:* Co-founder of pragmatism and analyzed the essential role of education in the maintenance of democratic government.
- *Antonio Gramsci:* Instigated the concepts hegemony and social formation. Fused the ideas of Marx, Engels, Spinoza and others within the so-called dominant ideology thesis (the ruling ideas of society are the ideas of its rulers).
- *Herbert Marcuse:* One of the principle thinkers within the Frankfurt School, and generally important in efforts to fuse the thought of Freud and Marx. Introduced the concept of repressive desublimation, in which social control can operate not only by direct control, but also by manipulation of desire. Analyzed the role of advertising and propaganda in societal consensus.
- *Friedrich Hayek:* Advanced an analysis under which any collectivism could only be maintained by a central authority. Advocated free-market capitalism in which the sole role of the state was to maintain the rule of law.
- *Hannah Arendt:* Analyzed the roots of totalitarianism and introduced the concept of the "banality of evil" (how ordinary technocratic rationality comes to deplorable fruition). Brought distinctive elements of and revisions to the philosophy of Martin Heidegger into political thought.
- *Leo Strauss:* Strauss is known for his writings on the classical and modernity philosophers and denouncement of the modern politics.
- *John Rawls:* Revitalised the study of normative political philosophy in Anglo-American universities with his 1971

book A Theory of Justice, which uses a version of social contract theory to answer fundamental questions about justice and to criticise utilitarianism.

- *Robert Nozick:* Criticized Rawls, and argued for Libertarianism, by appeal to a hypothetical history of the state and the real history of property.

BUREAUCRATIC POLITICS

Bureaucratic politics theories or explanations of why particular public policy decisions got made the way they did stress the motivation by the relevant officials in the government bureaucracy to protect or promote their own agency's special interests (in competition with other agencies) as a major motivating factor in shaping the timing and the content of government decisions. Each bureau (or other governmental sub-division) continually strives to maximize its budget and its authorized manpower, as well as to protect or extend its operating autonomy and discretion in decision-making in the area of its assigned responsibilities. Often this can be most readily accomplished by lobbying for an expansion of the scope of the bureau's responsibilities that are prescribed by Congress or the legislature. Because bureaucratic agencies are in competition with each other for budget shares and for personnel allocations as well as for gaining responsibility for juicy new programs justifying expansion, the policies and policy recommendations generated in the executive branch of the government and passed on to both the chief executive and the legislative authorities are often better understood as the by-product of bureaucratic turf-battles and expedient compromises between bureaucratic chieftains than as the product of reasoned analysis of how most effectively and efficiently to carry out the policy commitments of the elected chief executive or to serve the public interest.

Bureaucracy

In ordinary usage, "bureaucracy" refers to a complex, specialized organization (especially a governmental organi-zation) composed of non-elected, highly trained professional administrators and clerks hired on a full-time basis to perform administrative services and tasks. Bureaucratic organizations are broken up into specialized departments or ministries, to each of which is assigned responsibility for pursuing a limited number of the government's many official goals and policies -those falling within a single relatively narrow functional domain. The departments or ministries are subdivided into divisions that are each assigned even more specialized responsibilities for accomplishing various portions or aspects of the department's overall tasks, and these divisions are in turn composed of multiple agencies or bureaus with even more minutely specialized functions (and their own subdivisions). Bureaucratic organizations always rely heavily on the principle of hierarchy and rank, which requires a clear, unambiguous chain of command through which "higher" officials supervise the "lower" officials, who of course supervise their own subordinate administrators within the various subdivisions and sub-subdivisions of the organization.

Bureaucratic organizations are typically charcterized by great attention to the precise and stable delineation of authority or jurisdiction among the various subdivisions and among the officials who comprise them, which is done mainly by requiring the organization's employees to operate strictly according to fixed procedures and detailed rules designed to routinize nearly all decision-making. Some of the most important of these rules and procedures may be specified in laws or decrees enacted by the higher "political" authorities that are empowered to set the official goals and general policies for the organization, but upper-level (and even medium-level) bureaucrats typically are delegated considerable discretionary powers for elaborating their own detailed rules and procedures.

Because the incentive structures of bureaucratic organizations largely involve rewarding strict adherence to formal rules and punishing unauthorized departures from standard operating procedures (rather than focussing on measureable individual contributions toward actually attaining the organization's politically assigned goals), such organizations tend to rely very heavily upon extensive written records and standardized forms, which serve primarily to document the fact that all decisions about individual "cases" were taken in accordance with approved guidelines and procedures rather than merely reflecting the personal preferences or subjective judgment of the individual bureaucrat involved. The classic social scientific analysis of bureaucracy was that of the pioneer sociologist Max Weber in his

1922 book Economy and Society. Weber, like the good German he was, believed that a permanent, well-educated, conscientious, "non-partisan," Prussian-style bureaucracy professionally committed to implementing whatever decisions the legitimate rulers of the state might arrive at was the best organizational form yet discovered for the rational and efficient pursuit of collective social goals in a modern society with a specialized and highly complex division of labor. In his writings, Weber devoted considerable attention to showing ways in which the gradual evolution of modern bureaucratic methods and values helped to remove the formidable obstacles to economic development, social advancement and political stability that had been inherent in the much less professionalized and systematized practices of government administration in feudal Europe and most other premodern societies.

While most other social scientific students of bureaucracy have recognized the historical importance of bureaucratic organizational techniques in creating the powerful, centralized nation-states (and other very large organizations such as modern business corporations and labor unions) that predominate in the industrialized world of the 20th century, it is fair to say that they have generally been considerably less one-sidedly approving of bureaucracy than Weber was. Despite their many advantages for dealing efficiently and effectively with routine, recurring problems in a fairly stable and predictable environment, bureaucratic methods also have their dark side. Hired and promoted largely on the basis of educational credentials and seniority within the organization and protected by civil service personnel practices designed to provide a high degree of job security, bureaucratic officials tend to be very well insulated from responsibility for the external consequences of their decisions and actions as long as they stay formally within prescribed procedures.

Such sociologists as Robert K. Merton and Michel Crozier have shown that pressures on officials to conform to fixed rules and detailed procedures, when added to the narrow responsibilities of highly specialized agencies for pursuing only a select few of the many objectives that government has set, quite regularly leads bureaucrats to become defensive, rigid, and completely unresponsive to the urgent individual needs and concerns of the private citizens and outside organizations with which they come into professional contact. ("That's not my department. I cannot help you.") Because the salaries and promotion prospects of officials working in large bureaucracies seldom depend upon measurable success or efficiency by the organization in achieving its larger goals (which are often especially difficult to measure in government agencies and other non-profit oriented organizations that lack a clear "bottom line") and because any departure from established routines always requires permission from remote higher levels of the hierarchy, large bureaucratic organizations tend to be very slow and cumbersome in making important policy decisions (the "buck-passing" phenomenon) and are especially dull-witted in recognizing and responding to the consequences of major changes in economic, social and technological conditions and circumstances outside the organization itself.

In other words, individual officials working under bureaucratic incentive systems frequently find it to be in their own best interests to adhere rigidly to internal rules and formalities in a ritualistic fashion, behaving as if "proper procedure" were more important than the larger goals for serving their clients or the general public that they are supposedly designed to accomplish (the "red tape" phenomenon).

Incentive

Something that provides a motive for a person to choose a particular course of action. Organized cooperative activities in a social setting —such as cooperation for the purpose of economic production —depends upon each of the participants having some sort of incentive to behave in the required cooperative fashion. Different societies (and even different organizations within the same society) vary considerably in the nature of the incentive systems upon which they characteris-tically rely to organize their common projects. Incentives may be classified according to a number of different schemes, but one of the more useful classifications subdivides incentives into three general types: moral incentives, coercive incentives and remunerative incentives.

- A person has a moral incentive to behave in a particular way when he has been taught to believe that it is the "right" or "proper" or "admirable" thing to do. If he behaves as others expect him to, he may expect the approval or even the admiration of the other members of the collectivity and enjoy an enhanced sense of acceptance or self-esteem. If he behaves improperly, he may expect verbal expressions of condemnation, scorn, ridicule or even ostracism from the collectivity, and he may experience unpleasant feelings of guilt, shame or self-condemnation.

- A person has a coercive incentive to behave in a particular way when it has been made known to him that failure to do so will result in some form of physical aggression being directed at him by other members of the collectivity in the form of inflicting pain or physical harm on him or his loved ones, depriving him of his freedom of movement, or perhaps confiscating or destroying his treasured possessions.
- A person has a remunerative incentive to behave in a particular way if it has been made known to him that doing so will result in some form of material reward he will not otherwise receive. If he behaves as desired, he will receive some specified amount of a valuable good or service (or money with which he can purchase whatever he wishes) in exchange.

All known societies employ all three sorts of incentives to at least some degree in order to evoke from its members the necessary degree of cooperation for the society to survive and flourish. However, different societies differ radically in the relative proportions of these different kinds of incentives used within their characteristic mix of incentives. "Primitive" or "traditional" cultures such as those of hunter-gatherers tend to rely very heavily on moral incentives and make relatively little use of coercive and remunerative incentives to sustain social cooperation. More "advanced" or "modern" societies built around a much more specialized and complex division of labor tend to make much greater use of both coercive and remunerative incentives in organizing social activities, while still relying in very important ways upon moral or normative incentives.

Among the more "advanced" societies, liberal societies try to rely as much as possible on remunerative and moral incentives in preference to the use of coercive incentives, while authoritarian and totalitarian societies display much less reluctance to resort to coercive incentives in securing social cooperation.

State

1. A specialized type of political organization characterized by a full-time, specialized, professional work force of tax-collectors, soldiers, policemen, bureaucrats and the like that exercises supreme political authority over a defined territory with a permanent population, independent from any enduring external political control and possessing a local predominance of coercive power (always supplemented with moral and remunerative incentives as well) great enough to maintain general obedience to its laws or commands within its territorial borders. The first known states were created in ancient times in Egypt, Mesopotamia, India, China, Mexico and Peru, but it is only in relatively modern times that states have almost completely displaced alternative "stateless" forms of political organization of societies all over the planet. (Roving bands of hunter-gatherers and even fairly sizable and complex tribal societies based on herding or agriculture have existed without any full-time specialized state organization, and these "stateless" forms of political organization have in fact prevailed for all of the prehistory and much of the history of the human species.)
2. One of the component territorial political units in a larger federal state that are so called because, although they actually fall short of full independent statehood or sovereignty, they still possess a very large degree of autonomy in decision-making with respect to most of their internal affairs and are thus also legally allowed to exercise various forms of coercion over their regional populations.

Nation State

A form of state in which those who exercise power claim legitimacy for their rule partly or solely on the grounds that their power is exercised for the promotion of the distinctive interests, values and cultural heritage of a particular nation whose members ideally would constitute all, or most of, its subject population and all of whom would dwell within the borders.

Nation

A large aggregation or agglomeration of people sharing a

common and distinctive racial, linguistic, historical and/or cultural heritage that has led its members to think of themselves as belonging to a valued natural community sharing a common destiny that ought to be preserved forever.

Nationalism

An ideology, or rather a whole category of similar ideologies, based on the premise that each nation (or at least the ideologist's own nation) constitutes a natural political community whose members should all live together under the authority of "their own" independent nation state. When the people of one nation live in large numbers in a multi-ethnic state or in states with government(s) dominated by political elites drawn from another nationality, nationalism often becomes an ideology justifying rebellion or secession in order to create or recreate a nation state for the heretofore subjugated nation. When substantial numbers of people seen as belonging to the nation live outside the borders of their own nation state, nationalism often becomes an ideology justifying an aggressive foreign policy striving to expand the state's borders to include them. Nationalist ideologies usually claim that their respective nation possess special national characteristics or virtues that make them morally and intellectually superior to all other nations and should qualify their nation state for a special or privileged role in the world at large.

Ideology

A comprehensive and coherent set of basic beliefs about political, economic, social and cultural affairs that is held in common by a sizable group of people within a society. Such interrelated ideas and teachings purport both to explain how political, economic, social and cultural institutions really do work and also to prescribe how such institutions ought ideally to operate. Conservative ideologies seek to demonstrate a close correspondence between "the way things are" and "the way things ought to be," thus legitimizing the existing order in the eyes of those who can be convinced to believe in the ideology. Radical and revolutionary ideologies, on the other hand, set unconventional, higher, or even utopian standards with regard to what would constitute a legitimate and supportable social-economic-political system and then demonstrate in detail that the existing order does not even come close to meeting these standards, thereby de-legitimizing the existing system and helping mobilize believers in the ideology for concerted action to reform or overthrow the existing order. (In addition to their descriptive and prescriptive functions about existing and ideal social orders, ideologies may also include more specialized doctrines regarding the most suitable political strategies and tactics to be pursued by believers in their efforts to shore up or undermine the existing order.)

One useful way of categorizing ideologies from a political point of view focusses on differences in the ideologies' prescriptions for how much the government ought to be involved in directing or regulating economic, social and cultural affairs and how much individuals or voluntary organizations ought to be left alone to make their own (widely varied) decisions in these spheres of life. In this course, for example, we frequently employ a two-dimensional classification of ideologies proposed by Maddox and Lilie that is based on assessing people's preferences for government regulation versus non-regulation in:

1. Economic decisions
2. Non-economic or life-style decisions.

It should be noted that the term "ideology" often has a somewhat derogatory flavor, especially in Anglo-American societies, because it often carries the implication that "ideological" thought is unduly biased, dogmatic and distorted, an obstacle rather than an aid in perceiving how the world "really" works. ("You, sir, are an ideologue. I, on the other hand, am a pragmatic man of reason who sees things the way they really are.")

Legitimacy

The principle that indicates the acceptance of the decisions of government leaders and officials by (most of) the public on the grounds that these leaders' acquisition and exercise of power has been in accordance with the society's generally accepted procedures and political or moral values. Legitimacy may be conferred upon power holders in a variety of ways in different societies, usually involving solemn formal rituals of a religious or quasi-religious nature—royal birth and coronation in monarchies, popular election and "swearing in" in democracies and so on. "Legitimate" rulers typically require less use of physical coercion to enforce their decisions than rulers lacking in legitimacy, because most of the people are apt to feel a moral obligation to obey the former but not the latter. Consequently, people who gain or hold power by illegitimate means tend to work very hard to discover or create ways of endowing themselves with legitimacy after the fact, often by inventing a new ideology or religion and attempting to indoctrinate the people with its legitimating formulas through various forms of propaganda, thus creating moral incentives for the citizenry to obey their government.

Propaganda

Persuasive communications directed at a specific audience that are designed to influence the targeted audience's opinions, beliefs and emotions in such a way as to bring about specific, planned alterations in their behavior.

The information communicated by the propagandist may be true or false, the values appealed to may be sincerely held by the propagandist or cynically manipulated, and the presentation may be either logically and dispassionately argued or rhetorically tailored to arouse the most irrational emotions and prejudices - but the message content of propaganda is always deliberately selected and slanted to lead the audience toward a predetermined mindset that benefits the cause of the propagandist.

Socialism

A class of ideologies favoring an economic system in which all or most productive resources are the property of the government, in which the production and distribution of goods and services are administered primarily by the government rather than by private enterprise, and in which any remaining private production and distribution (socialists differ on how much of this is tolerable) is heavily regulated by the government rather than by market processes.

Both democratic and non-democratic socialists insist that the government they envision as running the economy must in principle be one that truly reflects the will of the masses of the population (or at least their "true" best interests), but of course they differ considerably in their ideas about what sorts of political institutions and practices are required to ensure this will be so. In practice, socialist economic principles may be combined with an extremely wide range of attitudes toward personal freedom, civil liberties, mass political participation, bureaucracy and political competition, ranging from Western European democratic socialism to the more authoritarian socialisms of many third world regimes to the totalitarian excesses of Soviet-style socialism or communism.

Communism

1. Any ideology based on the communal ownership of all property and a classless social structure, with economic production and distribution to be directed and regulated by means of an authoritative economic plan that supposedly embodies the interests of the community as a whole. Karl Marx is today the most famous early theoretician of communism, but he did not invent the term or the basic social ideals, which he mostly borrowed and adapted from the less systematic theories of earlier French utopian socialists —grafting these onto a philosophical framework Marx derived from the German philosophers Hegel and Feuerbach, while adding in a number of economic theories derived from his reinterpretation of the writings of such early political economists such as Adam Smith, Thomas Malthus, and David Ricardo. In most versions of the communist utopia, everyone would be expected to cooperate enthusiastically in the process of production, but the individual citizen's equal rights of access to consumer goods would be completely unaffected by his/her own individual contribution to production —hence Karl Marx's famous slogan "From each according to his ability; to each according to his need." The Marxian and other 19th century communist utopias also were expected to dispense with such "relics of the past" as trading, money, prices, wages, profits, interest, land-rent, calculations of profit and loss, contracts, banking, insurance, lawsuits, etc. It was expected that such a radical reordering of the economic sphere of life would also more or less rapidly lead to the elimination of all other major social problems such as class conflict, political oppression, racial discrimination, the inequality of the sexes, religious bigotry, and cultural backwardness-

as well as put an end to such more "psychological" forms of suffering as alienation, anomie, and feelings of powerlessness.

2. The specifically Marxist-Leninist variant of socialism which emphasizes that a truly communist society can be achieved only through the violent overthrow of capitalism and the establishment of a "dictatorship of the proletariat" that is to prepare the way for the future idealized society of communism under the authoritarian guidance of a hierarchical and disciplined Communist Party.
3. A world-wide revolutionary political movement inspired by the October Revolution (Red Oktober) in Russia in 1917 and advocating the establishment everywhere of political, economic, and social institutions and policies modeled on those of the Soviet Union (or, in some later versions, China or Albania) as a means for eventually attaining a communist society.

Capitalism

A form of economic order characterized by private ownership of the means of production and the freedom of private owners to use, buy and sell their property or services on the market at voluntarily agreed prices and terms, with only minimal interference with such transactions by the state or other authoritative third parties.

MARKET

In its original meaning, a physical coming together of a sizable number of merchants and prospective customers at a pre-arranged time and place (in medieval Europe, typically once a week on the main square of the largest village in the vicinity) for the purpose of striking deals to buy and sell a variety of goods and services. Large numbers of customers came to such organized markets because they found it convenient to be able to make many of their necessary purchases on the same day in one central location (minimizing their total travel time and other travel costs) and because the presence of many merchants offering similar wares made it much more practical to comparison shop for the best deals in terms of quality and price. Merchants were often attracted from considerable distances to participate in such markets because of the opportunity to sell so many of their wares to such large numbers of potential customers in such a short time. Modern day flea markets, farmers' markets, gun shows and crafts fairs are fairly close to the original concept.

In the language of modern industrial society, and especially in the language of professional economists, the concept of a market has been generalized and abstracted far beyond the original rather concrete and localized meaning of the term. In the more modern sense of the term, a market is the generalized name tag for the whole process that gets under way whenever a sizable number of people free to buy and/or sell a particular kind of good or service are in more or less close communication with each other (either personally and directly or else through the mediation of advertising, catalogs, news reports, postal carriers, telephone systems, computer networks, etc.) so that information about the terms of recent transactions and current offers to buy or sell is generally available to a large number of interested parties at relatively low cost—regardless of the participants' physical proximity or distance.

Such technological innovations of the industrial age as ever cheaper and more rapid transportation and communications over increasing distances both have dramatically increased the size of the areas from which buyers and sellers may be brought together to do business and have greatly reduced the need for them actually to meet face-to-face in one place in order to strike a bargain.

The markets for many consumers' durable goods like automobiles or TVs and major agricultural and industrial commodities like oil, natural gas, wheat, beef, steel, forest products and computer chips are now literally worldwide in extent. (Of course, for many markets there do still exist central gathering places or locations that play an especially important role in the local, national or even worldwide networks of buyers and sellers —for example, the New York Stock Exchange, the Chicago Commodities Exchange, the seasonal women's fashions shows in Paris and Milan, regional baseball card collectors conventions and so on but in nearly all such cases, it is not really necessary for an individual buyer or seller actually to travel to the relevant marketplace in order to participate in the broader markets of which these are nowadays only a part.)

Where markets exist and are allowed to function reasonably freely, there are certain predictable consequences for the way the economy will operate. Elaboration of these consequences is the primary purpose of most of the research in the theoretical subfield of microeconomics.

Market Economy

An economy in which scarce resources are all (or nearly all) allocated by the interplay of supply and demand in free markets, largely unhampered by government rationing, price-fixing or other coercive interference. In classifying real historical economies, the level of "marketization" is not primarily an either/or issue but rather a matter of degree. The greater the proportion of the goods and services produced in the society that are allocated by market processes (rather than by government edict or the operation of unchangeable custom), the more meaningful it is to refer to its economy as a market economy —and the more useful is the abstract economic theory of the operation of markets likely to be for understanding and even predicting economic behavior within that society.

Probably the most critical single distinction between "basically market" and "basically non-market" (socialist, feudal, hunter-gatherer, etc.) economies is whether or not the determinations of what is to be produced and of the corresponding allocation of producers' goods (land, raw materials, machinery, and other "capital," as well as the services of labor) are accomplished primarily through free markets rather than primarily through government command or unalterable custom.

The concept of a market presupposes the existence of certain sorts of property relations in the society involved. At least some goods and services must be legally or socially regarded as alienable property —that is, there must be ascertainable individuals (or group representatives) who are recognized as having not just the right to use particular scarce economic resources for their own purposes but also the discretionary authority permanently to transfer such rights of use to someone else in exchange for some mutually agreeable quid pro quo, such as money or other goods or services.

Not all human societies have recognized any such rights to transfer ownership, and most historical human societies have forbidden or placed stringent limits on the transferability of at least certain kinds of recognized property rights.

In many societies (including most of Europe during the Middle Ages), individual or family rights to the perpetual use of particular plots of land were well established and protected by law —but such rights only rarely could legally be sold to someone else because the land was socially regarded as fundamentally the inalienable property of either the local community as a whole or of the tribe or clan or church or perhaps of the reigning royal family. And even in the USA since 1865, while each person's ownership of his or her own body is well established, the law will still not allow you to make a binding contract to sell yourself into slavery or even to auction off your spare bodily organs for purposes of a surgical transplant.)

It is worth noting for clarity's sake that the concept of a market does not logically presuppose the existence of "private property in the means of production" in the sense that private individuals or family households are the owners of land and capital and thus the recipients of profits, interest, rent etc.

One may at least theoretically conceive of an economy of market socialism, in which workers' collectives, consumers' cooperatives, village communes or even autonomous state agencies leased from the state or held actual title to land, mines, factories, machinery and so forth —so long as the socialist production organizations were free to buy and sell their output and the use of their assigned land or capital assets to each other at freely negotiated prices responsive to conditions of supply and demand (assuming, of course, they are allowed to keep effective control of the bulk of the proceeds). There are, of course, both theoretical and practical problems with market socialism, and the costs and benefits of capitalist markets cannot be uncritically attributed to such a system. The larger point is that socialist economies have historically included varying proportions of "remnant" market elements in their make-up, and the theoretical possibilities for additional "hybrid" forms are numerous.

PROPERTY RIGHTS

A property right is the exclusive authority to determine how and by whom a particular resource is used. More broadly, property rights may be seen as a bundle of separate and distinct rights over a particular good -including at least the right of personal use, the right to demand compensation as a prerequisite for its use by other people, and the right to transfer any or all of these rights to others (either permanently by sale or temporarily through some form of contractual arrangement). Property rights may be exercised by governments through their designated officials (public ownership or public property) as well as by private individuals and other sorts of non-governmental organizations (private property).

Private Property Rights

The basic rights of individuals (and organizations or associations of people functioning as a single conglomerate "legal person" such as corporations, partnerships, churches, non-profit foundations, etc.) to the peaceful possession, control and enjoyment of the things they own as well as their rights to make contracts to rent, sell or give away all or part of their various ownership rights over these possessions (or these possessions' services) to any other people willing to accept the owners' terms. The possessions over which a person has property rights may be tangible (like real estate, factory machinery, livestock, automobiles or a jack-knife) or intangible (like contractual obligations to provide goods or services at some time in the future, shares of common stock in a corporation, bonds, insurance policies, the right to broadcast over a designated radio frequency, patents, trademarks and copyrights).

In highly specialized societies, property rights over particular resources may be "unbundled" and parcelled out among many individuals according to quite complex rules of division of authority over particular aspects or uses of the resource specified in written contracts -for example, separating mineral rights from surface rights to a parcel of land, utility easements over the same land, restrictive deed covenants and so on.

Contract

A legally binding agreement between two or more competent parties fixing the precise terms and details for a voluntary exchange of goods or services over which the contracting parties possess property rights. An agreement is a legally enforceable contract if and only if:

1. The agreement must be "mutual" (all parties have the

same understanding of the meaning of their agreement — there is a "meeting of the minds");

2. The agreement must be "voluntary" (none of the parties is agreeing under the influence of violent threats or fraudulent misrepresentation of the facts);
3. There must be actual "consideration" paid (that is, each party must be achieving a benefit by giving up something he controls to get something another party controls in exchange: a simple one-sided promise to give someone else a gratuitous benefit is not a contract);
4. All parties to the agreement must be "competent" (children and the severely mentally impaired or insane are assumed by the courts to be incapable of forming a coherent intent or determining their own best interests, so the courts will not enforce the agreements they make);
5. The substance of the agreement must not be "contrary to public policy" (for example, the U.S. courts will not enforce a contract that requires one or more of the parties to commit a crime, nor will they enforce a contract by which even a legally competent adult voluntarily sells himself into life-long slavery in exchange for, say, a ten million dollar payment to his children).

Factors of Production

The scarce resources that are useful not so much for direct and immediate satisfaction of human wants as for producing other goods or services. Economists often find it useful for purposes of theoretical simplification to group the millions of different sorts of factors of production into several very broad categories and then discuss them as though all the items within each category were perfectly substitutable for each other and therefore traded on a single market. The simplest such conventional categorization of the factors of production divides them into land, labor, capital, and sometimes also entrepreneurship and/or human capital.

Derived Demand

The demand for each of the factors of production is often referred to as a "derived" demand to emphasize the fact that the relationship between the factor's price and the quantity of the factor demanded by firms employing it in production is directly dependent on consumer demand for the final product(s) the factor is used to produce.

If for some reason (say, for example, a spontaneous shift in consumer tastes) the demand for men's hats increases (shifts to the right) so that more hats than before can be sold at any given price, then the "derived" demand for felt used in making hats will also increase (shift to the right) so that felt-makers will be able to sell more felt at any given price. (We would also expect the hat-makers' demand for the labor of hatters and for specialized hat-making machinery to shift to the right in a similar fashion in response to the public's greater demand for hats.)

What is the mechanism by which a shift in demand for the final product is translated into a shift in demand for the factors of production used in its manufacture?

The key is the change in the price of the final product brought about by the shift in demand for it. If the demand curve for hats shifts to the right and the (upwardly sloping) supply curve remains unchanged, then the equilibrium price and quantity in the hat market will now involve both a somewhat higher price for hats and a somewhat larger quantity of hats being produced and sold to the public. (Because of the price rise, the marginal revenues earned by the manufacturers per additional hat sold will be higher, so consequently their desire to maximize profits will lead them to produce additional hats until the marginal cost for the last hat rises to equal the new higher price.)

But producing more hats than before will require more of the relevant factors of production than before, which they will want to purchase from their suppliers, shifting the demand curves for each of the factors to the right. (This increase in demand for the factors in turn will tend to raise the factor prices somewhat and to increase the quantity of them sold, which then affects the factor producers' demand for their own necessary inputs and brings about further price-and-quantity adjustments throughout the economy in an ever-widening ripple effect.)

DEMAND

The willingness and ability of the people within a market area to purchase particular amounts of a good or service at a variety of alternative prices during a specified time period.

Other things being held constant, the lower the price of a good (or service), the greater the quantity of it that will be demanded by purchasers at any given time.

Demand Curve

A graphical representation of a demand schedule. Conventionally, the demand curve is usually drawn between axes with price plotted along the vertical axis and number of units of the good or service demanded plotted along the horizontal axis. Where the law of demand applies to the particular market under consideration, the demand curve will slope (either gently or steeply) downwards from left to right.

Demand Schedule

A table or listing showing the number of units of a single type of good (or service) that potential purchasers would offer to buy at each of a number of varying prices during some particular time period.

Demand schedules may be drawn up to reflect the behavioral propensities of a single unique individual, household, or firm or, more frequently encountered in microeconomic analysis, composite demand schedules for the particular good may be derived by adding up all the demand schedules of the large number of individuals, households or firms that are active or potentially active as purchasers in the market under consideration.

SUPPLY

The willingness and ability of potential sellers to offer various specific amounts of a good or service for sale at each of a variety of alternative prices during a particular time period. Other things being held constant, the higher the price of a good (or service), the larger the quantity of that good (or service) that will be offered for sale in a particular time period.

Supply Curve

A graphical representation of a supply schedule. Conventionally, the supply curve is drawn between axes with price plotted along the vertical axis and number of units of the good or service supplied plotted along the horizontal axis. Where the law of supply applies to the particular market under consideration, the supply curve will slope (either gently or steeply) upwards from left to right.

Supply Schedule

A table or listing showing the exact quantities of a single type of good (or service) that potential sellers would offer to sell at each of a number of varying prices during some particular time period. Supply schedules may be drawn up to reflect the behavioral propensities of a single unique individual, household, or firm — or, more frequently encountered in microeconomic analysis, composite supply schedules for the particular good may be derived by adding up all the supply schedules of the large number of individuals, households or firms that are active or potentially active as sellers in the market under consideration.

Law of Diminishing Returns

Sometimes also referred to as the law of variable proportions, this "law" is really a generalization economists make about the nature of technology when it is possible to combine the same factors of production in a number of different proportions to make the same product. The law states:

When increasing amounts of one factor of production are employed in production along with a fixed amount of some other production factor, after some point, the resulting increases in output of product become smaller and smaller. (That is, first the marginal returns to successive small increases in the variable factor of production turn down, and then eventually the overall average returns per unit of the variable input start decreasing.) Since the law assumes that the available quantity of at least one factor of production is fixed at a given level and that technological knowledge does not change during the relevant period, the law of diminishing returns normally translates into a statement about the short-run choice of production possibilities facing a firm (since in the longer run it is virtually always possible for the firm to acquire more of the temporarily "fixed" factor —building an additional factory building, buying additional land, installing additional machines of the same kind, installing newer and more advanced machinery, and so on.)

A simple example of the workings of the law of diminishing returns comes from gardening. A particular twenty by twenty garden plot will produce a certain number of pounds of tomatoes if the gardener just puts in the recommended number of rows and plants per row, waters them appropriately and keeps the weeds pulled.

If the gardener varies this approach by adding a pound of fertilizer to the topsoil, but otherwise does everything the same, he can increase the number of pounds of tomatoes the garden plot yields by quite a bit (notice the amount of land is being held fixed or constant). If he adds two pounds of fertilizer (rather than just one), probably he can get still more tomatoes per season, but the increase in tomatoes harvested by going from one pound to two pounds of fertilizer is probably smaller than the increase he gets by going from zero pounds to one (diminishing marginal returns). Applying three pounds of fertilizer may still increase the harvest, but perhaps by only a very little bit over the yields available using just two pounds. Applying four pounds of fertilizer turns out to be overdoing it —the garden yields fewer tomatoes than applying only three pounds because the plants begin to suffer damage from root-burn. And five pounds of fertilizer turns out to kill nearly all the plants before they even flower.

Another similar example of diminishing returns in an industrial setting might be a widget factory that features a certain number of square feet of work space and a certain number of machines inside it. Neither the space available nor the number of machines can be added to without a long delay for construction or installation, but it is possible to adjust the amount of labor on short notice by working more shifts and/or taking on some extra workers per shift. Adding extra man-hours of labor will increase the number of widgets produced, but only within limits. After a certain point, such things as worker fatigue, increasing difficulties in supervising the large work force, more frequent breakdowns by over-utilized machinery, or just plain inefficiency due to overcrowding of the work space begin to take their toll. The marginal returns to each successive increment of labor input get smaller and smaller and ultimately turn negative. The law of diminishing returns is significant because it is part of the basis for economists' expectations that a firm's short-run marginal cost curves will slope upward as the number of units of output increases. And this in turn is an important part of the basis for the law of supply's prediction that the number of units of product that a profit-maximizing firm will wish to sell increases as the price obtainable for that product increases.

Marginal Analysis

A concept employed constantly in microeconomic theory (and quite frequently in macroeconomic theory as well) is that of the marginal change in some economic variable (such as quantity of a good produced or consumed), or even the ratio of the marginal change in one variable to the marginal change in another variable. A marginal change is a proportionally very small addition or subtraction to the total quantity of some variable. Marginal analysis is the analysis of the relationships between such changes in related economic variables. Important ideas developed in such analysis include marginal cost, marginal revenue, marginal product, marginal rate of substitution, marginal propensity to save, and so on. In microeconomic theory, "marginal" concepts are employed primarily to explicate various forms of "optimizing" behavior. (Consumers are seen as striving to maximize their utility or satisfaction. Firms are seen as striving to maximize their profits.) The maximum value of such a variable is found by identifying a value of the independent variable such that either a marginal increase or a marginal decrease from that value causes the value of the dependent variable being maximized to fall. (The student of mathematics may recognize the opportunity to apply concepts from differential calculus here, with the various marginal concepts being special names given to first derivatives of particular functions.)

The valuation of the benefits (utility) and the costs of any good is determined "at the margin." For the (individual or collective) decision maker pondering how many units of a good to consume or provide to the market, net total benefits (benefits minus costs) will always be maximized at that level of consumption (or provision to the market) where the marginal benefit derived from adding the last unit equals the marginal addition to total costs of producing or acquiring that last additional unit.

Optimum

The very "best" possible situation or state of affairs according to some explicit objective that provides a precise standard of evaluation. For example, if a business firm's objective is to make the biggest profits possible (as economists generally assume it is), then the firm's optimal level of output at any given level of sales prices and production costs is that at which its profits will be the highest possible. Most of economics is concerned with analyzing how individuals or groups of people or even whole societies may achieve optimal use of available resources, and it is normally assumed that the maximum satisfaction of people's individual wants or desires is the objective of the economy that provides the relevant standard of evaluation. (Social critics, moral philosophers, religious thinkers, and political power-seekers in their various ways have often disputed the validity of this individualistic standard of evaluation, of course.)

Efficiency

In an economic sense, the ratio or proportionality between the value of the human end achieved ("benefits" or "satisfactions") and the value of the scarce resources expended to achieve it (opportunity costs). When an economist calls a situation or a practice "inefficient," he is claiming that we could achieve exactly the same desired goals with the expenditure of fewer scarce resources, or, put another way, that the amount of resources being employed could potentially produce even more of the beneficial results intended than they do. Efficiency simply means making the most we can of the limited resources we have.

Notice that "efficiency" in the economist's sense is an inherently evaluative term, not a matter of mere technical or scientific measurement of objective physical quantities, as the term might be used in an engineering context (as for example, the "efficiency" of various kinds of steam engine in transforming heat energy to useful kinetic energy). "Value of" always requires some sort of answer to the question "value to whom." When we assess the efficiency of any process or social institution or practice, just whose evaluations of the means and the ends are we using? In a well-developed market economy, assessment of economic efficiency makes heavy use of the monetary values placed on the various inputs and the resulting outputs in the open marketplace.

The valuations that count are thus the valuations of those who are willing and able to support their preferences by spending their money in the ways that seem to them most likely to maximize their own satisfactions or "utility" based on their own individual tastes and preferences. The evidence that any particular economic resource is being used efficiently is, in the end, the fact that no one finds it "worth his while" to bid up the price and pay more in order to divert it to some other use. The logical and philosophical elaboration of the idea that competitive market systems are highly efficient in a much broader sense even than this is the primary content of Adam Smith's classic work The Wealth of Nations (1776). Indeed the entire subdivision of today's economic science known as "welfare economics" specializes primarily in identifying and analyzing the necessary preconditions for voluntary market interactions to generate socially efficient outcomes (and in examining the possibilities for remedies by deliberate state economic policies where those necessary preconditions may not be fully met).

COST

In the widest sense, the measure of the value of what has to be given up in order to achieve a particular objective. In everyday language, people most often use the term rather like an accountant does, as synonymous with the total money outlays actually paid out to achieve the objective, but this is not precisely what economists mean by the term. Economists are concerned with rational decision-making, and the rational decision-maker needs to estimate in advance the full range of consequences of each of the various alternative uses of his time and resources open to him, not just the portion of the costs accounted for by money outlays. For the economist, the true cost of any decision is the value of the next best outcome (of all the other possible outcomes) that is given up because of that decision. Unless otherwise specified, when economists say "cost," they mean opportunity cost —that is, the highest valued alternative that must be sacrificed to attain something or otherwise satisfy a want. For example, the opportunity cost of a spur-of-the-moment decision to go to the movies Tuesday afternoon instead of going in to work is not just the six dollars for the ticket plus the gasoline and wear and tear on the car to get there. It also includes (at least) the four hours' wages not earned, diminished prospects for being promoted at work, and possibly such additional consequences as future hostility from co-workers who had to take up the slack, unpleasant feelings of guilt or shame, and so on. In a more extreme vein, the opportunity cost of committing suicide is not simply the money outlay for the necessary equipment, but rather the value of the total range of future satisfactions one might otherwise be able to achieve.

Transaction Costs

The costs other than the money price that are incurred in trading goods or services. Before a particular mutually beneficial trade can take place, at least one party must figure out that there may be someone with which such a trade is potentially possible, search out one or more such possible trade partners, inform him/them of the opportunity, and negotiate the terms of the exchange. All of these activities involve opportunity costs in terms of time, energy and money. If the terms of the trade are to be more complicated than simple "cash on the barrelhead" (for example, if the agreement involves such complications as payment in installments, prepayment for future delivery, warranties or guarantees for quality, provision for future maintenance and service, options for additional future purchases at a guaranteed price, etc.), negotiations for such a detailed contract may itself be prolonged and very costly in terms of time, travel expenses, lawyers' fees, and so on. After a trade has been agreed upon, there may also be significant costs involved in monitoring or policing the other party to make sure he is honoring the terms of the agreement (and, if he is not, to take appropriate legal or other actions to make him do so). These are the main sorts of transaction costs, then: search and information costs, bargaining and decision costs, policing and enforcement costs.

Elementary versions of economic theorizing often make the simplifying assumption that information and other transaction costs are zero (and, indeed, in a generally law-abiding society with a stable money system, cheap transportation and cheap communications, they are often pretty negligible). But realism nevertheless demands that we keep in mind the fact that the benefits to the participants in an exchange have to be high enough to cover their transaction costs if the trade is to take place at all. Indeed, many otherwise mutually advantageous trades do not take place because of the very high transaction costs that would be involved. High transaction costs are very often at the root of the problems discussed under the heading of externalities, especially in those situations where the external costs or benefits accrue to very large numbers of third parties and therefore a contractual agreement to internalize the externality is extremely costly to negotiate.

Externality

A situation in which the private costs or benefits to the producers or purchasers of a good or service differs from the total social costs or benefits entailed in its production and consumption. An externality exists whenever one individual's actions affect the well-being of another individual —whether for the better or for the worse —in ways that need not be paid for according to the existing definition of property rights in the society. An "external diseconomy," "external cost" or "negative externality" results when part of the cost of producing a good or service is born by a firm or household other than the producer or purchaser. An "external economy," "external benefit," or "positive externality" results when part of the benefit of producing or consuming a good or service accrues to a firm or household other than that which produces or purchases it. Example: If one neighbor decides to repaint his house and spruce up his yard so he can get a better price when selling it, he also at the same time is slightly improving the market value of other houses in the neighborhood, creating a "positive externality" benefitting his neighbors.

On the other hand, another neighbor who is a grade-A slob and lets the external appearance of his house run down creates a "negative externality" by depressing the attractiveness and thus the market value of the whole neighborhood.

Externalities of either the "positive" or the "negative" sort create a problem for the effective functioning of the market to maximize the total utility of the society. The "external" portions of the costs and benefits of producing a good will not be factored into its supply and demand functions because rational profit-maximizing buyers and sellers do not take into account costs and benefits they do not have to bear. Hence a portion of the costs or benefits will not be reflected in determining the market equilibrium prices and quantities of the good involved. The price of the good or service producing the externality will tend toward equality with the marginal personal cost to the producer and the marginal personal utility to the purchaser, rather than toward equality with the marginal social cost of production and the marginal social utility of consumption.

Thus, normal market incentives for the buyer and seller to maximize their personal utilities will lead to the over-or under-production of the commodity in question from the point of view of society as a whole, not the socially optimal level of production. Goods involving a positive externality will be "underproduced" from the point of view of society as a whole, while goods involving a negative externality will be "overproduced" from the point of view of society as a whole. In our example above, the individual homeowner pays all the cost of sprucing up his home but realizes only part of the benefits created —so consequently each homeowner will probably not keep his house up as well as he otherwise might if his neighbors could somehow be induced or required to pay him something for their share of the benefits from his labors.

Contracts often can be worked out as a means to "internalize" potential externalities because the existence of the externality implies there is at least the potential opportunity for mutual gains if the "third party" by-standers affected can offer compensation to the buyers or sellers in exchange for adjusting production or consumption levels of the good to a more acceptableble level. For example: If each homeowner in the neighborhood will agree to be legally responsible for maintaining a high common standard of upkeep in exchange for everyone else in the neighborhood also guaranteeing to do the same, then everyone can be financially better off than they would be without the agreement which is precisely why we observe such phenomena as homeowners associations and restrictive deed covenants.

Or other homeowners in the neighborhood might even band together and agree to finance jointly the entire cost of purchasing, fixing-up, and reselling some particularly run-down homestead in the neighborhood if the expected increase in their individual property values would be greater than their share of the cost of buying out their slovenly neighbor. Unfortunately, where externalities affect very large numbers of third parties (but only to a relatively minor degree in each case), the transaction costs of negotiating such many-sided contracts among them all may often be so large as to make this contractual solution impractical.

Where the transaction costs to arrive at contractual solutions to "externality" problems are prohibitively high, complex modern societies normally provide "second best" remedies to private persons through the courts. Nearly the whole area of "tort" law (including especially law suits for "nuisance" and for "negligence") deals with externality problems in one way or another. People adversely affected by other people's activities may go to court and sue them in an effort to obtain an award of financial compensation for the damages and/or a court injunction requiring their obnoxious neighbors to change their ways in the future.

Government regulations or tax policies are often justified to the public as a means of "correcting" the outcome of the market for goods involving especially sizable externalities, especially negative externalities.

The government might, for example, place a special tax or licensing fee on the production (or purchase) of a good or service believed to involve significant negative externalities, with the size of the tax or fee to be determined by some estimate of the total costs being imposed on third parties.

The government charges would force the sellers (or the buyers) of the good or service to begin to start taking into account these external costs along with their own and would effectively shift the supply curve (or the demand curve) to the left, resulting in somewhat smaller quantities of the good being sold at a somewhat higher price in the new equilibrium after inauguration of the tax—and thus, somewhat fewer costs will be imposed on third parties. (But note that it is the government that gets to keep the money, not the unfortunate bystanders still suffering the damage!)

In the case of a good or service involving a positive externality, government might cope in an analogous fashion by offering to pay subsidies to the producers or consumers of the good or service in question in order to encourage an appropriate expansion of production, or by using government's power to compel obedience without first negotiating mutually agreeable terms of cooperation among the affected parties, government might avoid the sizable transaction costs that would be involved in achieving a contractual solution to the problem by using its law-making or regulatory powers —for example, a city ordinance requiring all householders to keep their lawns mowed and their houses painted and forbidding them to allow trash or old automobile hulks to litter their front yards.

An important problem with the tax/subsidy approach to remedying externalities problems is, of course, that it may well be impossible or prohibitively expensive for the government to determine the size of the external costs or benefits involved and hence to determine even approximately what an appropriate tax or subsidy rate would be. More generally, there are bound to be transaction costs for all forms of government action, including regulatory or legal strategies for correcting externalities —costs of gathering information, costs of debating and making policy decisions, and costs of administration or policing once the policy has been made.

It will often be the case that the costs imposed on society by government taking corrective action would be larger than the decrease in welfare to society from the externalities that the government action is supposedly designed to cure. In any given case of externality, society may well be better off by simply leaving the externality in place, unless the third-party effects of the externality are truly massive. More precisely, government policy-makers need to devote their attention to the problem of lowering total transaction costs, rather than simply focussing on "fixing" this or that externality problem regardless of costs, if their intention is to maximize social welfare.

One area in which government has a great deal of control over the size of transactions costs throughout the economy is in the design and construction of the legal system.

The costs to private firms and individuals of enforcing their contracts and protecting their other property rights are largely determined by the government's arrangements for the legal system. If the legal system is costly and cumbersome and unpredictable, mutually beneficial trades may often not take place because of potentially high transactions costs involved in protecting and enforcing complex property rights and contracts once made. Moreover, negative externalities often arise because certain third party property rights have not been clearly defined or effectively enforced in some aspect of social life, and the law has mandated that social or common ownership will be imposed instead of conventional private ownership and control.

Excessive air and water pollution problems are often examples of such negative externalities from flaws in property law. For example, factory owners nearly always refrain from dumping waste products on neighboring privately-owned property for fear of the massive lawsuits they would surely lose —but they can often get by with dumping noxious waste products into "the public's air" or "the public's river" or "the public's ocean" without having to pay to secure the consent of those who later will be breathing or drinking or eating these poisons (or paying extra to remove them) precisely because the victims often have had no practical legal way of purchasing or selling a fully recognized exclusive property right in the portion of the air or rivers or the oceans (and their wildlife) on which they nevertheless depend.

TORT

Legal term. A wrongful or injurious act (other than breaking a contract) for which a civil suit may be brought in court by private persons. If the suit is successful, the court may award the victims cash compensation for damages, "punitive" damages above the actual cost of the injury in order to punish the defendent, and/or a court order banning any future repetitions of the kind of behavior giving rise to the suit.

For example, a householder might sue the owners of a nearby factory for creating excessive noise or pollution that interferes unreasonably with the householder's health or the peaceful enjoyment of his property. Tort law procedures are thus one of the principal mechanisms for defining and protecting property rights short of evoking criminal law and is an important governmental mechanism for trying to overcome the problem of negative externalities.

Judicial Activism

The view that the Supreme Court justices (and even other lower-ranking judges as well) can and should creatively (re)interpret the texts of the Constitution and the laws in order to serve the judges' own considered estimates of the vital needs of contemporary society when the elected "political" branches of the Federal government and/or the various state governments seem to them to be failing to meet these needs. On such a view, judges should not hesitate to go beyond their traditional role as interpreters of the Constitution and laws given to them by others in order to assume a role as independent policy makers or independent "trustees" on behalf of society.

Judicial Restraint

The view that the Supreme Court (and other lesser courts) should not read the judges' own philosophies or policy preferences into the constitution and laws and should whenever reasonably possible construe the law so as to avoid second guessing the policy decisions made by other governmental institutions such as Congress, the President and state governments within their constitutional spheres of authority.

On such a view, judges have no popular mandate to act as policy makers and should defer to the decisions of the elected "political" branches of the Federal government and of the states in matters of policy making so long as these policymakers stay within the limits of their powers as defined by the US Constitution and the constitutions of the several states.

Judicial Review

The power of the federal courts to overturn or limit the enforcement of Federal or state laws or regulations that the judges determine have violated the Federal constitution. The term also covers the power of the Federal courts to overturn or limit the enforcement of state laws or regulations that the judges determine are in direct conflict with Federal laws or regulations regarding a specific subject matter where the Federal constitution gives primary jurisdiction to the Federal government. Also the power of state courts to overturn or limit the enforcement of state laws or regulations that the judges determine have violated either the Federal constitution or the constitution of their own state.

Separation of Powers

One of the most important of the basic principles that guided the framers of the US Constitution in their design for America's future governance was the idea that the root cause and essence of tyrranical government is the concentration of control over all the powers and functions of government in the hands of the same individual or narrow political faction.

The corollary the Framers drew from this was the separation of powers principle: that free popular government can best be sustained by dividing the various powers and functions of government among separate and relatively independent governmental institutions whose officials would be selected at different intervals and through different procedures by somewhat different constituencies so as to make it unlikely that the same small faction could gain control of them all at the same time.

Thus, in the American federal republic the Framers designed, "the power surrendered by the people is first divided between two distinct governments the Federal government and the governments of the several states, and then the portion allotted to each subdivided among distinct and separate departments the executive, the legislative, and the judicial."

The idea that concentrated political power is a mortal danger to civil liberties and popular rights remains to this day one of the most persistent and characteristic features of American ideologies and popular thinking about politics. In comparison with other advanced industrial countries, the United States possesses one of the most complex governmental structures and perhaps the most broadly diffused distribution of governmental authority among independent agencies. Not only do American governmental arrangements still allocate power to separate executive, legislative and judicial branches at both the state and federal levels, but they also feature a great variety of forms of relatively autonomous and geographically overlapping governmental bodies at the local level —including not only general purpose county and municipal governments but also a wide variety of functionally specialized mini-governments such as elected district school boards, flood control district boards, water resource planning boards, transit authority boards and the like.

Autocracy

A system of government in which supreme political power to direct all the activities of the state is concentrated in the hands of one person, whose decisions are subject to neither external legal restraints nor regularized mechanisms of popular control (except perhaps for the implicit threat of coup d'etat or mass insurrection).

Dictatorship

Government by a single person (or group) whose discretion in using the powers and resources of the state is unrestrained by any fixed legal or constitutional rules and who is (are) in no effective way held responsible to the general population or their elected representatives.

Republic

Originally, any form of government not headed by an hereditary monarch. In modern American usage, the term usually refers more specifically to a form of government (a.k.a. "representative democracy") in which ultimate political power is theoretically vested in the people but in which popular control is exercised only intermittently and indirectly through the popular election of government officials and/or delegates to a legislative assembly rather than directly through frequent mass assemblies or legislation by referendum.

Democracy

A system of government in which effective political power is vested in the people.

In older usage (for example, in the writings of the classical Greek and Roman philosophers or in the Federalist Papers), the term was reserved exclusively for governmental systems in which the populace exercised this power directly through general assemblies or referenda to decide the most important questions of law or policy.

In more contemporary usage, the term has been broadened to include also what the American Founding Fathers called a republic—a governmental system in which the power of the people is normally exercised only indirectly, through freely elected representatives who are supposed to make government decisions according to the popular will, or at least according to the supposed values and interests of the population.

Oligarchy

Any system of government in which virtually all political power is held by a very small number of wealthy but otherwise unmeritorious people who shape public policy primarily to benefit themselves financially through direct subsidies to their agricultural estates or business firms, lucrative government contracts, and protectionist measures aimed at damaging their economic competitors -while displaying little or no concern for the broader interests of the rest of the citizenry.

"Oligarchy" is also used as a collective term to denote all the individual members of the small corrupt ruling group in such a system. The term always has a negative or derogatory connotation in both contemporary and classical usage, in contrast to aristocracy (which sometimes has a derogatory connotation in modern usage, but never in classical).

Elite (elitist) Theory

The theoretical view held by many social scientists which holds that American politics is best understood through the generalization that nearly all political power is held by a relatively small and wealthy group of people sharing similar values and interests and mostly coming from relatively similar privileged backgrounds.

Most of the top leaders in all or nearly all key sectors of society are seen as recruited from this same social group, and elite theorists emphasize the degree to which interlocking corporate and foundation directorates, old school ties and frequent social interaction tend to link together and facilitate coordination between the top leaders in business, government, civic organizations, educational and cultural establishments and the mass media.

This "power elite" can effectively dictate the main goals (if not always the practical means and details) for all really important government policy making (as well as dominate the activities of the major mass media and educational/cultural organizations in society) by virtue of their control over the economic resources of the major business and financial organizations in the country. Their power is seen as based most fundamentally on their personal economic resources and especially on their positions within the top management of the big corporations, and does not really depend upon their ability to garner mass support through efforts to "represent" the interests of broader social groups.

Elitist theoreticians differ somewhat among themselves on such questions as how open the power elite is to "new blood," the exact degree of agreement or disagreement that usually prevails within its ranks, and the degree of genuine concern (or lack thereof) for the broader public welfare that enters into their choices of public policy goals, but all such theorists broadly share the notion that it is these few thousand "movers and shakers" who really run the country and determine the basic directions of public policy, certainly not the manipulated and powerless masses of ordinary voters choosing among candidates at election time.

ARISTOCRACY

A privileged social class whose members possess disproportionately large shares of a society's wealth, social prestige, educational attainment and political influence, with these advantages having been acquired principally through gift or inheritance from a long line of similarly privileged and cultivated ancestors.

The term refers also to a form of government in which the state is effectively controlled by the members of such a class. The term tends to have a somewhat unsavory or derogatory connotation today in the light of democratic theories, but in classical political philosophy it meant rule by "the best people" of the society, who were expected to feel a paternalistic concern for the humbler members of the society that would keep them from ruling in a purely self-seeking fashion.

Pluralist Theory

The theoretical point of view held by many social scientists which holds that American politics is best understood through the generalization that power is relatively broadly (though unequally) distributed among many more or less organized interest groups in society that compete with one another to control public policy, with some groups tending to dominate in one or two issue areas or arenas of struggle while other groups and interests tend to dominate in other issue areas or arenas of struggle.

There tends to be little overlap between those leaders who participate most influentially in one policy area and those who are influential in other policy areas, and what linkage there is tends to come from popularly elected political officials (especially political executives and party leaders) who, by the nature of their jobs, must exercise leadership (or act as brokers) in a number of different policy areas.

There is no single, unified "power elite", but rather there are many competing power elites with differing backgrounds, values and bases of support in the broader society. Government tends to be depicted as a mechanism for mediating and compromising a constantly shifting balance between group interests rather than as an active innovator or imposer of policies upon society.

Interest Group

A group of people who share common traits, attitudes, beliefs, and/or objectives who have formed a formal organization to serve specific common interests of the membership. Examples of interest groups would include such disparate organizations as the Auburn Chamber of Commerce, the Society for the Prevention of Cruelty to Animals, the elementary school P.T.A., the Teamsters Union, the Southern Baptist Convention, the American Numismatics Association, the National Association for the Advancement of Colored People, the Brangus Breeders Association, the American Civil Liberties Union, the Cosa Nostra, and the Benevolent Order of Elks.

Interest groups typically have formal admission to membership, dues, elected officers, by-laws and regular meetings, and they often provide information and regular opportunities for communication through newsletters or magazines, sponsor recreational or educational activities, organize volunteer public service projects, make deals for group discounts or group insurance and so on. Larger interest group organizations may have full-time paid officers or professional staff to manage and to supplement the efforts of member-volunteers in furthering the work of the organization.

Many interest groups at least occasionally engage in some form of lobbying or other political activities with respect to issues that touch directly on the common interests that are the organization's reason for being —for example, the PTA may organize support for a bond issue election to pay for erecting a new school building. Some interest groups have political activity as their principal or only reason for being in the first place. Interest groups that exist primarily for exerting political influence as a means of affecting government policies or legislation are often referred to by the narrower term pressure groups.

Since more and more activities have become politicized with the expansion of the scope of activities of the government in the 20th century, more and more interest groups find themselves drawn into politics to protect or promote the interests of their membership, and the distinction in usage between the terms interest group and pressure group has accordingly become less significant in ordinary language.

Political Party

An organized group that has as its fundamental aim the attainment of political power and public office for its designated leaders. Usually, a political party will advertise a common commitment by its leaders and its membership to a set of political, social, economic and/or cultural values (an "ideology") that distinguish it from other political parties and which supposedly provide the basis for the policies the party proposes to implement or maintain through its members who obtain public office.

A political party differs from a pressure group in that a pressure group is primarily interested in influencing whatever government officials actually happen to be in office rather than in attaining office for its own leaders, and accordingly interest groups do not normally put forward candidates for public office under their own name (although they may sometimes endorse particular candidates put forward by party organizations).

In a democracy, political parties primarily function as agencies for recruiting suitable candidates to run for elective office and for organizing and conducting election campaigns. They may also become important in selecting candidates for appointive political office when winning the election has provided the party's leaders with power to appoint new officials to the cabinet and other top policy-making positions in the government bureaucracy. Political parties may also have another function as vehicles for coordinating the day to day activities and policy decisions of their elected and appointed office-holders so as to fulfill the party's policy platform, as for example, through an organized party caucus and a full-time party leadership machinery in the parliament or other legislative assembly.

However, unless the national party organization is in a good position to reward its members for "voting the party line" after they have been elected to office or to punish them for failing to support the party platform, the party organization's preferences may often not be the most important influence on the policy decisions made by its supposed representatives.

In the United States, neither the Democrat nor the Republican national convention (nor their standing national committees) have the power to deny renomination to their parties' uncooperative representatives in Congress so long as they can win renomination in local party primaries or party conventions back home in their states or districts.

The national party organizations' financial contributions to the campaign expenses of Congressional candidates (and usually those of state and local party organizations as well) tend to account for only a rather small proportion of what candidates need to be re-elected, so the party leaderships' financial leverage over their parties' office holders tends to be quite limited as well.

The dominant role of "seniority" in guaranteeing individual committee assignments and personal influence in the House and the Senate, as well as the fact that the House and Senate party leaderships are elected by their own House and Senate party caucuses rather than appointed by the national party organization, considerably insulate "non-conformist" representatives from retaliation by their national party organizations.

Fascism

A class of political ideologies (and historical political regimes) that takes its name from the movement led by Benito Mussolini that took power in Italy in 1922. Mussolini's ideas and practices directly and indirectly influenced political movements in Germany (especially the Nazi Party), Spain (Franco's Falange Party), France, Argentina, and many other European and non-European countries right up to the present day. The different "fascist" movements and regimes have varied considerably in their specific goals and practices, but they are usually said to be characterized by several common features:

1. Militant nationalism, proclaiming the racial and cultural superiority of the dominant ethnic group and asserting that group's inherent right to a special dominant position over other peoples in both the domestic and the international order
2. The adulation of a single charismatic national leader said to possess near superhuman abilities and to be the truest representation of the ideals of the national culture, whose will should therefore literally be law
3. Emphasis on the absolute necessity of complete national unity, which is said to require a very powerful and disciplined state organization (especially an extensive secret police and censorship apparatus), unlimited by constitutional restrictions or legal requirements and under the absolute domination of the leader and his political movement or party
4. Militant anti-Communism coupled with the belief in an extreme and imminent threat to national security from powerful and determined Communist forces both inside and outside the country
5. Contempt for democratic socialism, democratic capitalism, liberalism, and all forms of individualism as weak, degenerate, divisive and ineffective ideologies leading only to mediocrity or national suicide
6. Glorification of physical strength, fanatical personal loyalty to the leader, and general combat-readiness as the ultimate personal virtues
7. A sophisticated apparatus for systematically propagandizing the population into accepting these values and ideas through skilled manipulation of the mass media, which are totally monopolized by the regime once the movement comes to power
8. A propensity toward pursuing a militaristic and aggressive foreign policy

9. Strict regulation and control of the economy by the regime through some form of corporatist economic planning in which the legal forms of private ownership of industry are nominally preserved but in which both workers and capitalists are obliged to submit their plans and objectives to the most detailed state regulation and extensive wage and price controls, which are designed to insure the priority of the political leadership's objectives over the private economic interests of the citizenry. Therefore under fascism most of the more important markets are allowed to operate only in a non-competitive, cartelized, and governmentally "rigged" fashion.

TOTALITARIANISM

Domination by a single, like-minded governing elite of all (or virtually all) organized political, economic, social and cultural activities in a country by means of a single-party monopoly of power, police repression not only of all forms of dissent and opposition but also of all forms of independent private organizations as such, rigorous censorship of the mass media, centralized state planning and administration of the economy, and pervasive propaganda to inculcate the principles of the obligatory official ideology.

Totalitarian states differ from traditional dictatorships or despotisms primarily with respect to the broader ("total") scope of human behavior that the authorities seek to regulate in detail and with respect to their much more effective control mechanisms made possible by exploiting twentieth century breakthroughs in rapid communication and transportation, scientific psychology, pervasive mass media, surveillance technology, electronic information retrieval, and so on. The term is commonly applied both to fascist regimes and communist regimes, and occasionally by extension to other exotic cults, movements or regimes with ambitions for total control such as those led by various sorts of religious fanatics like the Rev. Jim Jones or the Ayatollah Khomeini.

Civil Rights, Civil Liberties

The rights of every citizen to freedom of thought, freedom of conscience, freedom of expression, freedom of movement, freedom to enjoy privacy and autonomy in the management of one's personal affairs, freedom of private individuals to associate voluntarily and to form organizations for pursuing common purposes, and freedom to participate politically in ways that do not infringe upon the similar rights of others. Although the two terms overlap considerably in ordinary usage (and are often difficult to distinguish in concrete instances), the term civil liberties generally refers more specifically to the protection of the individual's rights to form and express his or her own preferences or convictions and to act freely upon them in the private sphere without undue or intrusive interference by the government, while the term civil rights emphasizes more specifically the individual's rights as a citizen to participate freely and equally in politics and public affairs in order actively to promote his/her preferred public policy alternatives through lobbying policy-makers and/or through personal participation in the electoral process. Thus, civil liberties may be seen as the logical correlates of the goal of limited government, while civil rights are the logical correlates of the goal of popular or democratic government.

Liberalism

1. A 19th century political viewpoint or ideology associated with strong support for a broad interpretation of civil liberties for freedom of expression and religious toleration, for widespread popular participation in the political process, and for the repeal of protectionist legal restrictions inhibiting the operation of a capitalist free market economy.
2. In the 20th century US, the term has come to describe an ideology with similar views on civil liberties and personal freedom issues but now supporting a much stronger role for government in regulating and manipulating the private economy and providing public support for the economically and socially disadvantaged, though still stopping well short of full socialism.

In Europe, the term liberalism is still used more in its 19th century sense, and European liberals are rather more respectful of the values of the free market than their American namesakes, whose views sometimes more closely resemble those of Europeans styling themselves as social democrats.

Libertarianism

A contemporary 20th century political viewpoint or ideology derived largely from 19th century liberalism, holding that any legitimate government should be small and should play only the most minimal possible role in economic, social and cultural life, with social relationships to be regulated as much as possible by voluntary contracts and generally accepted custom and as little as possible by statute law.

In other words, libertarians believe that the individual should be as free as is practically feasible from government restraint and regulation in both the economic and non-economic aspects of life.

Thus, libertarians endorse stricter respect for private property rights, the establishment of a more laissez-faire laissez-faire capitalist economic system, rigorous separation of church and state, and greater respect for individual rights to freedom of expression and freedom of choice in personal lifestyles.

They oppose government programs for the redistribution of income, the inculcation of "politically correct" values through government schools and propaganda outlets, all forms of government-imposed censorship, the imposition of criminal penalties for the commission of "victimless crimes," and in general all forms of social, economic or cultural "engineering" by the government.

Laissez-faire

Literally, French for "Let do." The classical liberal (and modern libertarian) doctrine that the economic affairs of society are best guided by the free and autonomous decisions of individuals in the marketplace, to the near exclusion of government interference in economic matters. That is, the doctrine that government should almost always leave people alone and let them do as they please, so long as they respect the personal and property rights of others.

Welfare State

A state whose government devotes a very large proportion of its activities and expenditures to the direct provision of personal benefits to be consumed by qualifying individuals or families (as contrasted with such more traditional and less individually divisible government activities as national defense, law enforcement, controlling the money supply, economic regulation, maintaining transportation and communications nets, administering the public lands, etc.).

Welfare benefits to individuals may be in the form either of bureaucratically supplied professional services of government employees or in the form of government-issued stipends or allowances or subsidies (transfer payments) to help qualifying households pay for general subsistence or for specific categories of state-favored expenses (merit goods). Examples of such social welfare programs would include old age and disability pensions, unemployment benefits, aid to families with dependent children, income supplements for the poor, public housing and housing vouchers, health care provided in state hospitals or clinics and reimbursement for the costs of privately-provided health care, government-funded drug abuse rehabilitation programs, food stamps, public education and child care, etc.

Advocacy of extensive "welfare state" programs was at first associated mainly with socialist movements, but in most Western industrial societies today many welfare state programs are endorsed as well by non-socialist parties that nevertheless still continue to reject the socialists' traditional demands for much more extensive state ownership, state planning, and state administration of industry and commerce.

3

ORGANS OF THE GOVERNMENT

The branch of the social sciences that is primarily concerned with analyzing and explaining the functioning of political institutions (especially governmental institutions) as well as the political behavior of individuals, groups and organizations in their efforts to influence or resist the decisions and policies of government.

Whenever a group of people collectively decide about an issue the result does not only depend on the individual group members' opinions, but also, on the decision rule used. Different decision rules can thus give different results even if the group members' opinions about the issue do not vary. One aspect of this relationship, namely the purely formal one, is quite obvious. Let us, for instance, assume that 60 % of a group's members are in favor of a certain proposal.

If so, and if the group members just vote their minds, the proposal will pass if only a simple majority is required, but it will be refuted if a qualified majority of say 75 % is required. Apart from this formal aspect there is however another aspect which may be important, namely that decision rules affect more of the group members' behavior than just their voting. The rules may for instance affect the extent to which the individuals organize in various ways, their tendency to behave strategically, and so forth. The distinction made here is, by the way, the same one as made by Maurice Duverger (1964, p 224) when he discusses in particular electoral laws, namely the one between a "mechanical factor and a psychological factor". Duverger's distinction thus has a far wider application than he originally intended. Now, a democratic constitution can be considered as a decision rule, or rather as a system of such rules, and the population of a country as a decision making group. Within such a perspective the question about the constitution's impact on the resulting decisions obviously becomes pertinent. Do different kinds of constitutions, one may ask, give significantly different results, with different welfare effects and, if so, which are the differences? Is, for example, just to mention one important question, a society's public sector more likely to expand with one type of constitution than with another one? It is this kind of questions which the theory presented here deals with. When developing that theory it will obviously be important to consider not only "mechanical factors" but to a large extent also "psychological factors" in Duverger's sense.

The questions mentioned can also be phrased in a somewhat different manner. In all societies the citizens have individual opinions about various issues and some of these issues are, in fact, decided politically. The political decisions can thus be considered as aggregations of the individual opinions, but such aggregations can be related to the pattern of individual opinions in many different ways. It is therefore natural to ask about the relation between the original set of individual opinions and the emerging final political decisions, and about the constitution's impact on this relation. Questions like this have indeed been raised now and then.

Quite some time ago William Niskanen (1971, p 27) thus wrote that "The relation between the population's demands and the collective organization's expressed demands in a particular institutional setting is one of the more important problems of political science -and one, incidentally, that is not well understood." Some ten years later Bingham Powell (1982, p 186) wrote in a similar vein that "From the point of view of democratic process, it is important that the government be doing what citizens desire and that it be responsive to their changes in preference.... The analysis and comparison of such policy responsiveness is an extremely difficult problem, worth several books in its own right." Melvin Hinich and Michael Munger (1994, p 102), somewhat later still, stress the same issue again when writing that "The fundamental challenge to the development of a scientifically valid theory of electoral competition in a democratic society is to link the perceptions and preferences of voters on political factors that they care about with the actions of candidates before, during, and after an election." These problems, I think, are still about as unsolved as when Niskanen, Powell and Hinich & Munger expressed their concerns. The theory presented here aims at bringing them closer to a solution.

- My main concern is thus the impact of democratic constitutions of various types on the nature of the decisions taken, and on the welfare effects of those decisions. In the following I will present a number of hypotheses about these matters.
- In addition to this I am however also interested in differences in the politics, or political life, of different countries that are attributable to constitutional differences. The main reason for this interest is my contention that it is necessary, or at least highly helpful, to start by deducing differences in the political life, as an intermediary, in order to be able to deduce differences in the resulting decisions. This, however, does not preclude that the inferences about the political life may be interesting in their own right as well. Accordingly I will also present a number of hypotheses about these relationships.

Finally I should add that I will only treat constitutions that exist or have existed. Theoretically possible constitutions are not treated if they do not exist, however interesting some such constitutions may seem.

NATURE OF THE THEORY

The theory presented here, although verbal rather than formalized, aims at being a logical, deductive system. In essence this means that a number of propositions are logically derived from a limited set of basic propositions, which thus are used as axioms. Ultimately and ideally all propositions should, of course, be empirically tested. If this leads to verification that is good so far, if not that is a problem for the theory. Here, in this context, the theory should however rather be tested for logical consistency. It is of utmost importance that propositions which are presented as logical consequences of other more basic propositions really are so. To the extent that this is not case the theory, considered as theory, is a failure. If the theory does not form a logical system in the sense described it just is not a theory.

There are, I think, at least two dangerous pitfalls involved in an undertaking like this one. The first is the risk of presenting, without noticing it, circular arguments. The other is the risk of mistaking common knowledge of real matters for logical conclusions. In what follows I have, at my best, tried to be aware of these pitfalls, but I am not sure that I have succeeded in avoiding them everywhere.

At last it should be emphasized that a theory is more than an instrument for producing hypotheses. Even if it were possible, somehow, to produce hypotheses for empirical testing by other means than from a theory, the theory will still always be a necessary part of a scientific enterprise. The reason is that the logical order, and by that the predictive and explanatory power, which a theory brings to a set of empirical findings cannot be achieved in any other way. In this sense theory supports empirical results as much as empiricism supports theory. Perhaps it was something like this which the great British astronomer and physicist Arthur Stanley Eddington (1882-1944) had in mind when saying that "One should never believe any experiment until it has been confirmed by theory" (Quoted by Steven Weinberg, 1993, p 101).

LEGAL AND INFLUENTIAL POWER

In a democracy ruled by law the legally established institutions of the state, such as the legislature and the executive, have, in large and specified areas such as lawmaking, power in a very different sense than other actors in the community. That it is so is very important for a variety of reasons. In particular, in this context, it is this fact which makes possible the conception of a theory about constitutions and their effects. If legislatures and executives had not had power of a particular kind, which we may call legal power, such a theory had hardly been possible.

An important characteristic of the legal power is that it is specified by legally binding rules. If, for example, the constitution says that a majority of the legislature is entitled to institute laws of a certain kind, and a majority in fact decides to institute a law of that kind, then such a law really comes into existence. In that sense, and in this case, a majority in the legislature has all the power needed for instituting laws of the kind intended. Similarly a constitution usually stipulates the decisions or actions which can be undertaken by the executive alone, by the legislature alone, by the legislature and the executive in combination, and so on. All the power needed for these decisions is thus present in the various public institutions and the exact distribution of that power is spelled out in the constitution.

This, to be sure, does not preclude that public institutions can be influenced by other actors in the society. When for example the individual members of the legislature consider whether they, in their voting, shall favor or oppose a particular law, they are likely to take the opinions of people in their constituencies, of sponsors, of lobbying groups, and so on, into account. Of course I am not denying this. What I am saying is that if a majority of the legislature, if that is what is required by the constitution, votes in favor of a proposed law, then the proposal passes, otherwise not, independently of what lobbyists, sponsors and common voters think. Or, in other words, lobbyists, etc., cannot affect things in any other way than by influencing the relevant members of the legal public power structure. All analysis of power in a community ruled by law therefore has to start with a careful delineation of the legal power as determined by the constitution.

This principle of separating the legal power, and starting with it as a prerequisite for all other discussions about power, is at the same time so important and so overlooked, that it deserves a name of its own, for example the legalistic principle.

In order to clarify things further it is expedient to distinguish between different kinds of legal power. So far I have given examples of what might be called decision-making power. Actors who are explicitly mentioned in the decision rules enjoy that kind of power. In addition to this it is however also important to emphasize the importance of procedural power. Some actors may for example be authorized, formally, to make proposals to the decision-makers, and others may be entitled, again formally, to express their opinions about proposals. These kinds of rights related to the procedure do also constitute power, and since they are prescribed in the constitution they are examples of legal power. Some individuals have, of course, both decision-making power and procedural power.

The positions held by individuals in a legal power structure may be called legal power positions. In democracies, at the national level, there are two types of legal power positions which are particularly important, namely the positions as legislators in the legislature, and the positions in the executive. For countries which have a constitutional court, the positions as judges in those courts should be added to the legal power positions. All of these positions are associated with decision-making power. In addition, it is also common that some persons, for example heads of executives, speakers in the legislature, and chairmen of the committees in the legislature, have a considerable amount of procedural power. The constitutional rules often warrant certain competences to the incumbents of these positions.

It is important that power basically is attached to, or linked to, positions rather than to persons. Within such a structure a person thus has power only because he or she has been appointed to a certain position, and only for the period prescribed by the rules. This contrasts sharply to systems in which persons have power because they belong to a certain family, or because they have taken it, for example by violent means, and where they may keep that power for life, unless it is taken away from them by somebody else. In such systems the power is linked to a person, or a family, rather than to a position in a legal structure. This principle of linking power to positions, rather than to persons, is obviously immensely important for the functioning of democracy and for the legal security in a society.

Now, as I have already indicated, the holders of the legal power positions can, of course, be influenced, or even controlled, by outsiders such as for example unions, or big firms, or even influential individuals. Those influencing the holders of the legal power thus also have a kind of power, which we can call power of influence or influential power. Such power may be weak and partial, but it may also be complete in the sense that whenever the holder of influential power tells the holder of legal power to behave in a certain way, for example to vote in a specified manner, the holder of legal power does so. Even in this last extreme case the distinction between legal and influential power, and the existence of both, is still fundamental. This is so since the holder of influential power, according to our assumptions, can act only by influencing the holder of legal power he cannot himself do what the holder of legal power can do.

DECISIVE AND BLOCKING POWER

In part 2 I made a distinction between decision-making power and procedural power. Here, as a preparation for the subsequent discussion, I will continue by splitting decision-making power into the two concepts of decisive and blocking power.

For illustrating I will assume, as a very simple example, that we have a single decision making group consisting of 100 persons, and that a majority of 3/4 is required for an affirmative decision. If so, any set of 75 persons, or more, can make a proposal pass. Such a set is thus decisive, and it holds decisive power. Conversely any set of 26 persons, or more, can block the passage of a proposal -such a set is consequently blocking and it possesses blocking power. The concepts can also be described by saying that a decisive set is needed for changing the status quo, while a blocking set is enough for hindering a change of the status quo.

These concepts can, of course, also be used in more elaborated situations. Here we are for instance usually considering complexes including both an executive and a legislature, the latter possibly having two houses. In such situations it is always possible to describe exactly which composition a set must have in order to be decisive, and in order to be blocking. We just have to know the decision-rules exactly.

It is often easier to form a blocking set than a decisive one. Such, for instance, was the case in the example above, where a qualified majority was stipulated: 75 persons were required for dictating a decision whereas 26 persons were enough for blocking it. The same is true in a number of situations of interest for the discussion here. It is for instance true if there are two houses in the legislature, and a proposal, in order to pass, must be affirmed in both houses, even if only with a simple majority in each house. If so a majority in either house is enough for blocking a proposal, whereas a majority in each house is required for making it pass. Another example is a presidential system in which the affirmation of both the president and the legislature is required, even if there is only one house, and even if only a simple majority in the house is required. Obviously, in such a case, the president alone, or a majority in the legislature alone, is enough for blocking a proposal, whereas the acceptance of both the president and a majority in the legislature is needed for changing the status quo. There are, however, also situations, in which it is as difficult to form a blocking set as a decisive one. Consider for example a situation in which a simple majority in a one house legislature is enough for passing a proposal. In such a case the same kind of set, that is a simple majority, is obviously also needed for blocking the proposal.

The distinction between decisive and blocking sets is, of course, commonplace in social choice theory. Now and then it also appears in texts primarily devoted to constitutional problems. One example is Shugart & Mainwaring (1997, p 41) who call the power to change the status quo proactive power, and the power to block changes of the status quo reactive power. The concepts of positive and negative power may also be used.

THE LEGALISTIC PRINCIPLE DISREGARDED: EXAMPLES

I wrote in part 2 that the legalistic principle is often overlooked in political science, and a few examples may therefore be in order. The principle is obviously disregarded when the power of various actors, whether they belong to the legal decision-making system or not, is treated on equal terms.

The first example of this kind of disregard is taken from V. O. Key, Jr. He writes as follows about the "American democratic order" (1964, p 6 f): "Actual authority tends to be dispersed and exercised not solely by governmental officials but also by private individuals and groups within the society.... On one matter the President's decision may govern; on another, the wishes of the heads of a half-dozen industrial corporations will prevail; on a third, organized labor or agriculture will win the day; and on still another, a congressionally negotiated compromise completely satisfactory to none of the contenders may settle the matter. Even the journalists may cast the deciding vote on some issues."

Another, very recent, example is taken from Peter Esaiasson and Sören Holmberg. In their book "Representation from above" about the Swedish democracy they devote a whole chapter to "Power in Society" (1996, chapter 9).

There they discuss the power of 8 groups and institutions in exactly the same manner, and by using, for all groups, exactly the same terms. The groups or institutions are "The Cabinet", "Mass Media", "Trade Unions (LO)", "Parliament", "Civil Servants", "Employer Organisation (SAF)", "Private Business", and "The Electorate". This, again, constitutes a clear disregard of the legalistic principle.

Role of Political Parties

When exemplifying influential power in part 2 I mentioned unions, firms, and individuals, but not political parties. The reason is that political parties, although they certainly have influential power, are very special, or even unique, organizations. Political parties play a fundamental role in the theory presented here.

What makes the political parties special and unique is that they are directly engaged in the competition for the legal power positions, and there are several expressions of this basic contention in the political science literature. Schattschneider, for instance, wrote as follows (1942, p 35): "A political party is first of all an organized attempt to get power. Power is here defined as control of the government. That is the objective of party organization. The fact that the party aims at control of the government as a whole distingusihes it from pressure groups." A few lines later (p 36) Schattschneider adds that "Since control of a government is one of the most important things imaginable, it follows that a real party is one of the most significant organizations in society." Many years later Sartori (1976, p 63) wrote in a similar vein that "A party is any political group identified by an official label that presents at elections, and is capable of placing through elections..., candidates for public office". These conceptions of Schattschneider and Sartori correspond well to the party concept used here, and political parties are thus more directly attached to the legal power structure than any other type of organizations. Because of this role of political parties people holding legal power positions usually belong to a party, and are thereby also controlled by that party to some extent. This control can however vary considerably from being very strong to being quite weak. This is significant since the more control a party has over its representatives in the legal decision-making bodies, the more the party as such can be considered as an actor in its own right in the political game. This also means, in other words, that strong party discipline has the important effect of reducing the number of actors in the political game considerably.

Let us consider, as a theoretical extreme, a country in which the political parties are absolutely cohesive and disciplined. In such a case the party's control of its representatives in the executive and legislature is perfect. Whenever the party wants its representatives to behave in a certain way, for example to vote in a specific manner, they will do so. Although the representatives have all the legal power they are completely in the hands of the party with its overriding influential power. In such a situation it is quite reasonable to consider the party as a unitary actor. An illustrative example, which comes close to this extreme, is given by Key (1964, p 337) when he describes the old-fashioned machine organization of political parties in US cities as follows: "The classic machine took a clearly hierarchical form, with a boss at the head of an organization of workers held together by the spoils of politics and capable of determining the party's nominations and of exerting a mighty influence in elections as well. In its most fully developed form the urban machine became the government in that many major decisions, as well as minor matters, were decided by the party functionaries who managed their puppets in public office."

The other extreme, as theoretical as the former one, is a country in which there are no political parties at all. Such a country, it should first be noted, is perfectly possible since parties, although they are defined as organizations engaged in the political competition for positions in the legal structure, are nonetheless not necessary. A situation in which individuals compete for the legal power positions by themselves, without belonging to any organization, is perfectly thinkable. In such a situation there are obviously no party actors, but rather a considerable number of individual actors.

In reality we do perhaps not find any extremes like the ones just described but there are certainly cases approaching the one extreme or the other. Thus there are countries in which the parties are very well consolidated, cohesive and disciplined. There are also countries in which the parties are very loosely organized and which thus are rather close to the second extreme. There are also countries in the middle field between the two extremes. In the following I will present hypotheses about the constitutional conditions for these different patterns.

The observation that the influential power of political parties is of a special, interesting and consequential kind is certainly not new in the political science literature. In particular it has been noted that well consolidated political parties, at least to a large extent, may cancel or nullify the intended effects of constitutional rules. In his book Political Parties Maurice Duverger (1964, p 393 ff) has, for instance, a whole section on the subject where he writes, among other things, that "The degree of separation of powers is much more dependent on the party system than on the provisions of the Constitution. Thus the single party brings in its train a very close concentration of powers, even if the Constitution officially prescribes a marked separation: the party binds very closely together the various organs of government." This, of course, is a variation of the theme that the party structure is relevant for the functioning of the legal decision-making system.

The Party in the Legislature

In spite of their importance political parties are somewhat elusive and many-faced organizations. A first point to notice is that, although political parties appear and operate in all democracies, they are usually not highlighted in the constitutional texts. They may be mentioned, and their activities may also be regulated in various ways, but that is about all.

Thus, according to Sartori (1976, p 33), "(e)ven today, in most countries parties remain, juridically, private associations with no constitutional recognition. Among the few notable exceptions are the Bonn Fundamental Law and the French Constitution of 1958".

Another interesting exception, though negative in a sense, is the Austrian constitution in which the parties are mentioned mainly in the stipulation that the members of the constitutional court must not be party functionaries or employees (Müller, 1994, p 24). It is also interesting to quote Schlesinger (1991, p 10 f) writing that "The United States is unique among democracies in the extent to which it has sought to regulate and define party organization. ... In countries such as Great Britain or France ...parties have been free to organize as they see fit ...".

So, usually, the constitutions do not reveal the importance of the political parties. Still, the parties are important, and, furthermore, as will be outlined in the following, various constitutional elements play important roles in shaping the parties and the party-systems, and thereby also contribute in determining the exact roles played by the parties in the political process. Another important point is that political parties, since they work in both the legal decision-making structure and in society at large, and in a sense form links between these two worlds, have several appearances. V. O. Key has (1964, p 164), for instance, made distinctions between the party-in-the-electorate, the party-in-the-legislature, and the party-in-the-government.

- Using this terminology the kind of party I am mainly interested in here is the party-in-the-legislature. Thus, when I talk about cohesion and discipline of parties, I am primarily referring to the parties-in-the-legislature, and, in particular, I think about cohesion and discipline in voting.

THE NATURE OF THE POLITICAL PARTY

For the theory developed here it is enough, at least for a beginning, to state that there always are political parties in a democracy; that they are important; and that their organizational structures, and thereby their ways of acting, are significantly affected by various constitutional elements. Still it may be worthwhile, at least, to ask for the reason for the omnipresence of political parties. Why do political parties always appear?

A first comment to be made to this question is that parties may appear, or originate, in different contexts or arenas. Referring to the discussion in part 3.1 about the party-in-the-legislature and the party-in-the-electorate parties may, in fact, originate in the legislature or in the electorate. The distinction between these two kinds of origins is important and has been made, in particular, by Maurice Duverger (1964, p xxiii ff).

Having made that distinction we may however return to the question about why parties always appear, whether in the legislature or the electorate. This question has, in fact, considerable similarities with Ronald Coase's well-known question about firms. In his celebrated paper "The Nature of the Firm" he asked about the basic reasons for the existence of firms. He asked why markets, on which individuals freely operate, were not enough, and why it was advantageous also to have firms, whose inner operations are hierarchical and isolated from direct influences from the market. His answer was that the firm was advantageous since, and when, it entailed savings in transaction costs. Probably there is a similar rationale for the political party. But even so the exact and detailed answers, for parties originating in the electorate as well as for those originating in the legislature, are yet not formulated. The provision of those answers thus are important tasks still waiting for their fulfillment.

It may thus be a good idea to compare firms and parties but obviously there are not only similarities. One interesting difference has been highlighted by Harold Demsetz. According to him (1990) "a political party typically holds more stubbornly to its product mix than does a business firm". The reason is that the people active within a firm usually feel quite free to adjust the product as a means towards the end of profit maximizing. In a political party, on the contrary, the products of the party, that is its political ideas and its programme, and its candidates, are valuable in themselves for those working in the party, and therefore not likely to be basically changed in the efforts to get more votes. The products are, in Demsetz' words, laden with "amenity potential".

The Main Actor Concept

The theory presented here is strongly actor oriented. In particular the concept of main actor is important. A main actor is an actor operating in the legal system. An individual legislator may thus be a main actor, whereas a lobby group is just an actor. Things are however more complicated than this since a legislator is not necessarily a main actor, and also since a political party may be a main actor.

An individual holder of a legal power position is a main actor if he or she enjoys a significant amount of freedom in relation to his or her party. Such a person obviously has a capacity to act, in a real sense, on its own. It is for this reason, and since the person holds a legal power position, that I call such a person a main actor. Even political parties may however be main actors. If, for example, a party controls all its representatives in the legal structure, that party is a main actor (and the representatives are not main actors). The reason is that the party, in contrast to its representatives, enjoys a real freedom of its own. Obviously, however, a party need not necessarily control all its representatives, or none. Other patterns are quite conceivable. A party may, for instance, control some of its representatives, while some other ones may enjoy a considerable freedom. If so these latter representatives are main actors. As long as a party controls at least some of its representatives, to some extent, the party is however also a main actor, as the concept is used here.

- We thus have two types of main actors. An individual main actor is an individual who holds a legal power position

> and who, in that capacity, enjoys a substantial amount of individual freedom. A party main actor is a political party which is represented in the legal decision-making system, and which deprives at least one of its representatives there of a substantial amount of personal freedom and thus, to that extent, controls that individual.

A first obvious implication of this definition is that there is no rule saying "one main actor -one vote". A big party which controls all its representatives is for example a main actor with a lot of votes. Another implication is that the number of main actors will be big if the parties are weak and undisciplined, whereas the number will be small if the parties are cohesive and embracing in the sense of controlling all, or at least most, of their representatives. A third implication is that the voting result is known when the positions of all main actors on a particular issue, together with the decision rule, is known. Finally it should perhaps be said that a particular main actor may regularly happen to be a member of defeated minorities. A main actor is therefore not necessarily a powerful actor in this sense.

Main Types of Constitutions

In the preceding parts I have argued that a legal decision-making system's way of functioning to a large extent depends on its constellation of main actors, which in turn depends on the properties of the political parties. In the following I will furthermore show that some constitutional traits are important determinants of these properties. Thus we will see that it matters how the executive is appointed, and how the legislators are appointed.

There are two main methods for appointing the executive, the one used in parliamentary systems, the other one in presidential systems. According to the parliamentary method the people first elects the legislature, which, in turn, appoints the executive. In a pure parliamentary system the executive, furthermore, can remain in office only as long as it enjoys the support, or confidence, of a majority in the legislature. This requirement is often referred to as the parliamentary principle. According to the presidential method separate popular elections are held for appointing a president and, thereby, the rest of the executive. In a presidential country, there are thus two main types of popular elections, those for electing the executive and those for electing the legislature. As for methods for appointing the members of the legislature there are, again, essentially two types of methods. First there are the majoritarian methods using single-member constituencies and giving, in each constituency, the mandate to the candidate who, according to some set of rules, gets most votes. Second there are the proportional methods which use multi-member constituencies and distributes the mandates to the parties in proportion to their votes. Now, by combining the methods for appointing the executive, and the legislators, we get the following four types of constitutions.

- Parliamentary constitutions with proportional elections.
- Parliamentary constitutions with majoritarian elections.
- Presidential constitutions with proportional elections.
- Presidential constitutions with majoritarian elections.

This fourfold classification includes the main types of democratic constitutions dealt with in the theory presented here. The classification is thus of fundamental importance, and a few comments on it are in order.

First, the actual distribution of the different types of constitutions exhibits a discernible pattern. The main examples of parliamentary constitutions with proportionalism are found in Western Europe; parliamentarism combined with majoritarianism is characteristic for the United Kingdom and some other countries in the Commonwealth; presidentialism combined with proportionalism is mainly met with in Latin America; and finally, the main example of presidentialism combined with majoritarianism is the US.

Second, the classification is not completely exhaustive. In particular constitutions which simultaneously have elements of presidentialism and parliamentarism, as for example the French constitution, are not represented -although they are gaining popularity. I do however hope, and believe, that the classification is fruitful in spite of this deficiency. The reason is my contention that it is expedient to analyze the simple and clear-cut cases before turning to the more complex, mixed forms. Third, the fourfold classification of constitutions presented here is not totally absent in the political science literature. It is thus clearly indicated in for example Powell (1982) and Sartori (1994), and it is explicitly emphasized in Lijphart (1991). None of these authors do, however, stress the importance of the classification for the shaping of parties and party systems.

Majoritarian Elections

The plurality method, also called the first-past-the-post method, is used when the problem is to elect one member from each constituency, and it is the simplest method serving that purpose. The candidate which gets most votes, that is a plurality, wins. If for example candidate A gets 20 000 votes, candidate B 15 000 votes, candidate C 15 000 votes and candidate D 25 000 votes, then candidate D wins. The method has been criticized on the ground that a candidate who in reality enjoys only quite a weak support may be elected. Suppose, for instance, that all people who support A, or B, or C in the example above prefer anyone of these candidates to D. If so A, or B, or C would get 50 000 votes if put alone in a contest against D, who still would get just 25 0000 votes. D:s winning in the original example is thus, in a sense, due to the opposition's division.

Several methods have been designed in order to mitigate this problem and the double ballot method is one of them. As the name indicates the method stipulates the use of two ballots separated by some time, for example a week. If some candidate gets an absolute majority in the first ballot, then that candidate is elected. Otherwise there will be a second ballot, and in that second ballot plurality is enough for winning.

Illustrating with the same example as above, and assuming that the figures represent the result of the first ballot, we see that none of the four candidates A, B, C and D has an absolute majority. Therefore there will be a second ballot. What happens there is, however, impossible to predict without further assumptions. We may for example assume that the candidates B and C are politically rather close to each other, that both are somewhat distant from A, and that both are very hostile towards D. If so B and C may make the agreement that C shall withdraw from the second ballot and urge its supporters in the first ballot to vote for B in the second ballot. If they succeed with that A will get 20 000 votes in the second ballot, B 30 000 votes and D 25 000 votes. B thus gets a plurality and wins. There is a variant of the method, it should be mentioned, in which the second ballot is restricted to the two candidates with the highest number of votes in the first ballot, and thus it is ensured that the final winner gets an absolute majority of the votes. It is important to note that neither the plurality method, nor the double ballot method, presupposes any political parties. The candidates may be supported by, or even appointed by, parties, but they may, also, be free, independent individuals who, on their own, decide to compete. The methods work perfectly well in both cases.

Proportional Elections

Proportional methods are used when several representatives from each constituency are to be elected. They are motivated by a quest for proportional representation of existing political opinions, or fair representation as some would say. If, for example, there are 70 % socialists among the constituency's voters, and 30 % liberals, then the ambition is to elect representatives in the same proportions. Exact proportionality is not always possible but the larger the number of representatives from the constituency is, the easier it is, of course, to come close to that goal. From this point of view large, and consequently few, constituencies, is desirable. In the extreme the whole country may form one single constituency.

In principle the proportional methods are quite simple. Let us start by considering a method according to which the political parties, in each constituency, present lists with their candidates in sequence. Thus, on each party's list, there is a first candidate, a second candidate, and so on. The voters cast their votes on the parties, each voter voting for his or her favored party. The election result is thus, primarily, a distribution of votes on parties. Representatives are then, according to this method, taken from the parties' lists, in proportion to the number of votes they have got, starting, for each party, with its first candidate, and so on. Elections of this kind are usually called list elections. This general method may be varied, or complemented, in various of ways. In countries where the ideal is a very exact proportionalism it may thus be considered important to "correct", nation-wide, the perhaps somewhat erratic combined result of all the individual constituencies. Such a correction can be achieved by distributing a number of additional mandates in a proper way. In other countries it may, on the contrary, be considered desirable to make big parties' shares of the representatives somewhat bigger than their shares of the votes. This purpose may be achieved by using an appropriate formula, designed for the purpose, for the distribution of the mandates. In some countries it may also be considered expedient to discourage very small parties, which can be done by means of a threshold-rule of some kind.

Furthermore, it is sometimes considered desirable to give the voters a chance to express their feelings about particular candidates, for example by adding, or by erasing, names on the list of the party they are voting for. A candidate added, or erased, by a sufficient number of voters, may thus win, or lose, a place in the legislature in spite of the original list. Electoral systems like this may in fact be made completely independent of ordered lists of candidates. In Finland, for instance, the parties just nominate their candidates, without ordering them, and the voter then writes the name of one single candidate on his or her voting paper, which is blank from the beginning. Each vote thus becomes a vote both for a party and for a candidate. Within each party the candidates are then ordered according to the number of votes they have got, and each party becomes represented, from the top of the list determined by the voters and downwards, according to the number of votes it has got. This system thus gives the voters a very substantial influence over the composition, in terms of individuals, of the legislature.

But even if the proportional methods, as we have seen, can be varied in many ways, they all have one very important property in common, namely that they presuppose political parties. First the parties are needed for making the lists of candidates, or at least for nominating candidates. Second, and more basic, the very idea of proportionalism presupposes that there is something in the electorate, which can be proportionally represented in the legislature. It is the political parties which constitute that something. Proportional methods are therefore unthinkable without political parties.

Having said that it should however also be noted that there are electoral methods, which may be used in multi-member constituencies, and which do not presuppose parties. The single transferable vote method is an example. Certainly such methods are sometimes called proportional but, since there is nothing that is represented proportionally, that terminology is hardly appropriate.

Parliamentarism

The parliamentary principle, requiring that the executive enjoys a continous confidence from the legislature, may take slightly different forms. First there is a distinction between positive and negative parliamentarism, the former meaning that the executive must be actively supported by a majority of the legislature, the latter that it is enough for the executive not to be actively opposed by a majority of legislators. It may also be stipulated that the incumbent executive cannot be dismissed without the simultaneous appointment of a new one. This is usually referred to as a constructive vote of no confidence. The parliamentary principle can thus be varied within certain limits. For all of these varieties it is, however, for their proper functioning, of crucial importance that the political partygroups in the legislature are stable, centralised and cohesive.

This condition is, as far as I know, universally acknowledged. Some authors express it quite distinctly and I am not aware of anyone who objects. Sartori says (1994, p 94, his italics), for example, that "... parliamentary democracy cannot perform -in any of its varieties -unless it is served by parliamentary fit parties, that is to say, parties that have been socialized (by failure, duration, and appropriate incentives) into being relatively cohesive and/or disciplined bodies.... indeed, disciplined parties are a necessary condition for the 'working' of parliamentary systems."

But even if this is so it is hardly obvious why. The basic reason for the necessity of stable, disciplined, parties, is, I think, that the parliamentary confidence, in order to be reliable and lasting, cannot be anonymous. The confidence has to be expressed by a few stable and identifiable actors, which, in effect, means political parties. In such a case there are also substantial organisational links between the part of the legislature supporting the executive and the executive itself, which, of course, facilitates, the confidence problem. The relevant part of the legislature may even to some extent control the executive, should the need appear. All of this is, in fact, implicit in the concept fusion of power, which was introduced by Walter Bagehot (1826-77).

If, on the other hand, no political parties are present things become quite different. If, under such conditions, an executive gets a declaration of confidence from a majority of the assembly, that majority will necessarily be an ad hoc-majority which may perish at any moment, and because of any kind of dissatisfaction with the executive. This, in fact, means that the country really does not have an executive at all. Rather, the executive's functions are, in a sense, performed by ad hoc-majorities in the assembly, which is hardly in accordance with the ideas of parliamentarism.

In a parliamentary democracy it is thus important that political parties exist, and that they are stable, cohesive and disciplined enough, since otherwise a stable executive cannot be formed, and the system will not function as intended. This, by itself, does however not imply that such parties are likely to exist. There is no guarantee that a system, such as a parliamentarian one, automatically will function as intended. A system may obviously fail to work. What seems to be required therefore is that the properties which the parties acquire, when their functionaries and other supporters try to fulfil their ambitions, coincide with the properties required for the system's functioning. This may or may not be the case. I will return to this important topic in the following.

Here I will just finish by saying that the distinction between what parliamentarism requires for its functioning, and what in fact it brings about, is often disregarded. Peter Esaiasson, for instance, says (2000, p 51) that legislators in a parliamentary system may be looked upon "as more or less anonymous members of a cohesive party collective, and thus best analyzed as a group", and that the "main argument" for this position "of course, is that parliamentary systems require cohesive parties in order to function." Here, what is, and what is needed, is obvioulsy treated as one and the same thing. But there are also authors who honor the distinction. Michael Laver and Kenneth Shepsle thus write (1996, p 29 f, my italics) that "The effective operation of parliamentary democracy, in short, both depends upon and encourages disciplined behavior by political parties in the government formation process."

Presidentialism

Presidents can be appointed in popular elections in different ways. In essence, however, the whole country may, in a presidential election, be considered as one single-member constituency. The methods used are therefore usually variants of the plurality method or the double ballot method. When those methods are used there is, as we saw in part 5.1, and just considering the character of the method, no need for political parties at all, but still parties usually do play important roles. In part 5.3 we saw that parliamentary systems depend, for their proper functioning, on cohesive and disciplined parties. With presidential systems it is the other way round. There stable, cohesive parties, rather, are a problem since they may impede or block the proper decision-making. Such mechanisms will be further discussed when we come to the presidential systems in the following. The mechanisms, it should be noted, are observed by some political scientists. Sartori, for instance, remarks (1994, p 94, my italics) that in a presidential system "under conditions of divided government stalemate is avoided precisely by party indiscipline".

SIX HYPOTHESES ABOUT THE SHAPING OF PARTIES

In the preceding parts I have said that the constellation of main actors is dependent on the number of political parties, and their discipline and cohesion, in particular as manifested by the voting patterns in the legislature. Accordingly it is important to consider mechanisms which shape parties and party systems in these respects. In particular mechanisms with a constitutional basis, if there are any, are relevant in this context. Here, I shall present six hypotheses about such mechanisms -the first five are related to the constitutional traits identified. Then, I will discuss the hypotheses in more detail. This discussion will however be confined to the hypotheses' logical foundations, and their places in the logical structure, or theory, developed here. The issue about the hypotheses' empirical truth will, on the whole, not be dealt with.

- The first hypothesis says that majoritarian elections tend to reduce the number of parties. Or, in other words, a democracy with majoritarian elections should, under otherwise equivalent conditions, have fewer parties than one with proportional elections.

This hypothesis is often referred to as Duverger's law. The French political scientist Maurice Duverger was certainly not the first one to entertain the idea, but he was the first to give it a sharp formulation and, simultaneously, to maintain its status as a scientifically valid generalisation, and he also collected and systematically arranged a lot of empirical information in order to prove its truth (Riker, 1986, p 26). The hypothesis has been, and continues to be, extensively and explicitly discussed in political science, and it remains controversial.

- The second hypothesis (part 6.2) says that parliamentarism, in particular in combination with proportional elections, gives the political parties strong incentives for discipline and cohesion. In a presidential system there is no corresponding incentive-creating mchanism.
- The third hypothesis (part 6.3) says that proportional elections put strong means of discipline in the hands of the leaderships of political parties. Under otherwise equivalent conditions these means are thus more efficient than those in a system with majoritarian elections.
- The fourth hypothesis (part 6.4) says that parliamentarism, in contrast to presidentialism, also gives some means of discipline to the leaderships of the political parties.

These three last hypotheses, as we see, deal with the discipline of political parties -and, again, it is in particular the discipline in legislative voting which is at issue. These hypotheses are not at all discussed in the same systematic way as Duverger's law. Rather, there are just occasional references, in passing as it were, to the hypotheses or similar ideas. Furthermore the distinction made here between means and incentives is never, to my knowledge, done explicitly. Sometimes the distinction is not even made implicitly and the idea expressed is rather that parliamentarism leads to discipline, or something like that. A few examples may illustrate this.

Lipset, for instance, quoting a paper of his own from 1976, talks about "the tight national party discipline imposed by a parliamentary as compared with a presidential system" (1990, p 199). Some authors also hold that the cohesion of the parties in a parliamentary system is, indeed, so strong that the parties can be treated as individual, or unitary, actors. In a discussion mainly devoted to other matters Hinich & Munger (1994, p 134) thus suddenly claim that "The same model holds for parliamentary systems, where parties, rather than individual candidates, are the main actors in elections." Similarly Laver & Shepsle (1994), although they admit (p 309) that they "have not gone into the mechanisms of party discipline" emphasize (p 301) "the role of the parliamentary-party machine in enforcing party discipline, and hence in enhancing the party to function as a single monolithic actor." But even if most of the authors, who talk about the matter at all, thus seem to agree that parliamentarism enhances party discipline, there are also exceptions. Sartori, for instance, bluntly states (1994, p 95, his italics) that "... party solidification and discipline (in parliamentary voting) has never been a feedback of parliamentary government. If a system is assembly-based, atomized, unruly, magmatic, on its own intertia it will remain as it is. I cannot think of any party system that has evolved into a veritable 'system' made of strong, organization-based mass parties on the basis of internal parliamentary learning."

I do take side with those who claim that parliamentarism encourages discipline. In order to get deeper into the relevant mechanisms I have however found it productive to make a distinction between the incentives for discipline, and the means for enforcing it. Within this perspective discipline does not come about unless both incentives are present, and means available. The incentives are the subject matter of the second hypothesis, and the means are dealt with in the third and fourth hypotheses.

The two last hypotheses, number five and six, deal, without making the distinction between incentives and means, with mechanisms impeding party discipline.

- The fifth hypothesis (part 6.5) says that presidentialism is likely to impede party discipline somewhat.
- The sixth hypothesis (part 6.6) says that some popular democratic techniques are likely to impede party discipline.

The Number of Parties

When stating his law Duverger wrote (1964, p 217, his italics) that "Only individual investigation of the circumstances in each country can determine the real origins of the two-party system. The influence of such national factors is certainly very considerable; but we must not in their favour underestimate the importance of one general factor of a technical kind, the electoral system. Its effect can be expressed in the following formula: the simple-majority single-ballot system favours the two-party system. Of all the hypotheses that have been defined in this book, this approaches the most nearly perhaps to a true sociological law." Part of the controversies about Duverger's law are, I think, a consequence of his formulation that majoritarianism "favours" a two-party system. Since a law should be law this has been interpreted as a claim that majoritarianism leads to a two-party system. After that, since it is easy to find exceptions such as India and Canada, it is also easy to conclude that Duverger is just wrong.

But that is hardly sensible. What can be claimed is that majoritarianism, in contrast to proportionalism, involves strong forces tending to reduce the number of political parties. From this, by thinking in terms of equilibrium processes and taking countervailing forces into account, it is perfectly reasonable to conclude that, on the whole, we should expect fewer parties in countries with majoritarian elections than in those with proportional elections.

This is a strong and important statement, which is perfectly compatible with Duverger's text, and it is this statement which I here call Duverger's law. Our main interest here concerns the mechanisms behind Duverger's law. Why, other things being equal, should we expect fewer parties in a majoritarian system than in a proportional one? Duverger himself answered this question by referring (p 224) to "a mechanical factor and a psychological factor".

The first one consists in the pure mathematical effects of the application of the electoral rule -essentially the suppression of all parties but the biggest in each constituency. The second factor consists in the parties' and voters' reactions, and adaptations, to this suppression.

Duverger's idea about a mechanical and a psychological factor is of course perfectly reasonable even if the mechanisms behind the law can be described in a more detailed manner. In particular it is important to distinguish between the constituency level, where the important mechanisms work, and the national level where the result we are interested in is manifested. Duverger himself was well aware of this and wrote (1964, p 223) that "the true effect of the simple-majority system is limited to local bipartism."

Starting at the constituency level we can assume, as an example, that we have a constituency with five candidates representing the parties P1-P5. Let us furthermore assume that these parties, in an imagined first election, get 30, 25, 20, 15, and 10 % of the votes respectively. We shall also assume that these votes reflect the real preferences of the voters, and that these preferences remain constant over time.

P1	P2	P3	P4	P5
30 %	25 %	20 %	15 %	10 %

In the first election P1 thus gets a plurality and its candidate will consequently represent the constituency in the legislature. That result may make P1 and its voters happy, but the other parties, and their voters, are hardly likely to repeat their behavior exactly in the ensuing elections. Various adaptations are likely to take place.

Thus at least some of the voters, who are not satisfied by merely expressing their opinion, but really want to affect things, may change their votes from the most preferred party to their second or even third preference, if that party is considered better than the incumbent P1 and is also judged to stand a better chance than their first preference to beat P1. As the years pass, and the number of effectuated elections increases, this means that some parties, perhaps the initially smallest ones, will become still smaller, while a few, perhaps just two, main combatants will increase their vote support. In the long run the voters themselves, by departing from their initial first preferences, are thus likely to concentrate their votes on a few main combatants having real chances to win.

As for the parties and their candidates, assuming that they really want to take part in decision-making and thus are not content with just manifesting their existence, a corresponding behavior is likely. The parties, which remain small, and perhaps even decrease, as the years pass, are thus likely to withdraw from the competition altogether.

The combined behavior of the voters, and the parties, is thus likely to bring about a long term equilibrium with just a few parties, say two or three. If, at some time, there are considerably more parties than that, some of them are consequently likely to be eliminated in the long run.

After this the consequences at the national level may be considered. Let us assume that we have a country in which, initially, there are 10 parties. We shall also assume that all constituencies in important respects have the same properties. They thus have the same size, and the same patterns of political opinions. Initially all ten parties are thus represented in each constituency. After this we should thus expect, over the years and in each constituency, an equilibrium process of the kind. Since the constituencies have the same properties the process will be the same everywhere. Therefore, if it ends with for instance two parties in one constituency, it will end with the same two parties in each constituency, and thus also nationwide. In this case therefore, and due to the assumptions made, what happens in one constituency happens in the same way in the other ones, and consequently nationwide as well. Everywhere there is a reduction from 10 to two parties.

Things may however be different. Let us change the assumption that the constituencies have similar properties into its opposite, namely that all constituencies, due to important regional differences, are very different from each other. Let us also specify that there are five constituencies altogether. As for the rest everything is as before. From the beginning there are thus ten parties, which we may call p1-p10, all of which are represented in each constituency. Now, as in example above, and as the years pass, the number of parties will be reduced in each constituency. Since the constituencies are different in this example the reduction will however affect different parties in the different constituencies. We may for instance assume that, in the end, there will only be two parties in each constituency, and that these remaining parties are p1 and p2 in the first constituency, p3 and p4 in the second, p5 and p6 in the third, p7 and p8 in the fourth, and p9 and p10 in the final and fifth constituency. In this example therefore, and although the number of parties in each constituency has again been reduced from 10 to two, there is no reduction at all on the national level.

These two examples are, of course, extremes. What they have in common is that the number reducing process in the individual constituencies is the same in both cases, and the same as in the description of the mechanisms at the constituency level above. The difference is that in the first example, where all constituencies have the same properties, the national number of parties is reduced as much as the number in each constituency, whereas in the other example, where the constituencies are utterly dissimilar, the national number of parties is not reduced at all. In real situations, where there are some differences between different constituencies, but also a lot of similarities, the result is likely to be something in between. When the mechanisms operating in the constituencies reduce the number of parties there, the national number of parties is also likely to be reduced, but not as much as in the individual constituencies.

The discussion about the effects on the national level has, so far, only considered the logical effects of similarities, or differences, between constituencies. No further mechanisms other than the ones operating at the constituency level have been introduced. Mechanisms operating at the national level are, however, also imaginable. Economies of scale may for instance be important. The formation of parties, and of party opinions and positions, are thus likely to be demanding tasks requiring considerable basic investments which are independent of the number of constituencies involved. Therefore, and in order to make these investments pay off, a certain minimum number of constituencies may be required. If so, we have a mechanism which is likely to reduce the number of parties nationally as well. This mechanism, however, is as relevant for proportional as for majoritarian elections, and therefore we need not consider it further here.

Summing up we may say that the numbers of parties is likely to be smaller in a majoritarian system than in a proportional one, other things being equal. The basic mechanisms leading to this result operate at the constituency level. The result will however, even if attenuated, remain at the national level, provided that differences between the constituencies are not too many and too great.

A Corollary

Presidents, as we saw in part 5.4, are usually appointed by some kind of majoritarian method. In presidential elections there are therefore forces operating which tend to reduce the number of parties. Now, since the same political parties usually appear in presidential elections and in elections for the legislature, the forces affecting the parties in presidential elections are likely to be relevant for the elections to the legislature as well. Presidentialism will thus have some tendency to reduce the number of parties generally.

Incentives for Party Discipline

The second hypothesis, that parliamentarism gives political

parties strong incentives for cohesion and discipline, has not, to my knowledge been systematically discussed anywhere. I will therefore start from scratch with the logical foundations of the hypothesis as I see them.

Using the concepts of decisive and blocking sets it seems natural that legislators in general are trying to form, or become members of, decisive sets in favor of their own ideas or positions. If they do not succeed with that they will at least try to bring about sets which are able to block proposals they are against.

Now, it is an important property of a parliamentary system that most decisive constellations necessarily consist of the executive, or at least has the executive as a constituent part. It is thus not possible that the executive is excluded from most decision-making constellations since that would be tantamount to regular no-confidence votes, and thus against the parliamentarian principle. The legislators thus have incentives to make the system work, and therefore, since stable, cohesive and disciplined parties according to part 5.3 is a prerequisite for that, to form such parties.

The incentives may however be stronger in a proportional parliamentary system than in a majoritarian one, in particular if the majoritarian system (because of the operation of Duverger's law) comes close to being a two party-system. This is so because the majority, in a two party situation and for statistical reasons, often is considerably bigger than the minority. The majority which supports the executive therefore can afford some defectors and still deliver the necessary confidence. In proportional systems, on the contrary, where coalition executives are the rule the executive's marginals are usually much narrower and discipline therefore more important. (The nature of these reasons, both the statistical mechanisms in the majoritarian case, and the mechanisms behind the narrow margins in the proportional case, will be treated in more detail later on.)

Anyway, the existence of incentives among the legislators is not enough for cohesive and disciplined parties to appear. Without some further mechanism, such as reasonably effective means for enforcing discipline at the party leaderships' disposal, the parties are likely to remain rather loose and unconsolidated organizations. This is so since the parties, in spite of being parties, are likely to harbor, within themselves, considerable differences of opinions, which it is difficult to erase. The establishment of common clear-cut party positions is likely to require some kind of organizational power.

MEANS OF DISCIPLINE RELATED TO PROPORTIONALISM

There is, to my knowledge, no systematic discussion about the third hypothesis that proportionalism gives strong means of discipline to the party leaderships. Rather there are just occasional assertions of the hypothesis, or similar ideas. Duverger (1964, p 183), for instance, writes that "proportional representation with fixed lists and the ranking of candidates in strict order naturally makes parliamentary representatives dependent on the leaders within the party who prepare the lists and determine the order of the names." Similarly Matthew Shugart and John Carey (1992, s 173) write about "mechanisms, such as a closed party list, by which party leaders exert discipline over their rank and file." But even if the references to the hypothesis are scattered and few, they all seem to go in the same direction. I have not come across any denials of the hypothesis, and it is thus, as it seems, uncontroversial.

Still, the mechanisms behind the hypothesis can hardly be as simple as indicated in the quotations above, namely that those deciding about the lists easily can eliminate obstinate candidates. This argument applies equally well to the majoritarian case, since also there those responsible for the nominations obviously can exclude those who do not follow the group. We have to look for more fundamental mechanisms.

The main point seems to be that the incentives for campaigning are very different in the two types of systems. In a majoritarian system the efforts of the local party organization in the constituency, as well as the efforts, and the personality, of the individual candidate, are of great importance for the result. The campaigning efforts of a candidate in a single-member constituency will to a very large extent favor the candidate himself. If the candidate campaigns successfully the voters will vote for just him. Therefore, to a considerable extent, a legislator in a majoritarian context is the architect of his or her own fortune.

When considering the corresponding mechanisms in proportinal systems I will start with list systems. In such a system an imagined campaigning candidate in a constituency -which always is a multimember one -does not work for himself but rather, and necessarily, produces a collective good. The obvious reason is that the voters cannot reward an appreciated campaigner individually -they have to vote for his party rather than for the candidate himself. Things being like that it is interesting to ask more exactly about the nature of the collective good produced by the imagined local candidate.

At first it may then be stated that he works for his party rather than for himself. Furthermore, and to the extent that his constituency party organization is not a meaningful unit for the voters, he will be working for the national party rather than for the constituency organization. For that kind of work he is, however, because of his local, low level, position, probably most unfit. The amount of the collective good produced by his campaigning will therefore be quite small, and it will also be diffusely spread out, to a considerable extent beyond the borders of his own constituency. Thus, from the imagined candidate's own point of view, his efforts will in all likelihood seem wasted. The conclusion is that the imagined candidate will remain imagined. There will not be much local campaigning at all. This, incidentally, is exactly what the theory of collective action (Mancur Olson, 1965) tells us: the incentives for producing collective goods are notoriously weak.

At the summits of the parties in a proportional list system things are however different. For the party leaderships residing there campaigning may very well be profitable. Their campaigning is at first relatively effective since they are in the proper positions for that kind of work. Furthermore, on the whole, they will reap the fruits of their own efforts.

True, it may be argued that a party's candidates in all constituencies benefit from what the leadership is doing, but even so the leadership itself also benefits more the more candidates it really gets into the legislature. It is usually better to belong to the leadership of a big party than to that of a small one. It is this necessary dominance of the party leaderships in campaigning in proportional list systems, I would argue, which also supplies the leaderships with power over their legislators. If the leadership of a party wants control a certain legislator or candidate, by sticks or by carrots, the latter usually has no personal resources of his own, such as for instance popularity among voters, to mobilize for resistance.

This argument applies however, as I have said, primarily to pure list elections. In other kinds of proportional systems, in which the candidates' individual campaigns matter to some extent, for instance because the voters can add or erase names on the lists, or because (as in the Finish case as described in part 5.2) there are no lists at all, the effects described are more or less attenuated. Or, in other words, the means of discipline become weaker and more similar to those in majoritarian systems.

Means of Discipline Related to Parliamentarism

According to the fourth hypothesis there is also another mechanism of discipline, which is related to parliamentarism rather than to proportionalism. This mechanism has been discussed now and then since long.

Gary Cox (1987, p 80 ff) thus gives an account of an interesting discussion in which Walter Bagehot (1826-77) notices and explains the discipline of the British parties. According to Bagehot the legislators were afraid of voting against the executive, since thereby, through the dissolution of the Parliament, they might lose their places there. This explanation was however refuted in the discussion on the ground that it did not explain the cohesion of the opposition party. Duverger gives a slightly different version of the same argument when he asserts (1964, p 404) that the British government often uses the vote of confidence, and thereby the threat of dissolution, and a new election, as a disciplinary weapon within its own party. Later still Shugart & Carey write (1992, p 173) that "Where parliamentary systems have become fully developed, the existence of the institution of the vote of no-confidence has mandated an imposition of discipline. This party discipline in an archetypal parliamentary system (such as the United Kingdom, New Zealand, or Norway, for example) is sure to be far stronger than in a typical presidential system's assembly... ".

Obviously there may be a mechanism like this, even if it also seems correct that it does not explain the discipline of opposition parties. But perhaps the discipline of the opposition, in parliamentarian and majoritarian systems, really is lower than that of the party, or parties, in power.

Anyway, there is an interesting and important difference between the means of discipline discussed here and those related to proportionalism treated in part 6.3. The difference is that the latter are discriminating in the sense that they could be used against a single legislator or candidate, whereas those discussed here are non-discriminating and usable only against the governing party's parliamentary group as a whole.

A Mechanism Impeding Party Discipline Related to Presidentialism

Presidential elections may affect the inner structures of the parties. Since presidential candidates usually have to win a majority of the votes in order to be elected they may, one could suspect, modify or attenuate their parties' programs considerably in order to get more votes. This may lead to tensions within the parties, and to a degradation of the party programs.

Mechanisms Impeding Party Discipline Related to Primaries, Referendums and Initiatives

Some democratic techniques or institutions, such as primaries, referendums and initiatives, give additional power to the ordinary voter. For this reason these institutions also may impede party discipline. Popular primary elections, by which candidates for political posts are nominated, obviously deprive party leaderships of important power and thereby impede party cohesion and discipline.

The relation between referendums and party cohesion is a somewhat more complicated issue since referendums sometimes can be used in the service of party cohesion. Imagine for example that in a parliamentary country, in which party cohesion is essential, an important issue which divides the parties appears. If, in such a case, the referendum institute is used for the decision making, rather than the regular machinery, a potential threat to party cohesion is bypassed, which serves the system's functioning.

Referendums may however also be used frequently and regularly with the main purpose of reaching decisions, without any regards for party cohesion. If so the popular initiative is also an interesting institute, which may be made available for the citizens. Now, if referendums and initiatives are used without any regard for the parties, it is still interesting to ask whether, in fact, they are likely to affect the parties in any substantial way. I think they are, and the hypotheses is that the parties' consolidation and cohesion is likey to be undermined. The reason is that the parties, in order to be consolidated and cohesive also must have some importance, which means that they must be allowed to handle as many issues as possible. If a lot of issues are taken away from the parties' dominating influence, and are given away to people's direct initiatives and decisions, the parties will, I think, disintegrate.

Four main Actor Constellations

Using the hypotheses about party-shaping mechanisms it is now possible to derive conclusions, also hypothetical, about the constellations of main actors in the four constitutional systems.

The upper, left part illustrates the main actor constellation in parliamentary systems with proportional elections. Here, there is no strong constitutional mechanism reducing the number of parties, and hence we are likely to find considerably more than two parties, perhaps five to ten. Furthermore the incentives for upholding party discipline are strong, since the system is parliamentarian, and effective means towards that end are also available, due to the proportional elections. The parties are thus likely to be disciplined and cohesive. Looked at from outside they may be considered as unitary actors. This is the reason why the party-actors are indicated by solid circles in the figure.

In the upper, right part of the figure we have parliamentary systems with majoritarian elections. The number of parties shall, on the average, and because of the number-reducing tendency of the majoritarian elections, be smaller than in the former group of constitutions. The figure shows a case for which the reduction has been very effective, and where, as a result, there are only two parties. Obviously, and even with the number-reducing mechanism operating, there may however be more than two parties. Anyway, the parties are likely to be less disciplined than in the former case. One reason is that the incentives given by parliamentarism, according to the hypothesis in the preceding part, are weaker than in case of proportionalism. Another reason is that the means for enforcing discipline are weaker than in a proportional system. Since the discipline is less than perfect the party actors are indicated by broken circles in the figure.

Turning then to the lower parts of the figure, which show presidential systems, it may at first be noted that the actors are placed in two levels rather than one. The presidential executive is placed at an upper level, whereas the actors in the legislature are indicated at a lower level. The basic reason for placing the president at a separate level is that the rules regulating his or her actions usually differ in important respects from the rules for the legislative actors -particularly by giving the president much more power. Furthermore, as will be developed in the following, the president's general incentives may differ considerably from those of the legislative actors.

The president may, for instance, sometimes be endowed with incentives for favoring the common good rather than partisan interests. Now, the lower, left part of the figure, shows the constellation of actors in presidential systems with proportionalism. Here, in the elections for the legislature, there are no strong constitutional forces reducing the number of parties, and consequently we may expect quite a lot of them, as indicated. As for incentives for discipline, there are obviously no ones of the same nature as those in a parliamentary system, but perhaps there are other ones. Anyway, the means for discipline are there, since we are dealing with a proportional system. The parties may thus be disciplined and cohesive, but it may also be the other way round. In order to settle this issue additional assumptions about the incentives for discipline are required. So far, I have however not introduced any such assumptions, and the resulting ambivalence is illustrated in the figure by some broken, and some solid, circles.

The main Actors' Interactions

Having put the main actors on the stage it is now time to consider their actions, and the results of those actions. In this part, and the next two ones, I will introduce three topics related to these actions. These topics will then be treated in detail in the discussions about each one of the four main types of constitutions.

The topic introduced in this part concerns the main actors' interactions. How do the main actors relate to each other? What kinds of decision-making patterns will they form? And by which mechanisms or processes? And why? These are typical questions related to this topic. The answers to the questions, as we will see in the following, will to a large extent depend on the type of constitution considered. The concepts of decisive and blocking sets were introduced. Those concepts may, of course, be used for main actors as conceived here. Doing so it is now possible to state that a very important aspect of the political competition in a democratic society consists in the main actors' efforts, by positioning and bargaining and so forth, to form and enter, depending on the circumstances, decisive or blocking sets, and thereby further their ambitions.

The possibilities to act like this vary however considerably from case to case, depending among other things on the constitutional setting. For the discussion of these matters, which largely are of a behavioral nature, it may be useful to consider the degree of coordination among the main actors. Imagine, as an extreme example, a decision-making assembly which has so many main actors, and takes new decisions so often, that it is virtually impossible for the actors communicate with each other about what is going on. When a proposal is presented for such an assembly each actor thus have to vote for or against the proposal without any prior discussions with its fellow-actors. This voting behavior is thus completely uncoordinated. In the opposite extreme the number of main actors is so small, and other factors enhancing cooperation so favorable, that it easy for the actors to communicate extensively, and negotiate, about all proposals, and about the votes for the proposals. In such a case we should thus expect a very coordinated main actor behavior. When the conditions for coordination are favorable the coordination, it may be noted, is not necessarily limited to a single decision, or a few related decisions. If the interests of the actors concerned so dictate, the coordination may very well be extended over a considerable time period such as, for instance, a complete election period. The topic of coordination will be further discussed "Two kinds of compromises".

TWO KINDS OF COMPROMISES

In previous part I said that the actors' behavior was uncoordinated when they just voted their minds, whereas coordination involved discussion and negotiations between the actors. When coordinating, the actors are thus likely to adjust their positions and behavior in various ways in order to achieve benefits, for instance by forming and entering favorable decisive constellations, or at least blocking ones. That of course requires compromises, but political compromises may be of different kinds and the differences are of considerable interest. Here I will describe two kinds of compromises. Imagine two actors, A and B, which respectively have the opinions, or take the positions, a1-am and b1-bn. Now, for any pair of positions with one position from each actor, it is interesting to ask whether the positions are compatible or not. Each cell in the figure below represents one such comparison, and a few answers are also inserted as illustrations. Thus the positions a2 and bn, and a3 and b2, are compatible, whereas the positions a1 and b1, and am and b2, are not compatible. Now, in politics, both compatibility and non-compatibility are common. In principle the issue of compatibility has to be judged in each individual case, but two general rules, with possible exceptions, may however be hypothesized.

- Different ideological positions are likely to be in conflict with each other, and thus not compatible. A society can, for instance, not be built in accordance with both socialistic and capitalistic principles. It has to be the one way or the other. Socialism and capitalism are not compatible. Or, to take another example, a position on a spatial left-right scale is not compatible with another position on the same scale. Thus, an actor cannot adopt several positions on such a scale, it has to be just one.
- Positions about interests may, on the contrary, very well be compatible. The position that a certain group in society, say small farmers, should be supported is thus perfectly compatible with the position that another group, say widows with small means, should also be supported. There is no problem in adopting the two positions simultaneously.

Now compromises between political actors about political positions may be of two types.

- The first type of compromise consists in agreeing about a common program involving compatible positions from the actors concerned. Using the example in the figure the actors A and B may for example compromise about a program involving A's positions a2 and a3 and B's positions b2 and bn. The common policy or program thus is a2 + a3 + b2 + bn +.... Such a compromise is likely to be quite easy to reach, since no adjustments of original positions are needed. It is only required that all actors feel that a fair amount of their original positions are included in the final common policy.

- The second type of compromise, which in the general case should be much more difficult to reach, requires adjustments of positions which originally are incompatible. An example would be a compromise between A and B in the figure about the positions a1 and b1. If both actors adjust their positions they may finally become compatible, or perhaps even identical, and thus represent a possible compromise. a1 and b1 may for instance be two different positions on a spatial left-right scale, and the actors may agree to settle for a specific position between a1 and b1. This is however likely to be difficult since it requires that both actors change their original positions in favor of a new one.

A conclusion to be drawn from the reasoning here thus is that political compromises about interests are likely to be easier than compromises about ideological matters.

THE MAIN ACTORS AND THE VOTERS

In the preceding part I said that the main actor interaction constituted an important aspect of the political competition in democratic societies.

- Another equally important aspect of this competition is the fight for votes.

The voters obviously are of crucial importance for the main actors. A main actor without electoral support is unthinkable. Each main actor is supported by voters, and without that support the main actor would not be a main actor. For this reason electoral support can never be substituted completely by, or traded for, other goods appreciated by the main actor such as, for instance, beneficial relations with lobbyists or extensive and favorable publicity in media. Such goods are subordinated to votes, even if they may be used in the hunt for votes. Ultimately, and in the final count, a main actor depends on its electoral support.

- The topic introduced in this part concerns the relationships between the main actors and the voters. What will individuals and parties aspiring to get into the legal decision-making system, and thus to become main actors,

> do in order to get the necessary votes? What will the incumbent main actors do in order to keep their electoral support, and thereby their positions? How will the voters react to messages from campaigning individuals or parties, and choose between them? These are typical questions within this topic, and again we will see that the answers to a considerable extent will vary with the constitutional type considered.

Trying to attract voters a campaigning actor may use various ideological arguments, support various interests, or, if we are dealing with an individual actor, emphasize its own personal qualities. Furthermore, the actor may address the electorate at large, or, perhaps, particular target groups within the electorate. In these activities, however, the actor obviously also runs the risk of repelling voters, and it is therefore important to keep the net result positive. A good strategy attracts more voters than it repels.

As for the voter, the decision about which actor to vote for may be quite complex. The voter may consider the actors' positions on various ideological or interest-related issues, or the actors' personalities when the actors are individuals. The voter may also entertain ideas about the relative importance of these different aspects, and so forth. By weighing all this together the voter reaches a decision about how to vote. We may call this kind of voting compound voting. The contrast is voting on a single issue, for example in a referendum. In such a case the voting is straightforward rather than compound. The citizen just votes its position on the issue to be decided, and that is all. Voting, which aims at appointing main actors, is however usually compound.

In order to bring the analysis further ahead it is necessary to be more detailed about the relations between voters and politicians. In politics, and political analysis, it is common to talk about mandates from voters to politicians. Using another, and perhaps more modern terminology, it may also be said that the relationship between voters and politicians is a principal-agent relation, the voters being the principals and the politicians the agents (for an introduction to this terminology see, for instance, Milgrom & Roberts). The relation can take different forms. It is convenient to distinguish between two main types of such forms, namely delegation and instruction.

Delegation is, in a way, the simpler of the two relationships and many people have experience of it from everyday life. When people in typical voluntary associations like the local sports club or charity association elect presidents, cashiers, secretaries, and so on, they usually do not require more than having confidence in the persons elected. They just want to be able to rely on them to act in a way that is in accordance with common sense and the purposes of the club. Feeling such confidence they delegate the decision-making to the people elected. This rather simple kind of relationship is present not only in clubs and the like, but to a considerable extent also in politics.

Instruction, on the other hand, prevails when the voters do not limit themselves to a simple confidence in the ones elected but rather require that they shall execute a certain program, which may be worked out in a rather detailed way. Therefore, at the same time as people are elected, a program, or an instruction, which the ones elected shall realize, is adopted. It should be noted that the program may very well be, and often is, formulated by the people who wants to get elected. Different candidates for political positions thus offer voters to carry through different programs if elected. Even so, however, and as soon as a candidate is elected, the program can, from a formal point of view, be considered an instruction from the voters to the elected.

Here delegation and instruction have been presented as two rather pure, or archetypal, relationships. In reality, however, it is easy to see that mixtures of the two types often appear. Sometimes the element of delegation may dominate, sometimes the element of instruction, and it is interesting to ask about the reasons why. Before taking up that issue it should however be noted that instructions may be of different kinds. They may be specific or general. This distinction is closely is related to the one between generality and particularity made by Buchanan (1993).

General instructions may be based on ideological ideas about the ideal character or construction of society, or they may be derived from ideas about the common, or public, or general, interest. Often general instructions are about new rules or laws, and those supporting such new laws tend to emphasize the incentives created by the laws. The likely ambition is to create incentives which enhance the societal development, and people's general welfare, in the long run.

Specific instructions, on the other hand, are independent of notions about ideal societies, or about the common good. If general instructions often deal explicitly with rules and incentives, specific instructions are, rather, interventionistic. Their implementation usually means that some people, on purpose, satisfy their special interests at the expense of others. In these cases, therefore, the incentives created are not a main concern of those favoring the interests, and there is usually not much talk about incentives. But obviously some incentives will be affected, or created, as unintended side-effects of the instructions, and those incentives are worth investigating. They may very well be destructive.

Now, in their campaigning, the political actors may try to establish relationships of delegation, or instruction, or some mixture of the two. When considering what they are likely to do it is important to realize that the possibilities to effectuate instructions, that is to deliver, to a large extent depend on the constitutional setting. These matters will be dealt with in detail in the following parts, but generally speaking it may be said the possibilities to deliver are, on the whole, greater when the conditions for coordination are good than when they are not.

Furthermore, if the possibilities to deliver are slim, it is likely to be more prudent for the actor to strive for a relationship of delegation rather than instruction. From this point of view we should therefore expect delegation, at least to a large extent, to be associated with individual main actors and instruction with party main actors. In addition to this there is another argument which points in the same direction. The argument is that a consolidated party, with a recognizable identity over a considerable time span, has great, and perhaps even crucial, advantages in relation to individuals for developing and "marketing" instructions, and in particular such a bundle of instructions which constitute a political program.

- We should thus, on the whole, expect party main actors to rely on instructions, and individual main actors to strive for delegation.

The main Actors and the Lobbyists

It is commonplace in politics that various actors which do not belong to the legal decision-making system, and which in that sense are external, try to enhance their goals by influencing the main actors. Such actors are called lobbyists, and their activity is known as lobbying.

- The topic introduced in this part concerns the activities of the lobbyists, and the relationships between them and the main actors. Who are the lobbyists? How do they work in order to become effective and influential? Why do the main actors yield to their demands when they do so? These are typical questions within this topic, and the answers depend on the constitutional setting.

The actors engaged in lobbying may be of many different kinds. They may be single individuals, business firms, unions, interest groups or many other kinds of organizations (other than, by definition, political parties). The targets of lobbying are actors which have a potential for influencing the outputs of the legal decision-making system. This means, as I have already taken for granted in a few formulations above, that the lobbyist are likely to approach the main actors, which may be individuals or parties.

Furthermore the lobbyists may either try to influence incumbents, or to affect the appointment of new main actors. Both activities are important and common. In the latter case the lobbyists may for example, because of sympathy with their policies, add to their campaign efforts. There are also mixtures between these two activities. A lobbyist may thus, while supporting an actor's campaign, at the same time try influence the actor's future behavior.

The lobbyists, since they are not political parties, are likely to pursue interests rather ideologies or other general issues. Furthermore, within this general kind of ambition, the lobbyists are likely to limit their efforts to what can reasonably be achieved. If, for instance, it seems possible to influence decisive constellations of main actors, or to stimulate the creation of such constellations, and thus to change the status quo, the lobbyists are likely to do so. But if that is not within reach the lobbyists may confine themselves to stimulating the creation of blocking constellations, and thus to impede changes of the status quo.

It is interesting to note that, in constitutional settings where lobbyists are unlikely to be able to bring about changes of the status quo, and thus are restricted to blocking strategies, laws favoring various interests are likely to stimulate the creation of, and thus to precede, organizations defending them. In a setting where the lobbyists realistically may hope to change the status quo organizations are, on the contrary, likely to be created in order to bring such changes about, and thus to precede the changes.

It may also be noted that lobbying organizations sometimes may find it advantageous to form close relations, even in an organizational sense, with main actors. An obvious prerequisite for this is that we are dealing with party main actors rather than individual main actors, but this is not enough. It is also required, at least for organizational ties to develop, that the political parties themselves have enough of organizational structure, or, in other words, that they are cohesive and consolidated enough. It is difficult to imagine a close relationship between a well organized interest group and a party which is just a very loose conglomerate.

Sometimes lobbying organizations are called "pressure groups". This, I think, is a highly misleading term. It gives the impression that the organization uses some kind of almost physical force for driving the resisting main actor backwards, which is, I submit, a completely wrong idea about the nature of the relationship between the two parties. The lobbyists just do not have any power like that. When a main actor yields to a lobbyist's demand it does so rather because it finds its own interests enhanced thereby -if it were not for that it would not yield at all. We thus have to think about the two parties as reaching a mutually beneficial agreement. The understanding of lobbying is tantamount to knowledge about the relation between the two parties, which has to be analyzed in as detailed a way as is done, for instance, with sellers and buyers on a market in economic theory. Each party gives something away, gets something else in return, and comes out in a better state.

The benefits of the lobbyist always consist in favorable public decisions. The costs, on the contrary, may be of different kinds. One type of costs occur if the lobbyist, which in this case may be an organization, exercises its influence over its members to vote for the lobbied main actor. If so the costs do not only consist in the efforts made to get the members to change their votes, but also, for the members themselves, in the benefits foregone by not voting in the way they had originally intended to do. Another type of costs occur if the lobbyist provides money in cash in order to support the lobbied actor's election campaign. That, of course, is also a way of furnishing votes, albeit an indirect one. The lobbyist thus can fulfil his part of a bargain either by exercising influence over voters, or by supplying money, and it is, of course, of great interest to find out when and why the one or the other possibility is used. Finally it should be said that the lobbyist obviously also may supply money, or other valuables, for the lobbied actor's private use. Such manners, however, are obviously corrupt.

Within the perspective applied here the widely spread idea, which is given support by the term pressure group, that an organization is necessarily more effective the bigger, and the better organized, it is, seems dubious. Big and well administered organizations could quite conceivably lack influence, for example if the political counterpart does not see any benefits, such as votes, to result from yielding.

On the other hand even a very weak organization may get influence simply by informing legislators about its position, and thereby about ways to get votes. In fact, it seems quite possible for groups of citizens, for example marginal voters, to be influential without being organised at all, and one might therefore even speak about implicit organizations or lobbyists. So far I have just taken for granted that both political parties, and interest organizations, usually exist in a democratic system. Still it is important to ask why this is so. Which is the division of labor between political parties and interest organizations?

The Division of Labor Between Political Parties and Lobbying Organizations

Why, one may ask, are both lobbying organizations and political parties always present in a democratic political system? Why is it not enough with the organizations working close to the legal structure, that is the political parties?

Why are there, in addition to that, interest groups? Which functions do the latter have which cannot, at least not conveniently, be fulfilled by the parties? Which is the division of labor between them? The answers to these questions are, again, dependent on the constitutional setting and therefore not fit for a detailed treatment in this chapter. Two general points may, however, be made.

First, while political parties usually have at least some ideological inclination, although it may be weak, lobbying organizations focus strongly on interests. This point is emphasized by the fact that the majority rule, which is important in all democracies, makes it possible to further special interests of various kinds. In a context dominated by the unanimity rule interests would, on the contrary, usually be defeated, and there would thus not be any room for lobbying organizations.

Second, while political parties come and go from incumbency to opposition, lobbying organizations, by being free from the parties, can always direct their demands towards the incumbents.

Parliamentary Constitutions with Proportional Elections

In this constitutional setting the main actors are, as we have seen, likely to be cohesive and disciplined political parties. Some of these actors or parties are furthermore likely to form an executive, and they are also likely, to rely to a considerable extent on instructions, and bundles of instructions or programs, in their efforts to get votes.

Now, when discussing the formation of an executive it is essential that the number of main actors, although they are few, most likely are more than two. Each party therefore knows that in all likelihood it will have to make deals with other parties. Thus, the main actors must adopt strategies which are instrumental in bringing them into coalitions, and in affecting the policies of those coalitions.

What kind of strategies are these? What kind of matters are the parties to a coalition likely to agree about? In part 9 we concluded tentatively that the parties to a large extent will rely on instructions in their electoral strategies. This topic will finally be discussed in part 12, but assuming so far that the tentative conclusion is correct, the coalition agreements are likely to be about instructions as well. But what kind of instructions?

A first point is that specific instructions, rather than general, are likely to be particularly important in these agreements. There are two reasons for this contention. The first one is that it is easier for political parties to make deals about specific instructions than about general ones. If, for instance, one party is committed to a particular specific instruction, and another party to another one, they can easily agree about supporting each other -if you support my instruction, I support yours. General instructions, on the contrary, are often in conflict with each other and, if so, not easily reconciled. This first reason is thus related to the compatibility of various political positions as such.

The second reason, on the other hand, has to do with the acceptability for those concerned of a reconciliation. This problem, as it happens, is the subject matter of a theorem saying that a coalition executive cannot have a purely ideological foundation (Moberg, 2000). Following the terminology used here it may also be said that a reconciliation of two general instructions, even if such a reconciliation, in spite of the technical difficulties, is reached, is not likely to be accepted by the parties concerned.

But even if compromises based only on general instructions from the different parties are unlikely, there may be deals in which a general instruction of one party is knit together with a specific instruction of another party. They may agree that the first party supports the second party's specific instruction, if the second party supports, or perhaps just tolerates, the first party's general instruction. This, however, requires that the general instruction involved is not too offensive but rather attenuated or pragmatic enough. It may also be argued that general instructions, which give a prominent and far-reaching role to the state, are more easily reconciled with specific instructions than those giving a limited role to the state. The reason is that specific instructions often are natural parts of state interventionism. From these general arguments we can now infer the following hypotheses about the parties' programs:

- Specific instructions are likely to be frequent in all parties' programs.
- All parties do not necessarily have general instructions in their programs, and when such instructions appear they are likely to be pragmatic or attenuated.

We also get these hypotheses about the executive coalitions likely to emerge, and about their governmental programs:

- A governmental program containing only specific instructions is perfectly possible.
- A small party may be committed to some general instructions, but it is not likely to get them included in a governing coalition's program.
- If a governmental program contains general instructions, and in that sense has an ideological inclination, those

instructions are likely to have come directly from a big, dominating party's program. Either that party has been able to form an executive of its own, or it is the main participant in an executive involving one or a few small extra coalition members. In this latter case there may be a deal saying that the dominating party will support some specific instructions of the smaller parties, if they support, or tolerate, the dominating party's general instructions.

- Parties with articulated (in contrast to pragmatic or attenuated) and conflicting general instructions on their programs are not likely to be able to make deals about specific instructions with each other. The freedom of such parties is thus somewhat restricted.
- A party not having any general instruction in its program is completely free in choosing its partners, irrespective of their general instructions. Such a party is often able to play a pivotal role in coalition building processes. It can, for example, credibly threaten to leave, and thereby destroy, a coalition to which it presently belongs in order to join another one. Such threats can be used for enforcing concessions from the other members of the first coalition, or from the members of the second potential coalition, and thus for giving favors to the supporters of the party itself. For operating in that way a party need not be very big - in fact a moderate size may by an advantage since the party, thereby, fits into more places and thus gets more opportunities to have its specific instructions implemented.
- A party with strongly held, articulated and controversial general instructions in its program, for example a party with an extreme ideological inclination, may affront most other parties. If so the party may be excluded from all possible coalitions, and thus from all influence.

The purpose of the negotiating parties is, as I have mentioned above, to form a durable executive. This means that, in this constitutional setting, the main actor interaction, and thereby also the real decision making, to a large extent occurs in the government formation process. After that the executive will just go on presenting its agreed upon program, bit by bit, for the legislature. The real decision making is thus a batch process rather than a continuous process. The interval between the batches may be as long as the whole election period. This obviously also means that the majorities are fairly constant over the same long time periods. There is no constant recomposition of decisive majorities. Matters may, however, turn out somewhat differently if a minority executive, rather than a majority executive, is formed. Even such an executive depends, for its existence, on the support of a majority, but that majority, by definition, will contain parties which do not belong to the executive proper, and therefore the membership of that majority may. shift to some extent, for example from decision to decision in the legislature, or from time to time. This means that the decision-making will become somewhat more of a continuous process, and also that the composition of the majorities may change to some extent.

Another conclusion is that a big party may dominate the politics of its country for a long period even if it suffers occasional electoral recessions and, indeed, even if it never has a majority of its own. The party can stay in the executive all the time just by making deals about some specific instructions favored by one or two small parties, and then govern together with them. Most likely such a party continuously appoints the prime minister and the heads of a number of key ministries. This possibility for ideological influence may, in fact, be an important driving force for big parties to suppress internal divisions, or to live with them in one way or another, in order to remain big. If so we should expect to find an important ideological component in the programs of big parties like that.

We may also conclude that an organized opposition, in the form of for instance a shadow cabinet, is unlikely. The reason is that a new governing coalition, since the parties can combine in many ways, not necessarily consists exclusively of the former outsiders. Rather, some former outsiders may join some former incumbents in a new executive.

In order not to jeopardize any such possibilities the present outsiders are therefore not likely to form an organized group and thereby link their destinies. For a party aiming to develop and keep a pivotal position this consideration is particularly important. Finally it may be concluded that the executive coalitions formed are likely to be minimal winning in William Riker's sense (Riker, 1962). The reason is the important roles played by interests and specific instructions in the coalition agreements. Thus, and in other words, the executive coalitions are likely to exploit their outside minorities.

Some Conditions for the System's Proper Functioning

A parliamentary system depends, for its proper functioning on cohesive, disciplined political parties. Therefore some constitutional elements or constructions, which from a logical point may seem possible are, nevertheless, destructive in real politics.

First, it is important that the proportional technique used for appointing thé legislators is of a pure list character, or at least rather close to that. A system without any lists at all -such as the Finish system is hardly useful in a purely parliamentary setting. The reason, of course, is that it may be difficult for the party leaderships to maintain party discipline within such a system..

Second, it is important that the popular techniques of primaries, referendums and initiatives are not frequently used. The reason is that these techniques, as explained in part 6.6, are detrimental to party discipline. Still, and in some particular and rare cases, referendums may be used for upholding party discipline, as is also mentioned in part 6.6.

The Impossibility of a Coalition with a Purely Ideological Foundation

In previous part I said that a coalition executive cannot have a purely ideological foundation. This, in fact, is a theorem which says that it is impossible to account for the formation of the executive only in terms of a simple a left-right scale, or, in somewhat more technical terms, that it is impossible to account for the formation of the executive within the framework of the spatial model, at least in its one-dimensional version.

In the figure below we see a situation which can be used for proving the theorem. The figure represents a legislature with six political parties, P1-P6, each one with a certain position on the left-right scale and with a certain number of representatives in the assembly with altogether 300 members. Now, we may at first assume that there is no executive at all. If so the decisions taken by the legislature will be determined by the median voter theorem. This means that the decisions will become m, which is the ideological position of the party P3 and also the median position.

For proving the theorem we may compare this situation with one in which there is an executive. Clearly, if the executive is to make any difference at all, and thus to be of any interest for its members, its policy must diverge somewhat from m. We may for example think about an executive which has the policy indicated by l, and thus a leftist inclination, and which is supported by the majority composed of P2 and P3.

Now, it is easy to see that l is worse than m for P3. P3 is therefore in fact disfavored by belonging to the executive. Therefore, contrary to our assumption, P3 will not be member of the executive or support it. Our assumption that P3 belongs to the executive, since it is advantageous to do so, thus leads to a contradiction. This kind of argument is usually called a reductio ad absurdum. If it is possible to show that an assumption leads to a contradiction, then it is also fair to conclude that the assumption is unreasonable or absurd.

So far I have only dealt with the particular example in the particular figure above. Obviously we have to ask if other examples, with other possible party constellations in the legislature, also lead to contradictions for the same reasons. The answer is in the affirmative since the examples, however they are varied, will always have two crucial properties. First, the executive's policy must always diverge from m since otherwise the executive would not matter at all and, consequently, it would not be important to be a member of it. Second, since the constellation supporting the executive has to be a majority, it necessarily includes the median member of the assembly. (This, of course, presupposes that the coalition supporting the executive is connected, but departing from this assumption does hardly add anything of interest.) Thus, contrary to our assumptions, the executive will always include at least one party member for whom the membership is a unfavorable. We are thus entitled to draw the general conclusion that it is impossible to account for the formation of the executive within the framework of a simple, one-dimensional ideological model.

As a contrast, it is easy to account for a coalition executive in terms of interests. Thus, the parties belonging to an executive can, for instance, agree to tax those outside the coalition and share the spoils between themselves. Let us consider the following scenario. A party A tries, in an election campaign, to attract a particular group of voters by offering them some advantages at the expense of other voters. This offer, or proposal, which we can call P, is thus a specific instruction. Then some members of the target group, who appreciate the proposal, vote for A, which thereby becomes somewhat bigger than it otherwise would be. After the election A will be considered a possible executive member and, in the negotiations preceding the formation of the executive, A promises to support important points in the other prospective member parties' programs in return for their support of P. The parties reach an agreement along these lines and form an executive. P thus becomes part of the executive's program and will, accordingly, become implemented. Is this kind of scenario, we may ask, likely, or even typical, of a parliamentary democracy with proportionalism? My answer is in the affirmative.

A first prerequisite for this answer is that the parties are able to deliver in the way described, and this condition, as we have seen, is fulfilled. This, however, does not settle the issue. It is obviously not sufficient for the parties to be able to act in the way described -they must also find it expedient to do so, it must pay in terms of votes. More exactly, the behavior must be expected to result in a net gain in votes -the number of voters attracted from other parties must be greater than the number of voters repelled.

In principle this is quite possible. The negative effects may for example be spread out so thinly, and over so many people, that those hit hardly notice. With some shrewd maneuvering it may even be possible to allocate the negative effects mainly on voters who would not have voted for the party anyway. This is so since the campaigning politicians, in a setting in which specific interests are important, are likely to be able to recognize "their own people" to a considerable extent. In a presidential setting with plurality, on the contrary, and as I will later argue, such a behavior is hardly imaginable. There, as we will see, it is imperative for all campaigners not to hurt anybody.

In addition to these problems about the management of the negative effects it is, however, also necessary to consider the reactions of those favored by the proposal. Are they really likely to feel attracted and thus to change their minds in favor of the proposing party? Some may perhaps do so immediately, but there may also be those in the target group who, although favored by the particular proposal, generally dislike the system of politically distributed goods and clientelism, and therefore want to change the system rather than to use it. Such a voter, according to the terminology used here, favors some general instruction rather than the specific instruction at issue. But perhaps there is no party committed to the general instruction which the voter endorses, or if there is such a party its chances of becoming big enough for getting the instruction into a governmental program may be slim. Such dilemmas are, in fact, as we saw in part 11, quite likely. Our voter may thus find it best to play safe and vote for the party offering the favors. Voting for the second best may, after all, seem more prudent since it may give a payoff even if the favored party, after the election, still is quite small.

- The conclusion thus is that electoral strategies including specific instructions about favors to particular target groups may be quite profitable in the parliamentary, proportional setting.

From a methodological point of view it is, I think, important to note that I have not assumed any kind of rational ignorance among the voters in order to reach this conclusion. Rational ignorance, we remember, is the kind of ignorance that ordinary citizens have about public matters, since it does not pay to keep informed. The likelihood that a particular citizen voter will become pivotal in a general election is infinitesimal, and therefore the efforts needed for finding out about the campaigners programs are not worthwhile. The idea put forward here, that small target groups of voters may be favored at the expense of others, may thus be supported by the assumption that these others are rationally ignorant, and that, in fact, is often done. That assumption is however not necessary. The redistribution can, in fact, as I have shown, be explained as a consequence of perfectly enlightened and rational voter behavior within the institutional structures present. Such an explanation tells as much more about the situation than one relying on rational ignorance, and is therefore much more interesting. It is therefore, I would say, a good research strategy to avoid assumptions about rational ignorance as long as possible. In addition to this I would like to argue that ignorance, in the situation described, with several parties and a lot of interests involved, is more limited than usually assumed. People, in particular since they are not only voters but often also rent-seekers, are likely to know quite a lot about the favors offered by the political system. Another interesting point is that relations between voters and campaigners in the particular setting discussed here have important similarities with a market type contract relation.

Having said this it is however also important to emphasize, since we are dealing with compound voting, that other approaches to the voters than the one illustrated are by no means excluded. The campaigning parties may, for instance, try to attract ideologically committed voters with various ideological arguments, they may support various general instructions, or they may just refer to their achievements in the past hoping to get the voters confidence.

But even if various strategies thus may be useful, they can usually not be used without due regards. A party may for example be hurt if its various messages and promises do not form a reasonably coherent totality. If, for instance, some promise given to a group of marginal voters is to strikingly at odds with the party's ideology, some voters belonging to the party's core may leave the party. This importance of coherence has been emphasized by, among others, Downs (1957, pp 109 ff).

THE QUASI CONTRACTUAL RELATIONS BETWEEN PARTIES AND VOTERS

In the constitutional setting discussed here, the parties have a considerable capacity for delivering. It may also be said that they have a considerable capacity for credible commitment towards the voters, and from there it is not long to think about tacit deals, or quasi contracts, between the parties and their voters in various target groups.

In a real deal, or a contract, as we know, each of the parties undertakes to do something in return for the undertakings of the other parties. Here we may think of a contract like this: The party says that it will give favors to the members of the target group in return for their votes, and the members of the target group say that they will vote for the party in return for the favors. Obviously there is no contract like this, but there is something that may be considered as an approximation, and it is interesting to see how this approximation differs from the imagined real contract.

In the imagined real contract situation the party would not go ahead fulfilling its promises without making sure that the voters had fulfilled theirs. In the political situation there is obviously no such possibility -voting is anonymous and the party has no way of controlling the voters. A main rationale for anonymity, in fact, is to prevent parties and voters from bargaining. Joseph Schlesinger, for instance, writes (1991, p 146) that "... benefit seekers need some mechanisms to assert their claims.... One of the principal arguments for the secret ballot is that it makes it difficult for benefit seekers to prove their support and be paid for their vote". But even if anonymity certainly makes real contracts impossible it cannot prevent quasi contracts universally.

In such a quasi contract situation the party, in its own interest, is likely to go ahead in good faith once it has made its commitment. It will try to get into the executive, and it will try to get the promise incorporated in the executive's program. Or, in short, it will behave as in a real contract situation and thereby, for future needs, enhance its own credibility.

The voters, in contrast to the party, have not even made a public commitment, but just listened to the party. Still, even they, to the extent they are attracted by the offer, are likely to behave as in a real contract situation, and thus vote for the party. True, a voter might speculate that she will get the favor anyway, and therefore use her vote for some other purpose. But that means taking a risk and if the voter really wants to add the party in its efforts to fulfil its part of the deal, the best the voter can do is to vote for the party and thereby contribute to its chances of becoming a member of the executive, and to get the proposal included in the governmental program.

Obviously there is no real contract in the situation described. There is no formal agreement, no control, and no enforcement. Still the parts are likely to behave as if they were parts to a real contract, and it is therefore quite reasonable to talk about a quasi contract between the party and the attracted voters in the target group. The factor which mainly accounts for the possibility of such a quasi contract is the party's capacity for delivering, or for credible commitment. That capacity is linked to the particular constitutional setting dealt with here.

According to the discussion the main actors are the likely targets for lobbying. In this constitutional setting, it is thus the political parties, which essentially means the party leaderships at the summits of the party hierarchies, which will be approached by the lobbyists. Since these targets are few and powerful the lobbying will become a very concentrated, and possibly closed, activity. Furthermore, and since this constitutional setting to such a large extent is tuned towards interest politics, it should be a very fertile ground for lobbying activities. The lobbying is thus also likely to very effective.

- Our first conclusion thus is that the lobbying activities are likely to be concentrated, possibly closed, and very effective.

I argued that the lobbyists are likely to demand what they can reasonably get. Here, since that is possible, the lobbyists are likely to ask for changes of status quo -they will not be confined to merely blocking.

- From this -and following the argument in part 10 -it may be concluded that the interest organizations are likely to be long lasting and formed before the laws, which support their interests, are created.

One interesting possibility is that trade unions, which are formed for negotiating with their counterparts about wages and other conditions of labor, are likely to become important lobbyists as well. Since the unions are likely to be able to influence the voting behavior of their members to some extent, they may even, by playing a mediating role, enforce the contract character of the relation between parties and voters.

- Another conclusion, which follows form the fact that the prerequisites for organizational ties between parties and organizations as stated in part 10 are fulfilled, is that such ties are quite possible -and perhaps even likely.

This conclusion, it should be noted, is further supported by the fact that politics in the constitutional setting at issue here is likely to be strongly interest oriented. Thus not only the organizational prerequisites for alliances between parties and interest organizations are present, but also strong positive incentives for that kind of collaboration.

Parliamentary Constitutions with Proportional Elections: In this constitutional setting we are likely to get several political parties since the elections for the legislature are proportional. Furthermore it is important for the parties to get into the executive, since in a parliamentarian system most decisive constellations include the executive. Since there are numerous parties the executive is likely to be a coalition. A party aspiring for a place in a coalition executive is greatly helped by being cohesive and disciplined, and therefore the parties will be so, if effective means for discipline are available. In a proportional system that is the case, and thus the parties are likely to become cohesive and disciplined. The main actors will consequently be party main actors. As for their policies the basic important fact is that the parties are capable of delivering, or, in other words, have a capacity for credible commitment towards the voters. In their relations to the voters they are therefore likely to strive for instruction rather than delegation. Furthermore, and since it is much easier to agree about specific instructions than about general ones when forming a coalition executive, specific instructions are likely to be particularly important components of policies. Politics will to a large extent be interest politics. Since lobbyists are expected to approach the main actors they will, in this constitutional setting, turn to the leaderships of the cohesive political parties.

The lobbying activities will thus be very concentrated, and to some extent perhaps also closed or secret. Since politics to such a large extent is tuned towards interests, lobbying is also likely to be quite effective. The interest organizations, which may have organizational ties with the parties, are likely to get interests satisfied in exchange for votes from their members. This, so far, is a short summary of some earlier main points. In addition to this a few further conclusions may be added. I will start from the contention that the main actors, in this constitutional setting, are political parties, and that politics therefore, on the whole, is party politics. It may also be said that we are dealing with a partyocracy.

- Now, since the parties are just parties, this means that there is no democratically appointed main actor with a responsibility for the common good. All actors represent primarily, and basically, their own interests.
- Another related conclusion is that all proposals for decisions are made by those directly interested in them. The making of proposals, and of decisions, are in a sense inseparable aspects of one and the same process. Almost everything is done when the executive is formed, and by the parties taking part in that process.

The fact that the main actors are parties, does not, of course, mean that individuals are unimportant. The parties do obviously consist of individual human beings and this fact should certainly, and in accordance with methodological individualism, be recognized.

The individuals do however almost exclusively play their roles within, or on behalf of, the parties. Thus, and when it comes to dealings with actors outside the party, for example with other parties, or with the electorate in campaigns, or with lobbyists, it is usually the individuals belonging to the party leaderships which acts on behalf of their parties. Party positions on political issues are of course also determined by the individuals who belong to the party, usually with more influence the higher up in the party hierarchy they are:

- An important conclusion of this, since the individuals essentially play their roles within, or on behalf of, the parties, is that political careers, in this type of system, always are party careers..

Since the parties are likely to be well developed organizations, and to have an easily recognized identity over time, they will be able to develop successively, and to harbor, more and more elaborated, and more and more comprehensive, party programs.

- Furthermore, since the programs are likely to favour the interests of particular groups of voters, long-lasting, mutually supportive relations between parties and voters tend to develop. The party leaderships will thus to a large extent be able to recognise their own people in the electorate.

I have already said several times that politics in this constitutional setting tends to be focused on special interests.

- Another formulation of this conclusion, which alludes to the well known Gresham's law in economics ("cheap money drives out good"), is that specific instructions drive out general ones.

This does not mean that general instructions are altogether eradicated -we have for example seen that general instructions in a big party's program may prevail. Specific instructions are, however, much less threatened, and even encouraged by the system. Most parties, as it seems, will have to deal extensively with specific instructions in order to survive. Specific instructions are thus, in a sense, forced upon politics. This may also impede the voters from favouring ideological positions, and reduce them to interest seekers.

All of this, it may be noted, is to a large extent in agreement with Buchanan's contention (1993) that "Political players who might seek to further some conception of an all-encompassing general, or public, interest cannot survive". Buchanan is however discussing democratic constitutions in general, whereas the focus here is on parliamentary constitutions with proportional elections.

- One implication of this focussing on special interests is that the turnout in elections is likely to be high. Since people are stimulated to pursue their own private or personal interests by political means, the turnout is likely to be greater than in other types of democratic systems.
- Another implication is that the system is likely to exhibit the kind of properties which are usually associated with the so called "tragedy of the commons". There, we remember, the single farmer, since he is unable to affect the general handling of the common pasture, will have to put his cow on the pasture as quickly as possible if it shall get any grass at all. Consequently, and since all farmers are driven to behave in the same way, the pasture will be destroyed. In the political system discussed here the incentives of politicians and voters will bring them to treat common societal resources in a similar destructive way.

PARLIAMENTARY CONSTITUTIONS WITH MAJORITARIAN ELECTIONS

As I mentioned in previous part, there may also be more than two parties. Here, in this part, and in the following parts, I will however concentrate on the two-party case. The reason is that this case has important unique properties, since there will not be any coalition building. If, on the contrary, there are more than two parties we are likely to get coalition politics, and the analysis, although different in some respects, will also have important similarities with the analysis of proportional, parliamentary systems.

The most important fact in the two-party case is that there is normally no interaction at all between the main actors. The biggest party, that is the party which won the last general election, is likely have a safe majority of its own. That party will thus form the executive single-handedly. There will not be any need for the party to cooperate with the other party. The governing party will act alone. In this respect the system differs starkly from the three other main types of constitutional systems we are considering here.

There may, however, be exceptions to this general rule. Thus, if the biggest party's majority is narrow, relatively strong and independent, individual legislators of the governing party may be able to challenge the party leadership. Such legislators may for example force the party leadership to change some proposal in some way, or to deliver some other kind of favor, for example for the legislators' local constituencies. In these situations individual main actors thus become important, and the governing party main actor will have to deal with them. This, of course, is tantamount to main actor interaction.

Here, after having said what there is to say about main actor interaction in a narrow sense, I could end this part. It does, however, seem fitting to add a few consequences of the general rule of no main actor interaction at all, since they constitute contrasts to the preceding proportional variety of parliamentarism. Here are two consequences of that kind.

- First, the governmental process may be more continuous, and less of a batch process, than in the proportional variety of parliamentarism. The reason is that the proposals, which are presented for the legislature, are prepared by the governing party alone. The governmental program may therefore develop gradually during the electoral period.
- Second, in this system, there is always a clear-cut opposition. The party which does not govern is the opposition. There is no ambiguity in that sense, and there is nothing to be lost, such as valuable pivotal positions, by organizing the opposition. The establishment of a shadow cabinet should therefore cause no surprise.

The Cube Rule

In a majoritarian system the party getting most votes usually becomes over-represented in the legislature to a very considerable extent, and the party getting least votes is usually, and consequently, largely under-represented. The so called cube rule is the result of efforts to find a simple relationship, in a majoritarian system, between the quantities involved here. Originally it was formulated in 1909 by J. P. Smith in a report to the British Royal Commission on electoral systems. Let us assume that there are two parties which get V1 and V2 votes in an election, counted nationwide, and after that, using the plurality method, get M1 and M2 mandates respectively in the legislature. Then, according to the cube rule, (M1/M2) = (V1/V2)3. This rule has given a fairly good picture of the development in England during certain periods.

SOME CONDITIONS FOR THE SYSTEM'S PROPER FUNCTIONING

We saw that a parliamentary system, for its proper functioning, depends on disciplined and cohesive parties. This requirement is however probably more important in a proportional system than in a majoritarian one. The reason is that the dominating party in a two-party system usually represents a considerably greater majority in the legislature than a governing coalition in a multiparty-system. The somewhat lesser discipline which is likely in a majoritarian system may therefore be compensated for the smaller number of parties. It therefore seems reasonable to assume that both proportional and majoritarian electoral systems can sustain a parliamentary regime, but the requirement is that the electoral system is of an appropriate variety. We saw that a proportional system, when that is used, basically has to be of the list kind. Here, a similar condition is that the majoritarian method used probably has to be of the first-past-the-post type, whereas the double ballot method probably is unsuitable. The reason is that this latter method is likely to give a considerable number of parties with rather low discipline. The number of parties is thus likely to be greater than if the first-past-the-post method is used, and their discipline is likely to be considerably less than in the case of proportional list elections. A parliamentary system using the double-ballot method is thus likely to fail.

Furthermore, and for the same reasons as in the proportional, parliamentary setting, the popular techniques of primaries, referendums and initiatives are alien to the system and thus not likely to be used. Indeed, even the possibility of using referendums occasionally for saving the parties from dealing with potentially splitting issues, which was real in the proportional context. The reason is that, in this majoritarian context, it is important for the parties, in order to demonstrate a capacity for governing, to have a complete governmental program.

The Possibility of Purely Ideological Single Party Executives

As we saw it is impossible to account for the appearance of a coalition executive within the framework of an one-dimensional spatial model. If there are just two parties in the legislature, as we are now assuming (or if one party has a majority of its own), the executive may very well have an ideological foundation. Consider, for example, the situation. There P2 can easily, by itself, form an executive, and that executive is obviously able to pursue a policy equivalent to P2's position on the ideological scale. In a parliamentary-majoritarian context with two main parties it is thus perfectly possible to account for the executive formation in purely ideological terms.

Here, as always when we are talking about general elections in democracies, we have to do with compound voting. The parties may thus mix various specific or general instructions in their programs, and they may try to obtain some elements of delegation in the relations to the voters, and each individual voter will have to react to all this in his or her personal way. So far everything is the same as in the parliamentary, proportional.

Since we are dealing with parliamentary systems, with fairly cohesive and disciplined parties, it also seems reasonable to conclude that the parties, as in the proportional setting, have a clear capacity for credible commitment towards the voters in general, or towards particular segments of the electorate. A main problem, however, concerns the extent to which they are likely to make use of this latter capacity, the one related to specified target groups.

In the parliamentary, proportional setting, the voters, we remember, could be deterred from voting for general instructions, for example ideological ones, since such votes were easily wasted. In many situations the voters would rather settle for the second best and vote for some specific instruction. Here, these mechanisms are clearly different. Since we are dealing with one-party executives rather than coalition executives, the winning party will have no difficulty in implementing its general instructions, and therefore a voter, who likes a party's general principles, is not deterred from voting for it. The conclusion drawn in the previous chapter, that specific instructions tend to drive out general instructions, is thus not valid here. General instructions will obviously have a place in the election campaigns.

After that conclusion it is tempting to continue by asking whether, in fact, general instructions even tend to drive out specific instructions. I believe that there will be, at least, some such tendency. The reason is that the two parties in this setting, since either of them is going to form the executive single-handedly, must show some fitness for being able to govern, for statesmanship, or, in other words, for caring about general things, in order to get votes. The voters know that they are voting, directly, for a government. In the proportional setting that is not so. There the formation of the executive is, exclusively, a matter for the parties. The voters are devoid of means of influence in that respect, and to a large extent restricted to expressing their interests. Thus, in this situation, where the voters are, in fact, voting for a government, they are likely to be interested in, and to respond to, ideological signals from the campaigning parties. Ideology may thus be important and politics may therefore be quite well represented by models such as the one in the figure in part 15.3. The implication is that politics is mainly about ideological matters, and that the ideologies represented by the two parties are fairly close to each other, and also close to the median position on a single scale, which may be a left-right scale. The ideologies are thus not extreme. This kind of politics could be called median voter ideological politics. This leads to some important conclusions. A first one is that phrases such as "the winner takes all", or "majoritarian politics", which are sometimes used for describing the parliamentarian, majoritarian setting, are wrong, at least to the extent that we are dealing with median voter ideological politics. Rather, and since all voters in a sense contribute to determining the median position, it may be appropriate to talk about ideological consensus. Another conclusion is that we should not necessarily expect very narrow, or minimal, majorities in the legislature. Broad majorities, if they occur, should not be a surprise.

For countries characterized by median voter ideological politics we may, furthermore, conclude that a regular change of the governing party is likely to occur. The reason is that the parties take positions close to the median position and there will always, ex ante, be a considerable uncertainty about the electoral payoff of the positioning. In addition to that the mechanisms illustrated by the cube rule will usually make sure that small differences in electoral payoff are transformed into big differences in the legislature. The possibilities for a big party to dominate a country's politics for long periods, as in the parliamentary, proportional case, are consequently slim.

So far I have only talked about the parties' efforts to win elections but it is, since we are dealing with single member constituencies, and as I have already mentioned several times, also necessary to consider the individual candidates' efforts. These candidates, to the extent that they engage in campaigns of their own, will, as it seems, have to rely on emphasizing their own personalities in various ways. Consequently we shall expect, in this system, beside instructions, a certain amount of delegation as well.

PARLIAMENTARY CONSTITUTIONS WITH MAJORITARIAN ELECTIONS

Since we are dealing with a parliamentary system lobbying will, on the whole, occur at the summits of the party hierarchies. It is however likely to be less influential than in the parliamentary-proportional case, because interests plays a less important role in the politics of this system. In particular, since the governing party is likely to change, and since the programs of both parties are likely to be close to the median, and thus quite similar, fusions of interest organizations and parties are not likely to occur.

In this constitutional setting we are likely to get fewer parties than in the parliamentary, proportional setting. In the extreme case we will get just two dominating parties and that is the case I am dealing with here.

Since we are dealing with a parliamentary system it is important for the parties to be cohesive and disciplined. The requirements in this respect are, however, less far-reaching than in the parliamentary, proportional setting, since the bigger party usually, is considerably bigger than the smaller party in the legislature. Therefore it should not be a problem that the means of discipline are somewhat weaker than in the proportional case.

Furthermore, and since there are just two parties, the one or the other will single-handedly form the executive and we will thus not get any coalition politics. This is likely to be quite consequential since it opens the door for ideological politics concerned with general instructions rather than interest politics concerned with specific instructions. We are likely to get median voter ideological politics.

The fact that the parties try to occupy positions close to the median voter's position, in combination with the tendency for the bigger party to become grossly over-represented in the legislature, is also likely to lead to frequent changes of power. The mechanisms in the parliamentary, proportional setting which allow a party to dominate its country's politics over extended periods are not operating here.

Since there are just two parties, the one forming the executive and the other the opposition, we are also likely to get a shadow cabinet. This, again, is in contrast to the situation in the parliamentary, proportional context, where some parties' wish to obtain pivotal positions was likely to prevent the emergence of a shadow cabinet. Here, as in the proportional context, the lobbying organizations are likely to approach the party leadership's with their demands. Since the politics is less likely to be tuned towards interests, the politicians in the parties are, however, likely to be less inclined to listen to the lobbyists and make deals with them.

Presidential Constitutions with Proportional Elections

Here, as in the other systems we are studying, the main actors will try to further their ambitions by forming, or by just supporting, various decisive or blocking sets. In the presidential systems -this one as well as the majoritarian variety -the president has a particularly important role in these interactions. This is due to the following three aspects of the presidential power.

1. The inclusion of the president is often required for making a set decisive. Sometimes that requirement is dropped, but if so the requirements for a decisive set composed only of legislators is usually sharper. Some kind of qualified majority of legislators may for example be required.
2. The president is usually equipped with special, legal procedural power for making proposals.

3. The president may command resources of various kinds which may be used for giving favors, or compensations, to legislators in order to make them support a presidential proposal.

In the presidential, proportional system discussed here there may, as I have already mentioned, be some party main actors. Even so, however, there will also in all likelihood be quite a number individual main actors. The total number of main actors will therefore be rather great, and the conditions for coordination are consequently not the best.

The main actor interaction is therefore likely to be characterized by a lot of uncoordinated behavior. Furthermore, and from the legislators' point of view, coordination, to the extent that it is possible at all, will be considerably easier when it aims at creating blocking sets rather than decisive sets. In particular this is so if there are two houses in the legislature. Now, taking all of this, intc account, the following hypothetical conclusions can be drawn about the main actor interaction in proportional, presidential systems:

- The reactions to the proposals presented, whether they come from the president or the legislature, will to a large extent be uncoordinated. This means that the voting pattern, at least to a considerable extent, will vary from decision to decision. It also means that occasional majorities which are considerable larger than minimal winning should cause no surprise. It furthermore means that the political process will be continuous, rather than of the batch type. It also means that an organized opposition is unlikely.
- Proposals for new legislation require, in order to pass, the creation of decisive sets, and they will therefore, in fact, often come from the president. This is a consequence of the aspects 1 and 2 above. The president has an advantage in creating decisive sets.
- But even if it is difficult for the legislators to initiate new legislation, they may be successful in the much easier task of creating blocking sets. This is particularly so in this proportional setting, where some party groups in the legislature may be quite consolidated. The purpose may

be to bring about some wanted changes in the proposal blocked. The purpose may however also be obstructive - the proposal may be blocked even by legislators symphatizing with the proposal. If so the idea of the blocking legislators may be to blackmail the president -to force him to give favors to themselves, or to their constituencies, in exchange for an end to the blocking. What makes this kind of blackmail possible, and attractive, is, of course, the fact indicated in point 3 above that the president controls resources of various kinds. Thus, and since the legislature does not dispose of any resources of the kind mentioned, we will never see any blackmailing in the opposite direction -the president will not try to blackmail the legislature.

SOME CONDITIONS FOR THE SYSTEM'S PROPER FUNCTIONING

For the other three main types of constitutional systems treated in this theory it seems possible to consider some kind of functioning as the proper functioning, and therefore also to talk about the conditions for this proper functioning. In this case it is, however, not so clearly like that. I am rather inclined to say that this constitutional system, inherently, is inept and unlikely to function properly. The reason is that presidentialism, which requires party indiscipline is combined with proportional elections, which, at least if we are considering list elections, provide means for enforcing party discipline. Blocking and obstruction are thus likely to be frequent.

Pure list elections thus seem to be incompatible with the systems proper functioning, but perhaps it may work in combination with other kinds of proportional systems, which give the voters influence on the fate of individual candidates. The Finnish system is an example. The use of primaries may also, take power away from the party leaderships, and thus enhance the functioning of the system. Frequent use of initiatives and referendums may also have similar effects.

The upshot of all this is that presidential systems with proportional elections contain a kind of tension, or balance on a very thin edge. As we saw that proportional elections require that political parties of some kind exist. Still, and according to the argument just presented, the constitutional system treated here requires, for its proper functioning, that the parties are not too homogenous or too disciplined, or, in other words, that they are not too much of parties.

Presidential Constitutions with Proportional Elections: When discussing the relation between the main actors and the voters in this case it is, at first, necessary to distinguish between the presidential elections and the elections for the legislature.

The position for which presidential candidates are striving is, of course, even if the candidates belong to political parties, an individual main actor position. According to the final conclusion we should therefore expect the presidential candidates to strive for a relation of delegation, rather than instruction, with the voters. In their campaigns they will therefore concentrate on their own personalities and personal qualities rather on detailed political programs. Furthermore, since a candidate in order to win has to win a majority of the votes, or, depending on the circumstances and the exact rules, at least almost a majority, he or she has to treat all members of the electorate as potential supporters. The campaign messages are thus not likely to offend any voters, for instance by attacking their interests.

The nature of the election campaigns for the legislature will depend on whether we are dealing with pure list elections or not. In the case of list elections, the party leaderships are likely to do a main part of the campaign work. Furthermore, the campaigning will mainly be about instructions or political programs. These conclusions are valid, I think, independently of the extent to which the party leaderships choose to discipline their "troops" in the legislature. Thus, if we have pure list elections, the party leaderships will dominate the campaigns, and the message will be about instructions and programs, even if, after that, the party leaderships give the individual legislators a considerable amount of freedom in their activities in the legislature.

If, however, we are not dealing with pure list elections, but with some other proportional method which makes it possible for the voter to choose, to some extent, among individual candidates, things become different. If so we will also see some individual campaigning and consequently, also, more of delegation and less of instruction. Taking everything into account we are thus likely to see, side by side, very different kinds of campaigning in this constitutional setting, in particular if pure list elections are used for legislature. If so the presidential campaigns will emphasize delegation and personal qualities, whereas the campaigns for the legislature will emphasize instruction and party programs.

PRESIDENTIAL CONSTITUTIONS WITH PROPORTIONAL ELECTIONS

In this constitutional setting, as well as in the other ones, the lobbyists are likely to approach the main actors. Furthermore, the purposes of the lobbyists may either be to get new legislation into being, or to prevent the removal of existing legislation.

In the former case, since the problem is to bring about a decisive constellation, the lobbyist may find it best to approach the president. In the latter case, which is easier since the creation of a blocking constellation is enough, the lobbyist may however also find it worthwhile to approach party main actors in the legislature. Lobbyists approaching individual main actors in the legislature is, however, likely to be an infrequent phenomenon. At least this is so if there are any suitable party main actors in the legislature. Since the lobbyists thus may either try to initiate new legislation, or to prevent the removal existing legislation, we may, se both lobbying organizations, which are formed in order to bring changes about, and thus prior to any such changes, and organizations which are formed after some beneficial legislation, in order to prevent its removal.

Finally, and since some of the parties may be well consolidated, organizational ties between such parties and lobbying organizations should not be excluded. The main characteristic of this constitutional system is that its two main components -that is the president or the presidency on one side, and the legislature on the other -are likely to be ill-matched. The politics of the legislature is likely to be party politics to a large extent. This means that party main actors are likely to play dominant roles. It also means that all legislators, in all likelihood, are people making party careers.

Candidates aspiring for the presidency do not, however, necessarily have to belong to a political party. Their careers are not necessarily party careers. Still, of course, an elected president does have a personal mandate of some kind of his or her own.

The important main implication of this incongruous pattern is that clashes between the president and the legislature are likely and, in particular, that main actors in the legislature may try to blackmail the president.

In this system all main actors are likely to be individuals -we are not likely to find any party main actors. Therefore, although there are some similarities with the presidential, proportional system, there are also some differences.

The president's role is important for the same reasons as in the presidential, proportional setting, but it is considerably more difficult for the main actors in the legislature to co-ordinate their behavior. The reason, of course, is that individual main actors dominate in this system.

This means that the first two conclusions for presidential, proportional systems, as presented in part 19, will be the same here. Thus:

- The reactions to the proposals presented, whether they come from the president or the legislature, will to a large extent be uncoordinated. This means that the voting pattern, at least to a considerable extent, will vary from decision to decision. It also means that occasional majorities which are considerable larger than minimal winning should cause no surprise. It furthermore means that the political process will be continuous, rather than of the batch type. It also means that an organized opposition is unlikely.
- Proposals for new legislation require, in order to pass, the creation of decisive sets, and they will therefore, in fact, often come from the president. The president has an advantage in creating decisive sets.

The main difference concerns the third conclusion in part 19. Here -in contrast to the situation there -organized blocking, fund thus obstruction, will be less frequent.

SOME CONDITIONS FOR THE SYSTEM'S PROPER FUNCTIONING

Since the main actors in the legislature are likely to be individual main actors the threats to the system's functioning, in the form of clashes between the legislature and the president, that is blocking and obstructive behavior in the legislature, are much smaller here than in the presidential, proportional setting.

Still some such threats may exist. If so, the likely reason is that the legislators for some reason are dependent on political parties, and that the party leaderships somehow manage to discipline their troops. A corrective may be the introduction of primaries, and perhaps also of referendums and initiatives. Imagine a person running for the presidency, or for a seat in the legislature. In both cases everybody knows that the person, after the election, and however great the electoral success, will not, without anything further, be in a position to implement his or her delivered campaign proposals, since she also has to deal with the heterogeneous legislature. Exactly for that reason it would not be particularly clever, and perhaps even somewhat ridiculous, to let detailed proposals dominate the campaign. It seems more expedient for the candidate to emphasize his or her own personal very general political inclinations, and personal qualities, thereby indicating a capacity for prudent action in various future situations which, at the moment of the election, are impossible to foresee. The candidate's capacity for credible commitment towards the voters is very limited indeed. The relation between voters and politicians will thus be more of delegation than of instruction.

Furthermore, in this system, with no clear opposition, and without elaborated party programs, it is difficult, or impossible, for the politicians to distinguish between their own voters and the other ones. All citizens are potential supporters and it is therefore important to avoid repelling any voters. All policies which are distinctly harmful for specific groups of voters must be avoided. For this reason a politician may be ill advised to propose the canceling of favors which already happen to exist.

In contrast to the situation in parliamentary systems there is a very large number of targets for lobbying in this setting. The president is obviously a main target. There may also be key persons in the legislature with a lot of procedural power, for example chairmen of committees, which are likely to be approached. In addition to this all individual members of the legislature are also interesting targets. The lobbying activities are thus likely to be spread out, rather than concentrated, and therefore they are also likely to be very costly, or inefficient. If a lobbying organization, for instance, strives for getting a decisive constellation behind a proposal it favors, it will have to approach a great number of different individuals, one by one, rather than one or a few consolidated parties as in a parliamentary system.

This, in turn, may mean that it is considerably easier to lobby for blocking, than to lobby for changes of the status quo. The reason is not only that the constellations needed for blocking usually are smaller than the ones needed for a positive decision. In addition, as we saw in the preceding section, the politicians must be careful not to offend any voters. That should make it wise to abstain from supporting a proposal which a lobbyist wants to see defeated. Lobbying for change of status quo may preferably be directed towards the president.

Since the parties, considered as organizations, are too loose to be able to be parts in joint organizations, the lobbyists are likely to be free in relation to them. In contrast to the case in the parliamentary, proportional setting we will thus not see any fusions between political parties and interest organizations. There is also, a possibility that lobbyists form after reforms are implemented, rather than the other way round.

In this system political parties are significantly less important than in the other three system types. Political parties are not even necessary for the system's functioning since all elections, the presidential ones as well as those for the legislature, are majoritarian. Even so, parties may appear. The system's functioning is however not hampered, and it may indeed be improved, if the parties activities are constrained by for instance primaries.

An important consequence of this restricted role for political parties is that political careers do not have to be party careers, and that individual main actors are more important than in any other constitutional setting.

It may, in fact, be argued that this constitutional type, more than any other type, resembles an ordinary association, say a sports club or a charity association. In such an association, as we know, there are usually no parties. The main decision-makers, or decisions-making bodies, of such an association may be a president a board, and a general congress. These entities, and their workings may correspond quite closely to the president with his executive, and the legislature, in this constitutional setting.

4

NON-INTERNATIONAL ARMED CONFLICTS

ANSAs are often involved in internal conflicts restricted to the territory of a single State and involve at least one ANSA. These conflicts are defined as non-international armed conflicts by IHL as a contrast to wars of national liberation which have been internationalized with the adoption of Protocol I. The key to the identification of these armed conflicts is ANSA's concentrated use of violence under a relatively long period of time. This intensity is an established requirement which constitutes a threshold or a cut-off that hostilities such as internal disturbances, tensions, riots or other isolated and sporadic acts of violence do not cross and thereby are left beyond the reach of international law. This requirement has become a problem for the application of IHL since armed conflicts have always taken diverse appearances. Therefore, the scrutiny of each armed conflict is very essential in order to decide if IHL should apply. The question that imposes itself here is: at what point on the scale of intensity are we justified in designating an armed conflict as non-international? Unfortunately the transition from a common disturbance to an internal conflict of a non-international dignity is not like the freezing point of water.

There is also the problem of the emergence of new groups of armed conflicts. Globalization has not only internationalized the effects of internal armed conflicts, but also facilitated the transformation of internal armed conflicts into transnational conflicts. Adding to that the intervention of a third State in an otherwise internal armed conflict, to either stop or support one or both parties. IHL avoids dealing with this type of intervention although it is not a new phenomenon. This, nevertheless, does not mean that these rather complex situations are left unregulated. Such intervention might internationalize the conflict and in that case the entire IHL would be applicable, otherwise customary international law is always applicable.

RELEVANT PROVISIONS APPLICABLE TO NON-INTERNATIONAL ARMED CONFLICTS

Due to the frequency of these internal armed conflicts, the international community was forced to realise that some form of regulation of non-international conflicts was needed. The effort to extend IHL to non-international armed conflicts ultimately resulted in the bold and ambiguous Common Article 3. IHL applicable in non-international armed conflict is the result of a compromise between the concept of sovereignty and humanitarian concerns. Internal conflicts involve a high intensity of violence and cannot remain beyond the reach of international law providing protection to both civilians and combatants. Non-international armed conflicts are covered by Common Article 3, Protocol II (156 State Parties to date), several other treaties, as well as by customary law. Customary law acts both as a complement and a confirmation of the basic standards set by both Protocol II and Common Article 3. As already noted, many provisions applicable in international armed conflicts have also become applicable in non-international armed conflicts as customary international law. Under the following analysis you should have in mind that the part of IHL governing non-international armed conflict is the result of a compromise between the concept of sovereignty and humanitarian concerns.

COMMON ARTICLE 3

When Common article 3 was first adopted, it was considered a major step in the right direction in the development of the IHL. Indeed, it is the result of the first attempt ever to impose some basic humanitarian legal restraints upon both parties to an internal conflict carried out within the territory of a State Party to the Conventions. As is well known, States do not welcome any interference in their domestic security matters. So to agree upon imposing limitations in dealing with internal violence directed against? is still considered a great achievement. This "mini convention" is viewed as a part of *jus cogens*. The article states that: In the case of armed conflict not of an international character occurring in the territory of one of the High Contracting Parties, each party to the conflict shall be bound to apply, as a minimum, the following provisions:

1. Persons taking no active part in the hostilities, including members of armed forces who have laid down their arms and those placed *hors de combat* by sickness, wounds, detention, or any other cause, shall in all circumstances be treated humanely, without any adverse distinction founded on race, colour, religion or faith, sex, birth or wealth, or any other similar criteria.

   To this end the following acts are and shall remain prohibited at any time and in any place whatsoever with respect to the above-mentioned persons:

   a) violence to life and person, in particular murder of all kinds, mutilation, cruel treatment and torture;
   b) taking of hostages;
   c) outrages upon personal dignity, in particular, humiliating and degrading treatment;
   d) the passing of sentences and the carrying out of executions without previous judgment pronounced by a regularly constituted court affording all the judicial guarantees which are recognized as indispensable by civilized peoples.

2. The wounded and sick shall be collected and cared for. An impartial humanitarian body, such as the International Committee of the Red Cross, may offer its services to the Parties to the conflict. The Parties to the conflict should further endeavour to bring into force, by means of special agreements, all or part of the other provisions of the present Convention.

The application of the preceding provisions shall not affect the legal status of the Parties to the conflict.

Despite the undisputed significance of Common Article 3, as an improvement of the traditional international law approach to internal conflicts, it barely employs the most basic principles preserved in the Conventions onto non-international conflicts. It is true that the parties to the armed conflict are encouraged to apply all the provisions of the Conventions, but it fails to provide the full application of the entire body of IHL on its own. When governments have been reluctant to recognize the lower threshold in Common Article 3, namely that there is an internal conflict taking place within their territory, it seems rather unlikely that they would consider applying any additional provisions from the Conventions. To be clear, the application of Common Article 3 starts automatically when the objective criteria listed in this article are met.

Nevertheless, the government´s refusal to acknowledge this rule may contaminate the attitude of the armed group involved in the conflict, especially that they neither participated in the process that produced this rule, nor were allowed to become a party to the treaty. The reciprocity between the government and the ANSA remains important, though it is not a direct requirement for its application. Of course they may be other reasons why an armed group might refuse to comply with the law. Armed groups that do not have an aspiration to achieve international recognition and legitimacy, lack the intention to comply with international norms. They are merely interested in controlling economical/ natural resources or running criminal activities. On the other hand, a government´s reluctance to admit that an internal conflict existed within its territory had totally different reasons. It was grounded in its concern that such recognition would give legitimacy to the armed group´s cause and at the same time reveal the weak points of the State. It should be pointed out in this context that Common article 3 does not confer by any means recognition to the ANSA involved in the conflict, nor does it change their status in international law. It certainly does not provide any legitimization to their cause. By this provision, it is no longer required that the members of ANSA exercise control over any amount of territory or that they have the characteristic of a government. The threshold for the application of Common Article 3 is lower than that for recognised belligerency; such recognition would bring the whole corpus of IHL, not just the minimum rules of common Article 3, into application. As already mentioned, there are a lot of violent activities left outside the scope of this provision. Under this provision´s rather low threshold lies a range of conflicts, from passing sporadic challenges to State authority to insurgency, which could, conceivably, come within the scope of Common Article 3.

The greatest weakness in Common Article 3 is the absence of a clear definition of what is to be considered a non-international conflict. This ambiguity of its threshold makes it uncertain if and when violent actions in a State can be regarded as a non-international armed conflict and thereby trigger its application. Common Article 3 also lacks of the expression of the necessity or even better the formation of a competent authority who can decide if a certain conflict constitutes an 'Article 3 conflict'. As if all these deficiencies are not enough, Common Article 3 fails to take into account the special type of warfare involved in most internal conflicts, i.e. guerrilla warfare. Yet the article fails to take it into account. The Diplomatic Conference of 1949 failed to define the scope of the conflict which is covered by Common Article 3. A lot of difficulties and disputes had to be resolved by the committee of the non-international conflict at the Diplomatic Conference when the drafting of the provision of non-international conflicts came up for discussion. Judging from the conclusion of the article, they obviously had a hard time reaching a consensus. So the limitations and defects of this article's final composition must be regarded with this in mind. Indeed, Common article 3 has been the object of more attention and dispute than any other provision in the Conventions. In the end its conclusion can be regarded as an achievement despite the defects it holds.

ADDITIONAL PROTOCOL II

Protocol II, like Common Article 3, was considered innovative as it was the first separate treaty to establish standards for the protection of persons involved in internal armed conflicts. It provided basic rules on methods of warfare applicable by both States and ANSAs involved in non-international armed conflicts. Protocol II was meant to define and supplement Common Article 3. But the strong resistance it received from developing States that, although they supported a distinctive treatment for ANSAs fighting against colonial and racist regimes, strived to secure their fragile existence by decreasing the regulations in non-international armed conflicts that occurs within their territory and threaten their authority, led to the failure of this intention. The States severely limited Protocol II and introduced a high threshold for its applicability, since the status of ANSAs combating colonial and racist regimes was established, and they had no interest in adopting a comprehensive framework in Protocol II. It should be stressed at this point that a compliance with the provisions of Protocol II does not imply recognition of any particular status for armed opposition groups.

Protocol II turned out to be limited to ensuring the application of the basic rules of IHL to internal conflicts. Thereby, it does not limit the rights of the States or the means available to them to maintain or restore law and order. It cannot even be used to justify humanitarian intervention. A government faced with an insurrection can in no circumstances use the argument that the insurgents have illegally taken up arms to justify refusing to apply Protocol II, since the instrument was adopted precisely to govern situations of that nature. With respect to the obligations it creates, Protocol II therefore rules out any subordination of *jus in bello* to jus ad bellum. Nevertheless, Protocol II has had a significant influence on State Practice and the following formation of customary law applicable in non-international armed conflicts. As a result, many of its provisions are now considered to be part of customary international law. States practice has also created a significant number of customary rules that are more detailed than the elementary provisions in Protocol II. Customary law has a very important complementary role as it fixes the deficiencies and fills the gaps in both Protocol II and Common Article 3.

Both Article 3 and Protocol II can apply simultaneously to a conflict, providing for the minimum amount of protection. However, protocol II provides a much greater substantive protection, introducing new fundamental rules concerning the protection of civilians against the effects of hostilities, as well as the protection of medical personnel and transports.

Article 1

Article 1 of Protocol II comprises the foundation of the protocol as it lays down the scope of its application. In order to remedy the shortage of Common Article 3, mentioned earlier, and to improve the protection of victims of non-international conflicts it was necessary to develop rules and define objective criteria to determine the applicability of Protocol II. The uncertainty regarding definitions often led to the rejection of the applicability of Common Article 3. At the same time a strict and rigid definition would have also led to the same result. Article 1 is the result of many extensive and protracted negotiations. The outcome of the entire protocol hinged on this single provision.

The article states:

1) This Protocol, which develops and supplements Article 3 common to the Geneva Conventions of 12 August 1949 without modifying its existing conditions of application, shall apply to all armed conflicts which are not covered by Article 1 of the Protocol Additional to the Geneva Conventions of 12 August 1949, and relating to the Protection of Victims of International Armed Conflicts (Protocol I) and which take place in the territory of a High Contracting Party between its armed forces and dissident armed forces or other organized armed groups which, under responsible command, exercise such control over a part of its territory as to enable them to carry out sustained and concerted military operations and to implement this Protocol.
2) This Protocol shall not apply to situations of internal disturbances and tensions, such as riots, isolated and sporadic acts of violence and other acts of a similar nature, as not being armed conflicts.

While Common Article 3 does not provide a definition of "non-international armed conflict", Article 1 of Protocol II, clarifies that the Protocol applies to armed conflicts which take place (1) in the territory of a State Party to the protocol, (2) between its armed forces and ANSAs which (a) are organized under a responsible command, (b) exercise control over part of its territory, (c) are able to carry out continuous and intensive military operations and to implement the Protocol.

The condition of having a responsible authority and an organization does not imply that a hierarchical system of guerilla organization similar to that of regular armed forces is required. It simply points out the obligation of having an organization that exercise control over a certain amount of territory and capable of planning and carrying out continuous and concerted military operations. In addition to that, it should have a *de facto* authority imposing discipline on its members and capable of implementing this protocol. The amount of territory which should be occupied is not stated and in fact is not relevant: the occupation of the territory only has to be such as to allow sustained and concerted military operations and to apply the protocol. Therefore, internal conflicts resulting in a temporary occupation of a small territory without total control over another national territory do not fall under Protocol II. On the other hand being under command and in control of a large amount of the territory is a crucial requirement to be able to implement the protocol, for instance to set up of hospitals and prison camps.

So this rather high threshold is fairly realistic since the conditions provided in this article correspond with actual circumstances in which the parties may reasonably be expected to apply the rules developed in Protocol II. In practical terms, if the ANSA is organized in accordance with the requirements of the Protocol, the extent of territory it can claim to control will be that which escapes the control of the government's armed forces. However, there must be some degree of stability in the control of even a modest area of land for it to be capable of effectively applying the rules of the Protocol. This condition of territory control in the mother State is rarely achieved as most ANSAs have their base outside of the mother State. Obviously, these criteria restrict the scope of application of the Protocol to conflicts of a high intensity only. Therefore, only very few non-international conflicts are covered by Protocol II, unlike Common Article 3.

Once this threshold is passed, the Protocol applies to the conflict in question. The application of Protocol II is automatic, i.e. no declaration has to be made by the parties to the conflict as long as the requirements of Article 1 are met. Therefore, the question of the applicability of Protocol II can be answered differently in each case, according to the prevailing circumstances. Despite the efforts made to clarify the problem of the threshold of Protocol II, much ambiguity still surrounds its application. Protocol II does not clearly state how much territory must be under the control of the non-government party to the conflict. Even the implementation of this Protocol by the ANSA remains unclear. A lot is left up to the discretion of the State, which is not a very satisfactory position. If States are allowed to characterise a situation and in accordance with that dictates of their individual disposition, then the broader base of humanitarian concerns may be sacrificed in the process. The second paragraph of Article 1 reveals the exclusion of situations of internal disturbances and tensions, such as riots, isolated and sporadic acts of violence and other acts of a similar nature, from the scope of Protocol II. As already mentioned, these forms of hostilities are not considered as armed conflicts, not even in the framework of Common Article 3. A State may use armed force to maintain order caused by or even causing internal tensions or when force is used as a preventative measure to maintain respect for law and order without getting to be considered internal disturbances. However, situations of this kind are covered by regional and universal human rights according to the article.

Nevertheless, practice has laid down certain criteria to draw up the boundaries of non- international armed conflicts from internal disturbances. Firstly, the hostilities have to be carried out by force of arms and reveal such intensity that the government is compelled to utilize its armed forces against ANSA. Secondly, the hostilities are meant to be carried out by the entire ANSA, and not by a single group within. Additionally, the ANSA has to exhibit a minimum amount of organization. Its armed forces should be under a responsible command and thereby be capable of meeting humanitarian requirements. The conflict must demonstrate certain similarities to an armed conflict without fulfilling all conditions necessary for the recognition of belligerency. While in conflicts that come within the scope of Common Article 3, the ANSA and the State party involved are also encouraged to apply all the other provisions of the Conventions relating to international armed conflicts, thus offering a much broader base of protection to those involved in wars of national liberation, including a limit on the means and methods of warfare and on the conduct of hostilities.

Protocol II only applies to situations of conflicts between ANSA and the established government and not between two or more ANSAs, resulting in a scope of application that is much narrower than that of Common Article 3.

COMBATANT AND POW STATUS

The status of combatants in internal conflicts differs dramatically from the status of combatants in international conflicts. However, the restrictive combatant status offered in Common Article 3 can be accorded to both recognized and unrecognized ANSAs.

But Article 4 of the POW Convention, which automatically applies in international conflicts, does not apply to a non-international conflict unless the parties to such conflict choose to apply it, either by an expressed agreement or by concession. For instance, US Military command applied this article to the captured enemy in Vietnam.

The combatant status offered in Common Article 3 and Protocol II fail in providing any protection from prosecution to captured combatants. This is rather peculiar considering that both instruments establish a separation, if only to a limited extent, between *jus ad bellum* and *jus in bello*. The constraints on States provided by Common article 3 or Protocol II, such as the obligation to treat members of ANSAs in a humane manner, have been proven difficult to achieve. Indeed these instruments fail to achieve any constraints on the penalties these combatants are forced to endure for participating in the hostilities. This failure is extremely alarming bearing in mind the absence of specific rules and definitions with respect to the principles of distinction and proportionality that makes the distinction between combatants and civilians very minimal in Protocol II.

Article 44 (3, 4, and 5) of Protocol II states:

3. In order to protect the civilian population from hostilities, civilians are not to be harmed if they are not taking part in attacks or war activities or preparing attacks. Because in certain armed situations it is not possible to differentiate between the combatants and the civilians, people are to be granted combatants status if they: a) are openly carrying a weapon during a military manoeuvre; b) are openly carrying a weapon in view of the enemy while on a military march prior to an attack which they are supposed to take part in.
4. A combatant who falls into enemy hands and who is not covered by the provisions of Section 3/2 is to be considered a Prisoner of War; he is entitled to all rights guaranteed by the Third Convention and this Protocol.
5. A combatant who falls into enemy hands, not while taking part in an attack or preparing for an attack, is not considered a combatant or a Prisoner of War because of his prior activity.

To be regarded as combatants, members of ANSAs have to fulfill certain conditions. They have to be carrying arms openly either during the attack or in the preparation preceding the attack that they are participating in. If the combatants are caught participating in a military operation or preparing such but not abiding by the distinction rules they are still granted a POW status. Even civilians participating in these conflicts are granted both combatant and POW status under the same conditions. However unlike Protocol I, Protocol II does not grant either combatant or POW status on members of any armed group, for their mere membership. In addition to that domestic law still remains in force in situations where Protocol II is applicable. Obviously the protection offered by Protocol I regarding combatants and POW, is to be much preferred. However, Article 6, concerning penal prosecutions, lays down the judicial guarantees provided for in Common Article 3; independence of the courts, rights of defence, individual responsibility, non-retroactivity of penalties, presumption of innocence, information on judicial remedies. The fifth paragraph of this article contains a provision that even urge the established government to grant amnesty to the participants. There are also various resolutions granting POW status to members of ANSAs when captured, especially those fighting for a certain political objective, such as freedom. Most recently the US Supreme Court has declared the applicability of Common Article 3 with regard to trying individuals captured in Afghanistan during the conflict there between US and Al Qaeda. The Supreme Court declared that Common Article 3 applies even to that conflict. In the meanwhile, since neither common Article 3 nor Protocol II contains any provision on criminal responsibility for any violations of IHL in an internal armed conflict, the International Criminal Tribunal for the former Yugoslavia (ICTY) concluded in an important decision that horrific crimes committed in a non-international armed conflict are to be considered as international crimes. As a result, rules concerning international armed conflicts apply when trying a person prosecuted for a crime committed in a non-international armed conflict.

Both Common Article 3 and Protocol II apply simultaneously and automatically to internal conflicts when certain threshold criteria are reached. However, the ambiguity surrounding the application and scope of Common Article 3, caused by its lack of definition of what constitutes an internal conflict, made it difficult to distinguish between a non-international armed conflict and internal disturbances or other sporadic acts of violence. This has expectedly helped States escape their international obligation in applying these instruments by denying that such a conflict is taking place in their territory. Protocol II, however, describes its scope in considerable detail, excluding low-intensity conflicts. Article 1 makes the application of Protocol II dependent on the exercise of *de facto* control of part of the national territory and on the ability of on material circumstances linked to the nature of the hostilities, i.e. the ability to carry out organized and sustained acts of violence and to implement the Protocol. It applies to all armed conflicts in which these conditions are met, regardless of who triggered the conflict and why. Protocol II rules out any subordination of *jus in bello* to *jus ad bellum*. Protocol II, reaffirms the separation between *jus ad bellum* and *jus in bello* established by Common Article only as far as the obligations it creates are concerned and only to a limited extent as it fails to provide any protection from arbitrary persecution to the participants in these conflicts. It is fair to say that the protection offered by both Protocol II and Common Article 3, to captured members of unrecognized NSAs is very modest and in many cases non-existence.

CONCLUSION

Final Remarks

We stand at the dawn of the 21st century with so much violence and blood in our past, present and inescapably in our future too. To our consternation IHL has been proven repeatedly ineffective especially when dealing with the changed nature of global violence. The increase in armed conflicts generated by ANSAs presents both theoretical and practical challenges to international law. The impact of the violent activities of ANSAs on world politics is growing to such an extent that the traditionally exclusive role of States in international law must be reassessed. The first authoritative recognition of the existence and relevance of ANSAs from an international legal perspective came from ICJ. Even today when the existence of ANSAs is frequently acknowledged in international law books and journals, the State-centred conception of international law still prevails. It is rather obvious that ANSAs are not a new phenomenon; however our perception of them is much different today. Does this mean that the instruments provided by IHL are unsuited to the realities of today's conflicts? It should be remembered that IHL has always aimed at balancing between legitimate concern for the security of the State and its population on the one hand and the preservation of human life, health and dignity on the other.

This chapter sought to examine the rules that affirm the applicability of IHL on ANSAs and the armed conflicts in which they are involved. At the same time, it offers some explanation as to why these rules are not applied in such situations. Some light has even been shed over the international development that led to the current wording and form of these provisions to give a bigger picture when evaluating these instruments.

Traditional law allowed the applicability of the whole body of *jus in bello* only when a state of belligerency was recognized by the involved State or a third State. While such recognition of belligerency rarely occurred, the application of IHL was more of a political expediency with the involved State requiring the principle of reciprocity. Typically, this recognition came at a late stage of the conflict with much destruction and death already having taken place.

State sovereignty played a central role during the drafting period of the conventions, resulting in States refusal to adopt a comprehensive framework for internal armed conflicts since they regarded these conflicts as falling within their domestic jurisdiction and the members of ANSAs as criminals not deserving the protection of IHL. Ultimately this produced the ambiguous Common Article 3 that raised a lot of criticism. While some opine that the uncertainty surrounding the definition of an internal armed conflict as well as the confusion regarding its threshold and automatic applicability made it unpractical. Others argue that its scope covers all cases of armed conflicts not of an international character, especially in the absence of a clear definition for a non-international armed conflict. In any case, Common Article 3 still remains very significant as it is the first move towards legal intrusion of IHL into the conventional sphere of internal affairs of sovereign States.

By 1977 and as wars of national liberation became more frequent, Protocol I came to confer international status on these conflicts. If NLMS were viewed as a 'Power' under Common Article 2 (3), the possibility then existed that they could apply and agree to be bound by these Conventions under article 96, and the whole body of IHL would apply to the conflict in which they were involved. There are divergent opinions regarding the scope of the application of Protocol I as laid down in Article 1 (4), especially regarding inclusion and exclusion of some self-determination struggles, thus its scope has been seen to be very restrictive. However, our belief in the universality of human rights (HR) forces us to realize the inevitability of the transformation of a people's right to self-determination to even include people who are subject to apartheid, persecution, discrimination and other violations of HR by another group whether it is a minority or majority which prevents the affected group from the realisation of HR and fundamental freedoms. If it is of any comfort conflicts that do not fall within the scope of this article are rescued by Protocol II, and Common Article 3.

The other product of 1977 was Protocol II, which sought to extend the scope of Common Article 3 and present a definition of non-international armed conflicts making States definition or recognition of these situations irrelevant. Protocol II supplements and develops Common Article 3, but it does not substitute its provisions. In other words, Common Article 3 and Protocol II exist autonomously. Thus they can be applied simultaneously to a non-international armed conflict. However Protocol II provides more substantive protection for civilians. But, like Common Article 3, it does not offer any protection to the members of the ANSA. These would still be regarded as criminals and persecuted under domestic laws.

This paper shows that the applicability of IHL to ANSAs and the conflicts in which they are involved has been made unpractical by either the restrictiveness of the provisions or political reluctance. In theory State´s denial of the existence of an armed conflict within its borders, or their being a party to the conventions or the protocols is irrelevant. In practice, however, States prefer to classify internal conflicts of both international and non-international conflicts as internal disturbances or indeed manifestations of terrorism, and deal with them under municipal law, in order to preserve their State sovereignty and image. If they, against all expectations, concede to apply IHL, then it is just an act of "selective humanitarianism". IHL's restrictive applicability to armed conflicts, international and non-international, hinders its application to internal tensions or disturbances or other isolated acts of violence. At the same time, these supposedly unregulated hostilities are the ones causing most harm and the possibility of applying similar protection to these cases is very important to discuss. It has, therefore, been argued that the qualification of the conflict as international or non-international is declining in relevancy, since a considerable amount of customary rules applies regardless of that. However, customary rules cannot weaken the applicable treaty obligations of the Signatory Party. Customary international humanitarian law only fills in certain gaps in protection provided to victims of armed conflict by treaty law. These gaps result either from the lack of ratification of relevant treaties or from the lack of detailed rules on non-international armed conflicts in treaty law. The advantage of customary law is that it is not necessary for a State to formally accept a rule in order to be bound by it.

Bearing in mind that IHL strives to ease the suffering caused by armed conflicts, we have to admit that it is rather absurd that we still categorize armed conflicts as an international or a non-international conflict. This triggers different instruments offering different measures of protection to members of ANSA and civilians; when the scourges of the armed conflicts are virtually the same and sometimes even worse in non-international conflicts. If an armed conflict is considered to be an international conflict, the whole *jus in bello* would apply. But, if the same conflict is considered to be of a non-international character, then it is simply the basic rules of Common Article 3 or/and Protocol II which will be applicable, significantly limiting the protection offered to those involved in such conflict. On top of that States frequently tried to deny any applicability of IHL to the activities of ANSAs in their territory or in other territories for that matter, warring of granting legitimacy to ANSAs and their cause. The application of IHL does not confer any legal status on a group or their particular use of force. More important, the applicability of IHL cannot be judged upon the legality of the cause and conduct of hostilities. The rules of IHL apply equally to all parties to an armed conflict irrespective of which is the aggressor or the self-defender or which is a State or an armed group.

Many conflicts today are internal conflicts clashed between ANSAs without an obvious State involvement. These conflicts claim thousands of lives and affect millions of people every year. But because they are less politically sensitive than conflicts in which a State is a party to the conflict they do not get much attention in IHL or the international community. So if the nature of the conflict makes such a difference, maybe blurring the distinction between different categories would make the protection offered by IHL available to civilians and combatants against the barbarism that occurs in these conflicts.

In the end it should be stressed that there is no need to change the existing or to come up with new laws, because that will only lead to more confusion and additional inefficient laws. However let´s face it, States today are no longer capable of controlling ANSAs. Globalisation facilitated the expansion of ANSA´s activities and thereby helped create a space removed from the effective control of any State. This has allowed them to act with virtual impunity; escape their internationally recognized humanitarian obligations and the consequences of their actions. If ANSAs are to be held accountable for violations of humanitarian norms, they have to be addressed directly, even those designated as terrorists by the international community. Although there have been calls for measures to address "all parties" in armed conflicts, States remain reluctant to place ANSAs on their political agenda. International organizations engaging ANSAs are left to work in an often ad hoc manner without any international political support. The most important questions facing the world today are: Is the State still a central actor of international law? Is she the only one ruling and regulating on the national and international level? And of course whether the UN with its member States ignoring ANSAs can cope with the new era? Is it so that the UN ´s influence and good reputation is in decline?

The law ought to be made more effective and inclusive. Tomorrow´s mission should not be to determine what the rules are, or how to apply them to a specific situation, or even whether the existing rules are adequate or not, but rather how to secure or compel compliance with the law at all. It may be that we have now passed from the phase of law-making to a period where the focus is not on new substantive law but on how to make existing law effective.

5

POLITICS IN KOREA AND US

S.-North Korea relations developed primarily during the Korean War, but in recent years have been largely defined by the United States' suspicions regarding North Korea's nuclear programs, and North Korea's perception of an imminent US attack.

BACKGROUND

Although hostility between the two countries remains largely a product of Cold War politics, there were earlier conflicts and animosity between the US and Korea. In the mid-19th century Korea closed its borders to Western trade, much as North Korea has today. In the General Sherman Incident, Korean forces attacked a US gunboat sent to negotiate a trade treaty and killed its crew, after it defied instructions from Korean officials. A US retribution attack, the Sinmiyangyo, followed. Korea and the US ultimately established trade relations in 1882. Relations soured again when the US negotiated peace in the Russo-Japanese War. Japan persuaded the US to accept Korea as part of Japan's sphere of influence, and the US did not protest when Japan annexed Korea five years later. Korean nationalists petitioned the US to support their cause at the Versailles Treaty conference under Woodrow Wilson's principle of national self-determination, without success.

The US divided Korea after World War II along the 38th parallel, intending it as a temporary measure. However, the breakdown of relations between the US and USSR prevented a reunification. The North Korean government came to see the US as an imperalist successor to Japan, a view it still holds today. The United States maintains economic sanctions against the DPRK under the Trading with the Enemy Act.

DENUCLEARIZATION OF THE KOREAN PENINSULA

North Korea joined the nuclear Non-Proliferation Treaty (NPT) as a non-nuclear weapons state in 1985, and North and South Korean talks begun in 1990 resulted in a 1992 Denuclearization Statement. However, lack of progress in developing and implementing an agreement with the International Atomic Energy Agency (IAEA) for the inspection of the North's nuclear facilities led to North Korea's March 1993 announcement of its withdrawal from the NPT. A UN Security Council resolution in May 1993 urged North Korea to cooperate with the IAEA and to implement the 1992 North-South Denuclearization Statement. It also urged all member states to encourage North Korea to respond positively to this resolution and to facilitate a solution of the nuclear issue.

U.S.-North Korea talks beginning in June 1993 led to the U.S.-North Korea Agreed Framework in October 1994:

- North Korea agreed to freeze its existing plutonium enrichment program, to be monitored by the IAEA;
- Both sides agreed to cooperate to replace North Korea's graphite-moderated reactors with light water reactor (LWR) power plants, to be financed and supplied by an international consortium (later identified as the Korean Peninsula Energy Development Organization or KEDO);
- The United States and North Korea agreed to work together to store safely the spent fuel from the five-megawatt reactor and dispose of it in a safe manner that does not involve reprocessing in North Korea;
- The two sides agreed to move toward full normalization of political and economic relations;
- Both sides agreed to work together for peace and security on a nuclear-free Korean Peninsula; and
- Both sides agreed to work together to strengthen the international nuclear non-proliferation regime.

In accordance with the terms of the Agreed Framework, North Korea decided to freeze its nuclear program and cooperate with United States and IAEA verification efforts, and in January 1995 the U.S. eased economic sanctions against North Korea. North Korea agreed to accept the decisions of KEDO, the financier and supplier of the LWRs, with respect to provision of the reactors. KEDO subsequently identified Sinpo as the LWR project site and held a groundbreaking ceremony in August 1997. In December 1999, KEDO and the (South) Korea Electric Power Corporation (KEPCO) signed the Turnkey Contract (TKC), permitting fullscale construction of the LWRs.

In January 1995, as called for in the Agreed Framework, the United States and North Korea negotiated a method to store safely the spent fuel from the five-megawatt reactor. According to this method, U.S. and North Korean operators would work together to can the spent fuel and store the canisters in the spent fuel pond. Actual canning began in 1995. In April 2000, canning of all accessible spent fuel rods and rod fragments was declared complete.

In 1998, the United States identified an underground site in Kumchang-ni, which it suspected of being nuclear-related. In March 1999, North Korea agreed to grant the U.S. "satisfactory access" to the site. In October 2000, during Special Envoy Jo Myong Rok's visit to Washington, and after two visits to the site by teams of U.S. experts, the U.S. announced in a Joint Communiqué with North Korea that U.S. concerns about the site had been resolved.

As called for in Dr. William Perry's official review of U.S. policy toward North Korea, the United States and North Korea launched new negotiations in May 2000 called the Agreed Framework Implementation Talks.

NORTH KOREA POLICY UNDER GEORGE W. BUSH

Following the inauguration of President George W. Bush in January 2001, the new Administration began a review of North Korea policy. At the conclusion of that review, the Administration announced on June 6, 2001, that it had decided to pursue continued dialogue with North Korea on the full range of issues of concern to the Administration, including North Korea's conventional force posture, missile development and export programs, human rights practices, and humanitarian issues. In 2002, the Administration also became aware that North Korea was developing a uranium enrichment program for nuclear weapons purposes. U.S.-D.P.R.K. tensions mounted, when Bush categorized North Korea as part of the "Axis of Evil" in his 2002 State of the Union address.

When U.S.-D.P.R.K. direct dialogue resumed in October 2002,

this uranium- enrichment program was high on the U.S. agenda. North Korean officials acknowledged to a U.S. delegation, headed by Assistant Secretary of State for East Asian and Pacific Affairs James A. Kelly, the existence of the uranium enrichment program. Such a program violated North Korea's obligations under the NPT and its commitments in the 1992 North-South Denuclearization Declaration and the 1994 Agreed Framework. The U.S. side stated that North Korea would have to terminate the program before any further progress could be made in U.S.-D.P.R.K. relations. The U.S. side also made clear that if this program were verifiably eliminated, the U.S. would be prepared to work with North Korea on the development of a fundamentally new relationship. In November 2002, the members of KEDO agreed to suspend heavy fuel oil shipments to North Korea pending a resolution of the nuclear dispute.

In December 2002, Spanish troops boarded and detained a shipment of Scud missiles from North Korea destined for Yemen, at the United States' request. After two days, the United States released the ship to continue its shipment to Yemen. This further strained the relationship between the US and North Korea, with North Korea characterizing the boarding an "act of piracy".

In late 2002 and early 2003, North Korea terminated the freeze on its existing plutonium-based nuclear facilities, expelled IAEA inspectors and removed seals and monitoring equipment, quit the NPT, and resumed reprocessing of spent nuclear fuel to extract plutonium for weapons purposes. North Korea subsequently announced that it was taking these steps to provide itself with a deterrent force in the face of U.S. threats and the U.S.' "hostile policy". Beginning in mid-2003, the North repeatedly claimed to have completed reprocessing of the spent fuel rods previously frozen at Yongbyon and later publicly said that the resulting fissile material would be used to bolster its "nuclear deterrent force". There is no independent confirmation of North Korea's claims.

President Bush has stated that the United States has no plans at this time to invade North Korea now or in the forseeable future. He also stated that the United States intends to make every effort to achieve a peaceful end to North Korea's nuclear program in cooperation with North Korea's neighbors, who have also expressed concern over the threat to regional stability and security they believe it poses. The Bush Administration's stated goal is the complete, verifiable, and irreversible elimination of North Korea's nuclear weapons program. North Korea's neighbors have joined the United States in supporting a nuclear weapons-free Korean Peninsula.

In the last months of 2005, relations between the countries have been further strained by US allegations of North Korean counterfeiting of American dollars. The US alleges that North Korea produces $15 million worth of 'supernotes' every year, and has induced banks in Macau and elsewhere to end business with North Korea.

SIX-PARTY TALKS : SIX-PARTY TALKS

In early 2003 multilateral talks were proposed to be held among the six most relevant parties aimed at reaching a settlement through diplomatic means. North Korea initially opposed such a process, maintaining that the nuclear dispute was purely a bilateral matter between themselves and the United States. However, under pressure from its neighbors and with the active involvement of the People's Republic of China, North Korea agreed to preliminary three-party talks with China and the United States in Beijing in April 2003.

After this meeting, North Korea then agreed to six-party talks, between the United States, North Korea, South Korea, China, Japan and Russia. The first round of talks was held in August 2003, with subsequent rounds being held at regular intervals. However, since the last round (5th round, 1st phase) was held in November 2005, North Korea has refused to return to the talks. This was in retaliation for the US freezing offshore North Korean bank accounts in Macau.

In early 2005, US government told its East Asia allies that Pyongyang had exported nuclear material to Libya. This backfired when the Asia allies discovered that US government had concealed involvement of Pakistan; a key U.S. ally was the weapon's middle man. In March 2005, Condoleezza Rice had to travel to East Asia in an effort to repair the damage.

2006 Nuclear Test

U.S. intelligence agencies have been unable to confirm that a test has occurred, but are presently looking into the situation.

Tony Snow, President George W. Bush's White House Press Secretary, said that the United States would now go to the United Nations to determine "what our next steps should be in response to this very serious step."President Bush stated in a televised speech Monday morning, that such a claim of a test is a "provocative act" and U.S condemns such acts. President Bush stated that the United States is "committed to diplomacy" but will "continue to protect America and America's interests."

Press Say About This.

WASHINGTON North Korea said Monday that it had set off its first nuclear test, becoming the eighth country in history, and arguably the most unstable and most dangerous, to proclaim that it has joined the club of nuclear weapons states.

The test came just two days after the country was warned by the United Nations Security Council that the action could lead to severe consequences.

American officials cautioned that they had not yet received any confirmation that the test had occurred. The United States Geological Survey said it had detected a tremor of 4.2 magnitude on the Korean Peninsula.

China called the test a "flagrant and brazen" violation of international opinion and said it "firmly opposes" North Korea's conduct.

Senior Bush administration officials said that they had little reason to doubt the announcement, and warned that the test would usher in a new era of confrontation with the isolated and unpredictable country run by President Kim Jong-il.

Early Monday morning, even before the test was confirmed, Bush administration officials were holding conference calls to discuss ways to further cut off a country that is already subject to sanctions, and hard-liners said the moment had arrived for neighboring countries, especially China and Russia, to cut off the trade and oil supplies that have been Kim's lifeline.

In South Korea, the country that fought a bloody war with the North for three years and has lived with an uneasy truce and failed efforts at reconciliation for more than half a century, officials said they believed that an explosion occurred around 10:36 p.m. New York time - 11:36 a.m. Monday in Korea.

They identified the source of the explosion as North Hamgyong Province, roughly the area where American spy satellites have been focused for several years on a variety of suspected underground test sites.

That was less than an hour after North Korean officials had called their counterparts in China and warned them that a test was just minutes away. The Chinese, who have been North Korea's main ally for 60 years but have grown increasingly frustrated by the its defiance of Beijing, sent an emergency alert to Washington through the United States Embassy in Beijing. Within minutes, President Bush was notified, shortly after 10 p.m., by his national security adviser, Stephen Hadley, that a test was imminent.

North Korea's decision to conduct the test demonstrated what the world has suspected for years: the country has joined India, Pakistan and Israel as one of the world's "undeclared" nuclear powers. India and Pakistan conducted tests in 1998; Israel has never acknowledged conducting a test or possessing a weapon. But by actually setting off a weapon, if that is proven, the North has chosen to end years of carefully crafted and diplomatically useful ambiguity about its abilities.

The North's decision to set off a nuclear device could profoundly change the politics of Asia.

The test occurred only a week after Japan installed a new, more nationalistic prime minister, Shinzo Abe, and just as the country was renewing a debate about whether its ban on possessing nuclear weapons - deeply felt in a country that saw two of its cities incinerated in 1945 - still makes strategic sense. And it shook the peninsula just as Abe was arriving in South Korea for the first time as prime minister, in an effort to repair a badly strained relationship, having just visited with Chinese leaders in Beijing. It places his untested administration in the midst of one of the region's biggest security crises in years, and one whose outcome will be watched closely in Iran and other states suspected of attempting to follow the path that North Korea has taken.

Now, Tokyo and Washington are expected to put even more pressure on the South Korean government to terminate its "sunshine policy" of trade, tourism and openings to the North - a policy that has been the source of enormous tension between Seoul and Washington since Bush took office.

The explosion was the product of nearly four decades of work by North Korea, one of the world's poorest and most isolated countries. The nation of 23 million people appears constantly fearful that its far richer, more powerful neighbors - and particularly the United States - will try to unseat its leadership. The country's founder, Kim Il-sung, who died in 1994, emerged from the Korean War determined to equal the power of the United States, and acutely aware that Gen. Douglas MacArthur had requested nuclear weapons to use against his country.

But it took decades to put together the technology, and only in the past few years has the North appeared to have made a political decision to speed forward. "I think they just had their military plan to demonstrate that no one could mess with them, and they weren't going to be deterred, not even by the Chinese," a senior American official who deals with the North said late Sunday evening. "In the end, there was just no stopping them."

But the explosion was also the product of more than two decades of diplomatic failure, spread over at least three presidencies. American spy satellites saw the North building a good-size nuclear reactor in the early 1980's, and by the early 1990's the C.I.A. estimated that the country could have one or two nuclear weapons. But a series of diplomatic efforts to "freeze" the nuclear program - including a 1994 accord signed with the Clinton administration - ultimately broke down, amid distrust and recriminations on both sides.

Three years ago, just as President Bush was sending American troops toward Iraq, the North threw out the few remaining weapons inspectors living at their nuclear complex in Yongbyon, and moved 8,000 nuclear fuel rods they had kept under lock and key. Those rods contained enough plutonium, experts said, to produce five or six nuclear weapons, though it is unclear how many the North now stockpiles.

For years, some diplomats assumed that the North was using that ambiguity to trade away its nuclear capability, for recognition, security guarantees, aid and trade with the West. But in the end, the country's reclusive leader, Kim Jong-il, who inherited the mantle of leadership from his father, still called the "Great Leader," appears to have concluded that the surest way of getting what he seeks is to demonstrate that he has the capability to strike back if attacked.

Assessing the nature of that ability is difficult. If the test occurred as the North claimed, it is unclear whether it was an actual bomb or a more primitive device. Some experts cautioned that it could try to fake an explosion, setting off conventional explosives; the only way to know for sure will be if American "sniffer" planes, patrolling the North Korean coast, pick up evidence of nuclear byproducts in the air.

Even then, it is not clear that the North could fabricate that bomb into a weapon that could fit atop its missiles, one of the country's few significant exports.

But the big fear about North Korea, American officials have long said, has less to do with its ability to lash out than it does with its proclivity to proliferate. The country has sold its missiles and other weapons to Iran, Syria and Pakistan; at various moments in the six-party talks that have gone on for the past few years, North Korean representatives have threatened to sell nuclear weapons. But in a statement issued last week, announcing that it intends to set off a test, the country said it would not sell its nuclear products.

The fear of proliferation prompted President Bush to declare in 2003 that the United States would never "tolerate" a nuclear-armed North Korea. He has never defined what he means by "tolerate," and on Sunday night Tony Snow, Bush's press secretary, said that, assuming the report of the test is accurate, the United States would now go to the United Nations to determine "what our next steps should be in response to this very serious step."

Nuclear testing is often considered a necessary step to proving a weapon's reliability as well as the most forceful way for a nation to declare its status as a nuclear power.

"Once they do that, it's serious," said Harold M. Agnew, a former director of the Los Alamos weapons laboratory, which designed most of the nation's nuclear arms. "Otherwise, the North Koreans are just jerking us around."

Networks of seismometers that detect faint trembles in the earth and track distant rumbles are the best way to spot an underground nuclear test.

The big challenge is to distinguish the signatures of earthquakes from those of nuclear blasts. Typically, the shock waves from nuclear explosions begin with a sharp spike as earth and rock are compressed violently. The signal then tends to become fuzzier as surface rumblings and shudders and after shocks create seismologic mayhem.

With earthquakes, it is usually the opposite. A gentle jostling suddenly becomes much bigger and more violent.

Most of the world's seismic networks that look for nuclear blasts are designed to detect explosions as small as one kiloton, or equal to 1,000 tons of high explosives. On instruments for detecting earthquakes, such a blast would measure a magnitude of about 4, like a small tremor.

Philip E. Coyle III, a former head of weapons testing at the Pentagon and former director of nuclear testing for the Lawrence Livermore National Laboratory, a weapons-design center in California, said the North Koreans could learn much from a nuclear test even if it was small by world standards or less than an unqualified success.

"It would not be totally surprising if it was a fizzle and they said it was a success because they learned something," he said. "We did that sometimes. We had a missile defense test not so long ago that failed, but the Pentagon said it was a success because they learned something, which I agree with. Failures can teach you a lot." William J. Broad contributed reporting from New York, and Thom Shanker from Washington.

WASHINGTON North Korea said Monday that it had set off its first nuclear test, becoming the eighth country in history, and arguably the most unstable and most dangerous, to proclaim that it has joined the club of nuclear weapons states.

The test came just two days after the country was warned by the United Nations Security Council that the action could lead to severe consequences.

American officials cautioned that they had not yet received any confirmation that the test had occurred. The United States Geological Survey said it had detected a tremor of 4.2 magnitude on the Korean Peninsula. China called the test a "flagrant and brazen" violation of international opinion and said it "firmly opposes" North Korea's conduct.

Senior Bush administration officials said that they had little reason to doubt the announcement, and warned that the test would usher in a new era of confrontation with the isolated and unpredictable country run by President Kim Jong-il.

Early Monday morning, even before the test was confirmed, Bush administration officials were holding conference calls to discuss ways to further cut off a country that is already subject to sanctions, and hard-liners said the moment had arrived for neighboring countries, especially China and Russia, to cut off the trade and oil supplies that have been Kim's lifeline.

In South Korea, the country that fought a bloody war with the North for three years and has lived with an uneasy truce and failed efforts at reconciliation for more than half a century, officials said they believed that an explosion occurred around 10:36 p.m. New York time - 11:36 a.m. Monday in Korea.

They identified the source of the explosion as North Hamgyong Province, roughly the area where American spy satellites have been focused for several years on a variety of suspected underground test sites.

That was less than an hour after North Korean officials had called their counterparts in China and warned them that a test was just minutes away. The Chinese, who have been North Korea's main ally for 60 years but have grown increasingly frustrated by the its defiance of Beijing, sent an emergency alert to Washington through the United States Embassy in Beijing. Within minutes, President Bush was notified, shortly after 10 p.m., by his national security adviser, Stephen Hadley, that a test was imminent.

North Korea's decision to conduct the test demonstrated what the world has suspected for years: the country has joined India, Pakistan and Israel as one of the world's "undeclared" nuclear powers. India and Pakistan conducted tests in 1998; Israel has never acknowledged conducting a test or possessing a weapon. But by actually setting off a weapon, if that is proven, the North has chosen to end years of carefully crafted and diplomatically useful ambiguity about its abilities.

The North's decision to set off a nuclear device could profoundly change the politics of Asia.

The test occurred only a week after Japan installed a new, more nationalistic prime minister, Shinzo Abe, and just as the country was renewing a debate about whether its ban on possessing nuclear weapons - deeply felt in a country that saw two of its cities incinerated in 1945 - still makes strategic sense. And it shook the peninsula just as Abe was arriving in South Korea for the first time as prime minister, in an effort to repair a badly strained relationship, having just visited with Chinese leaders in Beijing. It places his untested administration in the midst of one of the region's biggest security crises in years, and one whose outcome will be watched closely in Iran and other states suspected of attempting to follow the path that North Korea has taken.

Now, Tokyo and Washington are expected to put even more pressure on the South Korean government to terminate its "sunshine policy" of trade, tourism and openings to the North - a policy that has been the source of enormous tension between Seoul and Washington since Bush took office.

The explosion was the product of nearly four decades of work by North Korea, one of the world's poorest and most isolated countries. The nation of 23 million people appears constantly fearful that its far richer, more powerful neighbors - and particularly the United States - will try to unseat its leadership. The country's founder, Kim Il-sung, who died in 1994, emerged from the Korean War determined to equal the power of the United States, and acutely aware that Gen. Douglas MacArthur had requested nuclear weapons to use against his country.

But it took decades to put together the technology, and only in the past few years has the North appeared to have made a political decision to speed forward. "I think they just had their military plan to demonstrate that no one could mess with them, and they weren't going to be deterred, not even by the Chinese," a senior American official who deals with the North said late Sunday evening. "In the end, there was just no stopping them."

But the explosion was also the product of more than two decades of diplomatic failure, spread over at least three presidencies. American spy satellites saw the North building a good-size nuclear reactor in the early 1980's, and by the early 1990's the C.I.A. estimated that the country could have one or two nuclear weapons. But a series of diplomatic efforts to "freeze" the nuclear program - including a 1994 accord signed with the Clinton administration - ultimately broke down, amid distrust and recriminations on both sides. Three years ago, just as President Bush was sending American troops toward Iraq, the North threw out the few remaining weapons inspectors living at their nuclear complex in Yongbyon, and moved 8,000 nuclear fuel rods they had kept under lock and key. Those rods contained enough plutonium, experts said, to produce five or six nuclear weapons, though it is unclear how many the North now stockpiles. For years, some diplomats assumed that the North was using that ambiguity to trade away its nuclear capability, for recognition, security guarantees, aid and trade with the West. But in the end, the country's reclusive leader, Kim Jong-il, who inherited the mantle of leadership from his father, still called the "Great Leader," appears to have concluded that the surest way of getting what he seeks is to demonstrate that he has the capability to strike back if attacked.

Assessing the nature of that ability is difficult. If the test occurred as the North claimed, it is unclear whether it was an actual bomb or a more primitive device. Some experts cautioned that it could try to fake an explosion, setting off conventional explosives; the only way to know for sure will be if American "sniffer" planes, patrolling the North Korean coast, pick up evidence of nuclear byproducts in the air.

Even then, it is not clear that the North could fabricate that bomb into a weapon that could fit atop its missiles, one of the country's few significant exports.

But the big fear about North Korea, American officials have long said, has less to do with its ability to lash out than it does with its proclivity to proliferate. The country has sold its missiles and other weapons to Iran, Syria and Pakistan; at various moments in the six-party talks that have gone on for the past few years, North Korean representatives have threatened to sell nuclear weapons. But in a statement issued last week, announcing that it intends to set off a test, the country said it would not sell its nuclear products.

The fear of proliferation prompted President Bush to declare in 2003 that the United States would never "tolerate" a nuclear-armed North Korea. He has never defined what he means by "tolerate," and on Sunday night Tony Snow, Bush's press secretary, said that, assuming the report of the test is accurate, the United States would now go to the United Nations to determine "what our next steps should be in response to this very serious step." Nuclear testing is often considered a necessary step to proving a weapon's reliability as well as the most forceful way for a nation to declare its status as a nuclear power.

"Once they do that, it's serious," said Harold M. Agnew, a former director of the Los Alamos weapons laboratory, which designed most of the nation's nuclear arms. "Otherwise, the North Koreans are just jerking us around."

Networks of seismometers that detect faint trembles in the earth and track distant rumbles are the best way to spot an underground nuclear test.

The big challenge is to distinguish the signatures of earthquakes from those of nuclear blasts. Typically, the shock waves from nuclear explosions begin with a sharp spike as earth and rock are compressed violently. The signal then tends to become fuzzier as surface rumblings and shudders and after shocks create seismologic mayhem.

With earthquakes, it is usually the opposite. A gentle jostling suddenly becomes much bigger and more violent.

Most of the world's seismic networks that look for nuclear blasts are designed to detect explosions as small as one kiloton, or equal to 1,000 tons of high explosives. On instruments for detecting earthquakes, such a blast would measure a magnitude of about 4, like a small tremor.

Philip E. Coyle III, a former head of weapons testing at the Pentagon and former director of nuclear testing for the Lawrence Livermore National Laboratory, a weapons-design center in California, said the North Koreans could learn much from a nuclear test even if it was small by world standards or less than an unqualified success.

"It would not be totally surprising if it was a fizzle and they said it was a success because they learned something," he said. "We did that sometimes. We had a missile defense test not so long ago that failed, but the Pentagon said it was a success because they learned something, which I agree with. Failures can teach you a lot."

William J. Broad contributed reporting from New York, and Thom Shanker from Washington.

WASHINGTON North Korea said Monday that it had set off its first nuclear test, becoming the eighth country in history, and arguably the most unstable and most dangerous, to proclaim that it has joined the club of nuclear weapons states.

The test came just two days after the country was warned by the United Nations Security Council that the action could lead to severe consequences.

American officials cautioned that they had not yet received any confirmation that the test had occurred. The United States Geological Survey said it had detected a tremor of 4.2 magnitude on the Korean Peninsula.

China called the test a "flagrant and brazen" violation of international opinion and said it "firmly opposes" North Korea's conduct. Senior Bush administration officials said that they had little reason to doubt the announcement, and warned that the test would usher in a new era of confrontation with the isolated and unpredictable country run by President Kim Jong-il.

Early Monday morning, even before the test was confirmed, Bush administration officials were holding conference calls to discuss ways to further cut off a country that is already subject to sanctions, and hard-liners said the moment had arrived for neighboring countries, especially China and Russia, to cut off the trade and oil supplies that have been Kim's lifeline.

In South Korea, the country that fought a bloody war with the North for three years and has lived with an uneasy truce and failed efforts at reconciliation for more than half a century, officials said they believed that an explosion occurred around 10:36 p.m. New York time - 11:36 a.m. Monday in Korea.

They identified the source of the explosion as North Hamgyong Province, roughly the area where American spy satellites have been focused for several years on a variety of suspected underground test sites.

That was less than an hour after North Korean officials had called their counterparts in China and warned them that a test was just minutes away. The Chinese, who have been North Korea's main ally for 60 years but have grown increasingly frustrated by the its defiance of Beijing, sent an emergency alert to Washington through the United States Embassy in Beijing. Within minutes, President Bush was notified, shortly after 10 p.m., by his national security adviser, Stephen Hadley, that a test was imminent.

North Korea's decision to conduct the test demonstrated what the world has suspected for years: the country has joined India, Pakistan and Israel as one of the world's "undeclared" nuclear powers. India and Pakistan conducted tests in 1998; Israel has never acknowledged conducting a test or possessing a weapon. But by actually setting off a weapon, if that is proven, the North has chosen to end years of carefully crafted and diplomatically useful ambiguity about its abilities.

The North's decision to set off a nuclear device could profoundly change the politics of Asia.

The test occurred only a week after Japan installed a new, more nationalistic prime minister, Shinzo Abe, and just as the country was renewing a debate about whether its ban on possessing nuclear weapons - deeply felt in a country that saw two of its cities incinerated in 1945 - still makes strategic sense.

And it shook the peninsula just as Abe was arriving in South Korea for the first time as prime minister, in an effort to repair a badly strained relationship, having just visited with Chinese leaders in Beijing. It places his untested administration in the midst of one of the region's biggest security crises in years, and one whose outcome will be watched closely in Iran and other states suspected of attempting to follow the path that North Korea has taken.

Now, Tokyo and Washington are expected to put even more pressure on the South Korean government to terminate its "sunshine policy" of trade, tourism and openings to the North - a policy that has been the source of enormous tension between Seoul and Washington since Bush took office.

The explosion was the product of nearly four decades of work by North Korea, one of the world's poorest and most isolated countries. The nation of 23 million people appears constantly fearful that its far richer, more powerful neighbors - and particularly the United States - will try to unseat its leadership. The country's founder, Kim Il-sung, who died in 1994, emerged from the Korean War determined to equal the power of the United States, and acutely aware that Gen. Douglas MacArthur had requested nuclear weapons to use against his country.

But it took decades to put together the technology, and only in the past few years has the North appeared to have made a political decision to speed forward. "I think they just had their military plan to demonstrate that no one could mess with them, and they weren't going to be deterred, not even by the Chinese," a senior American official who deals with the North said late Sunday evening. "In the end, there was just no stopping them."

But the explosion was also the product of more than two decades of diplomatic failure, spread over at least three presidencies. American spy satellites saw the North building a good-size nuclear reactor in the early 1980's, and by the early 1990's the C.I.A. estimated that the country could have one or two nuclear weapons. But a series of diplomatic efforts to "freeze" the nuclear program - including a 1994 accord signed with the Clinton administration - ultimately broke down, amid distrust and recriminations on both sides.

Three years ago, just as President Bush was sending American troops toward Iraq, the North threw out the few remaining weapons inspectors living at their nuclear complex in Yongbyon, and moved 8,000 nuclear fuel rods they had kept under lock and key. Those rods contained enough plutonium, experts said, to produce five or six nuclear weapons, though it is unclear how many the North now stockpiles.

For years, some diplomats assumed that the North was using that ambiguity to trade away its nuclear capability, for recognition, security guarantees, aid and trade with the West. But in the end, the country's reclusive leader, Kim Jong-il, who inherited the mantle of leadership from his father, still called the "Great Leader," appears to have concluded that the surest way of getting what he seeks is to demonstrate that he has the capability to strike back if attacked.

Assessing the nature of that ability is difficult. If the test occurred as the North claimed, it is unclear whether it was an actual bomb or a more primitive device. Some experts cautioned that it could try to fake an explosion, setting off conventional explosives; the only way to know for sure will be if American "sniffer" planes, patrolling the North Korean coast, pick up evidence of nuclear byproducts in the air.

Even then, it is not clear that the North could fabricate that bomb into a weapon that could fit atop its missiles, one of the country's few significant exports.

But the big fear about North Korea, American officials have long said, has less to do with its ability to lash out than it does with its proclivity to proliferate. The country has sold its missiles and other weapons to Iran, Syria and Pakistan; at various moments in the six-party talks that have gone on for the past few years, North Korean representatives have threatened to sell nuclear weapons. But in a statement issued last week, announcing that it intends to set off a test, the country said it would not sell its nuclear products. The fear of proliferation prompted President Bush to declare in 2003 that the United States would never "tolerate" a nuclear-armed North Korea. He has never defined what he means by "tolerate," and on Sunday night Tony Snow, Bush's press secretary, said that, assuming the report of the test is accurate, the United States would now go to the United Nations to determine "what our next steps should be in response to this very serious step."

Nuclear testing is often considered a necessary step to proving a weapon's reliability as well as the most forceful way for a nation to declare its status as a nuclear power.

"Once they do that, it's serious," said Harold M. Agnew, a former director of the Los Alamos weapons laboratory, which designed most of the nation's nuclear arms. "Otherwise, the North Koreans are just jerking us around."

Networks of seismometers that detect faint trembles in the earth and track distant rumbles are the best way to spot an underground nuclear test.

The big challenge is to distinguish the signatures of earthquakes from those of nuclear blasts. Typically, the shock waves from nuclear explosions begin with a sharp spike as earth and rock are compressed violently. The signal then tends to become fuzzier as surface rumblings and shudders and after shocks create seismologic mayhem.

With earthquakes, it is usually the opposite. A gentle jostling suddenly becomes much bigger and more violent.

Most of the world's seismic networks that look for nuclear blasts are designed to detect explosions as small as one kiloton, or equal to 1,000 tons of high explosives. On instruments for detecting earthquakes, such a blast would measure a magnitude of about 4, like a small tremor.

Philip E. Coyle III, a former head of weapons testing at the Pentagon and former director of nuclear testing for the Lawrence Livermore National Laboratory, a weapons-design center in California, said the North Koreans could learn much from a nuclear test even if it was small by world standards or less than an unqualified success.

"It would not be totally surprising if it was a fizzle and they said it was a success because they learned something," he said. "We did that sometimes. We had a missile defense test not so long ago that failed, but the Pentagon said it was a success because they learned something, which I agree with. Failures can teach you a lot."

NORTH KOREA – THE NUCLEAR STATE

North Korea is a country in the Far East occupying the northern part of the peninsula of Korea. North Korea was formed in 1948 when Korea was partitioned along the 38th parallel. Its official language is Korean. Its capital is Pyongyang while its complete name is Democratic People's Republic of Korea.

In 1950, a war began between North and South Korea. North Korea attacked South Korea. United States of America dominating the UN troops countered the attack by invading North Korea from South Korea. North Korea, was however sided by China in this war. In 1951, peace negotiations started and eventually it was attained after 2 years in 1953. The previous borders were restored, thus, the war left no results.

According to recent CIA investigations, North Korea is on the verge of testing its nuclear weapons probably in a cave or mine shaft somewhere in the barren northeast of the country. It is also believed that a small amount of breakout nuclear material will fallout of the test site and drift towards Japan. This good news is really going to incite excitement in the financial markets of South Korea and Japan. Foreign investors in South Korea will move forward to decisions of pulling out their money from the market or minimizing the range of operations. This is a very bad news for the South Korean administrators since they will lose their strong economies after such a repatriation of money from their markets. Meanwhile, US will look forward to impose a blockage or other tough measures to control North Korea's nuclear tests. It is commented that North Korea is working out on plans of testing its nuclear capabilities within a short time. Its is said that these nuclear weapons had been under preparation since last 50 years. This country has already been declared as a nuclear state as it has disclosed its nuclear weapons. The aim of North Korea behind developing nuclear weapons is believed that it wants to be a "recognized" nuclear state just like China, India and Pakistan. To attain these motives, it first needs to demonstrate its nuclear capabilities. Now lets see how was it able to develop such nuclear weapons right from the beginning through all these 50 years.

According to CIA's investigation, North Korea started its nuclear proliferation in 1956, just after 3 years of the Korean War. The programme commenced when North Korea signed a pact with USSR who agreed to train its nuclear scientists. It was with the help of USSR, with which North Korea established its first ever nuclear reactor in 1965. Then, in 1974 North Korea also signed a nuclear training agreement with China. Then North Korea built another small nuclear reactor in 1986 at Yongbyon. This time, America played its sinister role and detected the third larger nuclear reactor of North Korea in 1989. According to estimates, the nuclear proliferation ability of the nuclear reactors of North Korea was enough to enrich plutonium fuel rods to the necessary levels to make a nuclear bomb. United States considering this state of affairs predicted a future devastation and hazard within Asia. United States offered North Korea with aids and trade treaties at the cost of suspending its nuclear proliferation. In 1994, a pact was signed between North Korea and US after which North Korea put her 8000 fuel rods at Yongbyon under seal. However, they clandestinely treaded on their path, using highly enriched uranium prepared in special centrifuges allegedly supplied by Pakistan (A.Q. Khan Network).

North Korea has been openly alluding about that fact that it is going to join the Nuclear Club. United States, in 2002, found evidence of their clandestine nuclear enrichment programme and North Korea didn't decline this fact and accordingly resumed the reprocessing of Plutonium fuel rods which was suspended in 1994. Soon after the worldwide disclosure of the fact about North Korea's nuclear enrichment programme, North Korea declared that she was willing to expose her nuclear capabilities, infact pointing to the Nuclear Test programmes. Later officials from

North Korea displayed the reason of "self-defence" for retaining the Nuclear Weapons. Subsequently it was announced that North Korea had developed nuclear weapons and will retain them under any circumstances. North Korea performed some nuclear tests in 1998 using the three-stage Taedopong-I missile over Japan and the Pacific Ocean. North Korea openly announced this and its also believed that the ones that are due to take place soon will also be announced. North Korea has been alleged to have the technology to produce an actual warhead that could fit atop missiles which, by U.S. intelligence estimates, could reach parts of the United States. North Korea has not objected to this claim also.

The rivalry between North Korea and US has been since long. Bush calls Kim Jong-II, the leader of North Korea, as "tyrant and a dangerous person who starves his own people and has a high concentration of camps". North Korea, on its stance has been right. North Korea has already seen the fate of Baghdad and Kabul. Now it has two options. Either wait for America's invasion or adopt to pre-emption for its preparation to face the invasions and pressurize the Big Brother. North Korea looks inclined towards the other option much. Showing the nuclear cards is the only option to perpetuate her regime and stay unharmed. There are so less chances that North Korea will switch to negotiations regarding its Nuclear Programme any more.

North Korea, has now earned a new identity in Asia. According to it, China and South Korea should rise from their illusions and accept the reality. North Korea's nuclear capability is a tremendous threat to all the Asia. Asia needs to co-operate in this regard, with the Big Brother to explain North Korea about the repercussions and solve the problem peacefully.

6

POLITICAL DIVERSITY

Developing nations are the nations predominantly situated in the southern hemisphere. They are characterized by civil strife, political instability, hunger, high population growth, and other social misfortunes. It is however clear that they are walking away from this state towards advancement as they attain political maturity. The level of development of these countries however differs remarkably. Some are experiencing an economic boom while others are sinking deep into political oblivion, disappearing from the ladder scales. Examples include Burma and Somali which have been classified as failed states. However, there is some light at the end of the tunnel. With the current trend of globalization and the formation of political blocs, democratic governance characterized by openness in society is cropping in, all for the better of society.Political Diversity within Developing World

Politics is an aspect of social science concerned with leadership and policy making and its implementation in society. It is the exercise of power in a desired manner. Often misinterpreted as a dirty game without rules of procedure, politics is manifested in all aspects of society. Any society needs a clear political structure, lest it is a state of nature as presented by Thomas Hobbes, where life is short, brutish, disorganized and of a war of all against all. Aristotle defined it as the search for the good life. In this sense, politics is meant to bring order in society; sine man is a political animal, social in nature.

Different societies have different systems of politics. The political system in application at a given time is greatly dependent on the culture of the people in the society in question. Culture may be defined as a way of life of a people. Thus the political systems of the western advanced nations would differ greatly from that of the less developed countries.

A developed nation refers to an industrialized nation, one where the major export products are finished goods. The opposite of this would therefore be a political system whose major exports are primary produce. The 'three worlds theory' attempts to classify the world into three classes: the capitalist developed world; the socialist world; and the third world, comprising newly found states resulting from independence struggles. The theory is however controversial, as the level of development is measured to the western standards, and again very many countries whose economic positions are different by far are lumped together. The theory, again, is only applicable to states, not the people or the societies in the states (Ahmad 1992). Developing nations are the countries found predominantly in Asia, Latin America and Africa. They are over 100, comprising a population of a third of the total world population.

Developing countries suffer a great deal on issues of pervasive poverty, rapid population growth, ethnic conflict, famine, disease, revolutions, and corruption. The politics of developed and developing nations has been raging for quite some time and the fact that the developed nation reached their status as a result of under-developing the developing nations is a hot debate. During colonization the developing world was the victim of the process. Inhabitants were taken as slaves to go and develop the western world, of course using resources from the developing nations. Natural resources were exploited from the third world countries at no cost to the whites. They competed in the scramble until they decided to divide the African continent among themselves as was the case during the Berlin conferences (Rosenberg).

The whites brought in their education which was so basic and naked for the third world. It was education meant to make it easy for communication between natives and the foreigners as to indoctrinate the natives to think that they are lesser beings who need white supervision and guidance. Native cultures were also dismissed as archaic and demonic that they were retrogressive. All these combined had the natives developed a negative attitude against themselves.

The idea of terming some countries as under developed is totally unacceptable. There are developed and developing nations, not the other argument. Underdevelopment would indiçate that the development is retrogręssing which is not the case. All countries are developing and from the foregoing it is also wrong to claim that the developing world is trying to catch up with the developed world. It is ridiculous because as the third world is developing, the industrialized states are still industrializing. To get the facts right, development of the third world should be pegged on its own unique society and culture. Foreign concepts of development should not be imposed on these countries. For instance, due to the rot in the west on morality, these countries do not consider morality as an aspect of development. They are instead quick to extend indoctrination by having the less developed countries to use their language and education system. They introduce economic policies and governance principles, some of which are not compatible with the native way of living.

Developing nations are found in the southern hemisphere of the globe. They include the continent of Africa, Southern Asia and Latin America. At one time or another, these countries were under colonial administration, an era characterized by slavery and exploitation. Natural resources were exploited to Europe and America. The masters made maximum use of the available free resources to a point that they partitioned the continent of Africa among themselves for their economic gains. Australia is however exempted because it is in the Southern hemisphere but is classified among the advanced countries.

The developing nations were once under a colonial rule. Latin America Africa and Asia were all being ruled at some point in time by European powers. This was the height of exploitation perpetually perpetrated by the developed countries for their political and economic gains. The United Kingdom of Great Britain and Wales dominated almost the whole world that it was once said the sun never sets in its empire. This was the depth of the imperial dominance that reflected the might of the Kingdom, and any other dominant country. The colonial administration left a legacy of use of brute force and gross violation of human rights. Divide and rule was one of the methods of containing the unrest of the native communities.

Independent struggles led to most of these countries to attain their independence after bloody struggles. They inherited the political system of former colonial masters which had some points of incompatibility with the native social systems. Poorly trained officers took over apparatus of governance, proving a disaster to some newly-found states like the Zaire. The constitu were hurriedly amended to empower one institution in the name of national cohesion. There followed periods of coups and countercoups, with the leadership consolidating even more powers to absolute levels. Lord Acton's opinion on the absolute corruptibility of absolute power became a reality. The accumulation of power in one institution, mostly the presidency proved counterproductive, as imperial presidencies sprung up.

The economic front of developing nations is characterized by low pa capita incomes and high poverty rates. Unemployment is high due to scarcity of both jobs and skills. A concerted effort is made by some governments urging its citizens to look for jobs in other countries. These countries major in the export of raw materials both agricultural and mineral resources. They are known to be pawns of the richer nations. Patron-client relation characterized the smuggling by weaponry to sponsor wars in the developing world. Infrastructure is usually poor, complicating further the cycle of poverty.

Health wise, these countries are known to suffer from malnutrition and diseases related to this problem. The poor hygienic conditions and general state of poverty reduces the life expectancy rates. Medical care is not easily accessible as is clean water safe for consumption.

The political leadership of these nations is weak and often dictatorial. Most of governmental authority is vested in an individual who would misuse by appointing cronies to positions of influence. This would then promote corruption in the system which may turn to be an issue of political instability due to dissatisfaction by a section of society feeling neglected. It would then foment an uprising or a coup. Somali Republic is an example in Africa with Haiti in Latin America. Civil society is not free to operate in such systems. Media censorship is practiced with some countries having the media being monopolized by the state. There is no independent media. They hold regular 'selections' in the name of upholding the rule of democracy. Such 'democratic' practices are only meant for cosmetic reasons as the electoral bodies are appointed by a player in the election.

In the international front, these countries have a lesser say. Major policy decisions are made by the major economic powers, through their manipulative abilities by use of briefcase diplomacy.

Legislative authorities of the developing world often act as rubber stamps to executive decisions. The executive overshadows the legislature and the judiciary in their operation, thus defeating the logic of having a system of checks and balances. Any discontents are treated harshly, often with impunity. Torture and political assassinations thus become a norm rather than an exception. The civil servants work at the mercies of the president, thus subjecting all state machinery at the hands of an individual.

COMPARISON WITH THE DEVELOPED WORLD

The political systems of developed countries are a product of long term experience. Distinct systems are presidential as in America, parliamentary as in the UK or a mixture of the two as in the case in France. The long tradition has made the system part of the culture of the society a reason for a strong political orientation.

The developed nations as mentioned earlier owe their success to the developing world. The level they have reached allows them a variety of opportunities. They have accumulated capital and so development is not an issue. They talk of economic growth while the developing nations think of economic development.

Some of the countries in the advanced world category are welfare states. This would eliminate any talk of poverty as the state is committed to the welfare of its population. The state is in a position to take care of its entire population unlike the crippled economy of the developing world.

A robust civil society and clear separation of powers make it difficult for corruption to thrive. The high rate of literacy is a further resource. Technology grows faster due to scientific innovation. Funding is readily available for research work, a factor that remains a nightmare in the developing world.

Despite these differences, the developing world is showing some remarkable progress especially in the sphere of governance and economy. Globalization has opened the world, exposing populations to different challenges facing people in similar situations in the globe and how they got themselves out of political bondage to a free society. The Orange Revolution of Ukraine, for instance, was a clear lesson that the incumbent cannot remain in office illegitimately. The people decided to use their civil rights and had the person of their choice in the political office. This is however the opposite of what happens in Zimbabwe after President Mugabe shamelessly competed with his shadow in a run-off presidential election after unleashing terror to the opposition supporters. On the economic front, the 'Asian Tigers' are far much ahead of other developing nations. They have reached a level almost close to that of the developed world. In this category is also included China, South Africa, Brazil, Argentina, among others, said to be the emerging markets of the world. All this is happening as Zimbabwe is reeling into a pit, with inflation rates reported by the Central Bank to be 2.2 million percent.

The different developing countries practice different political systems. Some are parliamentary, while others presidential. South Korea is presidential executive system, India a Prime Ministerial system, and Kenya is a mixed system, with the executive comprising of both an executive president and prime minister.

The Kenyan system of dual executive was brought about after a disputed election in December 2007 after both the incumbent Mwai Kibaki and the leader of opposition Raila Odinga claimed victory in the election, which was later declared by the electoral commission in an enclosed place, with only the state media being allowed to air the coverage. It followed the worst political violence Kenya witnessed in its post independence history. International attention was attracted and the former United Nations Secretary General led a team that negotiated for a power sharing deal that recommended the amendment of the Constitution to provide for the office of an executive prime minister and two deputies. This is an example of political expedience in developing world. The Ugandan case involved the President taking a bill to Parliament to amend the national Constitution to allow him a further term in office. His two constitutional terms had expired but he was not ready to leave office. President Obasanjo of Nigeria attempted but was embarrassed by his vice president at the time Atiku Abubakar. This is just an indication that the leadership in the developing world is not ready to relinquish power after their constitutional terms in office. This is however contrasted by the former South African President Nelson Mandela who voluntarily retired after leading his country into black majority rule.

Political systems of the advanced world are characterized by a robust civil society movement. This aspect has begun showing prominence in the developing world as well. However, in countries like Cuba and China, the civil society is not as pronounced as in Nigeria, South Africa, India, Brazil, just to mention a few. China has been known to contain the media through censorship. Democratic space is limited by stringent legal provisions. In Cuba, it was until the retirement of the long-serving Fidel Castro that his brother Raul allowed the open use of the internet and mobile phones. The media has also been allowed some breathing space, and the civil society can speak, though still with some utmost caution. With the current trend of globalization, promoted by the wide use of the internet, most societies are going to be opened up. The dynamism of the political play in the international level would force the conservative societies to tore the line of openness and accountability. Internationalism and transnational are fast diluting cultures which were tightly held by some societies.

From the foregoing therefore, all countries are moving the development paths, and it is the purpose of comparative politics to shed more light on the best form of political and economic leadership to embrace in order to achieve the golden Millennium Development Goals by 2015.

INTERNATIONAL RELATIONS INVOLVING A PARTICIPATORY SOCIETY

This essay seeks to explore the issues that would face a participatory democratic society when relating to other countries. It is assumed that some of the other countries the participatory society deals with are not participatory societies. It is assumed that there could exist a country whose economy was governed by participatory democratic structures as envisioned by Hahnel and Albert in their vision of "Participatory Economics" (parecon). Also, it is assumed that this country has a "Participatory Polity" (parpolity) as envisioned by Stephen Shalom. There would be other important characteristics of this society, dealing with such issues as kinship, culture, and religion, but they will not be specified here.

The purpose of this essay is not to provide vision about how a participatory society should manage its international affairs. Rather, I am seeking to address the likely scenarios a participatory nation will face, and how it will likely deal with them, given my understanding of participatory structures and institutions. Some questions along this line are: With what structures would a participatory society manage its relations with other countries? How would the institutions of a participatory society motivate it to help (or hinder) the development of other countries? Would it have an army? Would it have conscription? Would it be motivated to commit an aggressive war to conquer other nations? Would be motivated to never go to war? How would it negotiate economic deals with capitalist countries? Would it deal with capitalist countries? Would it try to "export revolution" (encourage - or force - other countries to adopt its institutions and systems)? How would foreign policy be decided? Would it have ambassadors? How would immigration be handled? How would its unique monetary system coexist with international currencies?

There are many questions to answer, and I honestly do not know how to answer them all. By interpreting the writings of parpolity and parecon, I will attempt to address some major issues.

As a bit of a preamble, I would first like to establish a basic principle of a participatory society, namely that the policy of the participatory nation, based on the wishes of the majority of its citizens, is most often fair and reasonable. I will use this idea throughout the essay. Since we are dealing with an imagined participatory society, where the opinions and beliefs of the majority of the population should reflect (for the most part) the foreign policy of the nation, it seems reasonable to think that the foreign policy will be fair minded. Evidence for this is given in polls of ordinary citizens conducted in the modern age. Polls show that most Americans think resorting to military force to promote democracy is wrong4, that the Kyoto protocols on the environment should be honored5, etc. despite what their government actually does regarding these issues. There are numerous examples of the majority of people in a democratic society (let us call representative democracies "democratic" even though it is arguable that there is very little real democracy in such societies) believing in fairly socialist values, like Medicare7, universal education, universal suffrage, etc. This is often contrary to policy delivered by elected representatives. There are exceptions of course, Americans appear to be divided on the issue of socialized medicine. One wonders what the result would be if the US media was not corporate owned. However, it is possible for the majority to be irrational and nasty, for example, consider witch burning and slavery. It is probable that instances of the "tyranny of the majority" may crop up in a participatory society. Fortunately there are proposed methods for dealing with this, discussed below. Hopefully such instances where the majority of citizens want unethical things to happen to a subgroup or foreign group of people would be rare. It is of course, impossible to predict, but since there would be much debate in this society, free and non corporate media, and people would often be considering the opinions of others, one would hope and expect that the majority of people in a participatory society would be convinced by the voices of others to support ideas that are fair minded and reasonable.

I will now briefly summarize the economic system of parecon and the political system of parpolity. For more background, please see the writings of Robin Hahnel and Michael Albert on participatory economics, also see Stephen Shalom on "parpolity." People already familiar with these proposed systems are invited to skip the next bit.

Participatory Economics seeks to set up an entirely different economic system by fundamentally changing work life, and how goods and services are allocated (no markets and no central planning). By law, productive property would be owned by all citizens, no private ownership of factories of farms etc. would be allowed. Work life would be democratic, each worker would be able to vote on issues in the workplace in proportion to how much the issue effects them. Further, each worker would have a "balanced job complex." This means that each worker has a mix of tasks, some empowering, and some rote and perhaps unpleasant. Through sharing both the empowering and unempowering work, one class is established, and the economy is more fair. For instance someone might be an airplane pilot (empowering) some of the time, and a baggage handler at the airport for the rest of their work week. Surgeons would spend some of their time sweeping floors or sorting mail. Also, if it is necessary for someone to be in charge in the workplace, then this job is rotated. For instance, if you are in charge of baggage handling at the airport, then on some other day, you are one of the baggage handlers. Finally, in a parecon one gets paid according to how much effort and sacrifice one does at work. If you work longer hours, or at a hard job, you get paid more. Balanced job complexes should have roughly the same effort and sacrifice.

Money in a participatory society is also different. A worker in a parecon gets "credits", a sort of record of how much they work. They can then use these credits to buy goods and services, but when they buy things, some of their credits disappear. They do not go into a till or a bank, they are gone. To get more, one must work more. Credits are not transferable to other people. I could not give you any of my credits no matter what you might give me. There are no banks, no stock market, and no interest rates. Investment still happens, but differently. If the parecon nation wants to invest in infrastructure, everything else gets more expensive, but no loans are given.

Allocation in a participatory society would also be very different from today. Each year, all citizens would engage in a participatory planning procedure, the goal of which would be to set prices for all goods and services for one year. At the beginning of the procedure, consumers would enter proposals on what they plan to consume for the coming year on an individual, neighborhood, city wide, provincial, and country wide basis. For instance, an individual might order a new bicycle and stereo for the new year, and a city might order a sewer system upgrade. Proposals involving more than one person would be accomplished by any citizen submitting a proposal to a facilitation board, which would be a service to help develop the proposal for approval by the rest of the population. The sum of proposals would then be approved by interested people in that region, then submitted during the participatory planning procedure. In a similar way each worker (who would also be a consumer) would propose how much they want to work in the coming year, and at what they want to work. Workplaces would also propose changes to their workplaces, such as upgrades. This proposed supply and demand will be summed up, and factors such as environmental damage involved in producing goods and the toll on workers will be added to the price of a good, making it more or less expensive. This generates prices to be reviewed for all goods and services. Since the prices incorporate information about the impact of the goods on society, it is said that the prices reflect the "social opportunity cost". After reviewing the prices, people then resubmit proposals, as prices might not be what they expected. This process is repeated several times, and less deviation is allowed each time, whittling down the proposals into something beneficial to all. After this, prices are set for a year. Note that though this might seem like a demanding process for the population, there are mechanisms to make it easy on consumers, such as getting time off work to do it.

Parecon describes how economic life would work, but this leaves out the creation and enforcement of laws. This is a job for a parpolity2. To make laws, Shalom proposes that a nested council structure be created. Each person would belong to a council of 25 to 50 other citizens. Each council would elect a representative to go to the next level council, which would then represent 625 to 2500 people, and each of these would send representatives to the next level, and so on. At five or six levels, you can represent billions of people. Each council would be deliberative, that is, capable of making independent decisions for the sum total of its constituents. Laws passed could involve new work safety standards, outlawing practices that are very harmful to the environment, etc. However, the decisions of each higher level council would be easily challengeable by a referendum. Also, the lower level councils would be asked to give general preferences for issues that come up, leaving the details to be worked out by the appropriate council.

For instance people could vote that they are generally in favor of allowing stem cell research, with provisions like no babies are to be brought to maturity just to get their stem cells, but leave the exact details to a higher level council. People interested in the details could follow the deliberations of the higher level councils and comment on them as well, and perhaps petition for a general vote if many observers are unsatisfied.

Courts in parpolity would not be changed a great deal, however, there might be more juries. Presumably police would still be needed, as this is a skilled profession, and police would work in a balanced job complex. Prisons might be needed as well for seriously violent people. Hopefully the need for police and prisons would be much diminished, and prisons would focus on reform and creative ways to help people who have trouble living in a society. Courts would also be used to check tyranny of the majority. If one group tries to oppress a smaller group through voting some legislation, courts would be used to block these violations of the constitution. Courts can also assist on ruling which group of people gets to vote on what issue. It is assumed here that there would be a constitution, though Shalom has not made this explicit, since it seems to be the only way to aid court rulings. Countries like the UK, who have no constitution, rely on precedents to aid court rulings. Since there would be no precedents for many of the actions of a participatory society, it would seem a constitution is in order.

Now that each system is summarized, let us move on to international relations.

ECONOMIC RELATIONS BETWEEN COUNTRIES

Fortunately, Robin Hahnel has recently clarified how economic relations would work both between parecon countries and also parecon and non-parecon countries in his recent book "Economic Justice and Democracy". Previous to this, how this might work was something of a mystery.

ECONOMIC RELATIONS BETWEEN PARTICIPATORY SOCIETIES

For relations between two parecon countries, it is first important to understand a few points about parecon. In a parecon, every able worker has a balanced job complex.

In implementing the balanced job complex, though, it is proposed that not every worker work at the same place for their entire job complex. Some workers could perhaps perform their tasks all under one roof, but others will have to spend some part of their work in one place (say a coal mine) and another part somewhere else (such as a research institution). In this way, jobs are balanced amongst workplaces.

Another point to understand is that there is freedom of movement anywhere in a parecon. If you want to live somewhere within the parecon, you may live there (as long the work you can do is needed, and you can get to your workplace). If some parts of a country are much more desirable to live in, then many people will want to live there. If too many people want to live there then the resources of that region are strained, and the environment is strained. What can be done to mitigate the undesirable (and unstoppable) effects of too much migration to more desirable parts of the country? The solution is to not develop one part of the county beyond other parts, so that each part is as desirable to live in as possible. To put it another way, if two countries go parecon at the same time, and one is less technologically advanced than another, the first priority of the more advanced former nation (now a part of a larger nation) is to help develop the less advanced region. Otherwise, too many people will move to the more advanced region and overwhelm it. Also, because jobs would be balanced across workplaces, then people from the more advanced areas of the country would be motivated to improve the less advanced regions, else they will have to work in worse conditions. The interesting (and laudable) thing is that the parecon nation is seriously motivated to aid underdeveloped regions, otherwise its own progress is hindered. Two parecon countries geographically adjacent to each other would most likely become one country economically. The more developed country would be obligated to help the less developed country until they are on equal terms, as above. Councils would order projects that would affect both countries, effectively becoming a single entity, as there should be unrestricted trade between each. However, the farther apart each country is, the higher the price of goods would be if the good would have to be shipped all the way from one end of the country to another. Two parecon countries separated by water would presumably be able to order goods freely from each other with no restrictions, but transportation costs would factor in by raising the social opportunity cost of each item.

It is of course possible that many regions in a parecon country could be culturally and politically distinct, and might be named differently and so on. However, if both are parecon, there is no reason to assume that these differences would impede the free flow of goods between each other, and that there would be any trade restrictions. In fact any restrictions would be detrimental to the economy of each, as it would seem to hurt efficiency, and decrease the diversity of goods, and would make workers in each country work harder and longer hours. If consumer councils cannot order goods and services from other regions just because of cultural differences, then there is an unfortunate dispute between the two regions, something for the polity to resolve. In any case, restricting trade between two parecon countries would be in the economic interest of neither.

ECONOMIC RELATIONS BETWEEN PARTICIPATORY SOCIETIES AND NON-PARTICIPATORY SOCIETIES (CAPITALIST OR COMMUNIST)

Leaving aside for the moment that a participatory society would likely face hostility from non-participatory societies, there is a possibility that a "capitalist" or "communist" countries might wish to have economic relations with a participatory country. Robin Hahnel has also recently proposed how this might work as well.

Hahnel states that if a parecon country can deal with a more advanced economy (technologically speaking presumably) then it is fine to get the best deal it can get. The parecon country should sue for the most "efficiency gains" it can get, since nobody will be worse off in either country.

In physics, more efficiency means that the work or energy you get out of a device is greatest compared to how much energy or work was put into a device. A car is not very efficient if much of the energy produced by the engine goes into making heat, (typically only 10% goes into moving the car). In an economy, transposing this concept would define an efficiency gain as putting the least amount of labor and resources into producing a good for the greatest amount of the good produced and the greatest social benefits as well (including worker satisfaction, not impacting the environment etc.). If you can produce enough toothbrushes for all with 10 people in a small factory, then you shouldn't use 100 people and vast resources to do it. Also, if infrastructure is already existing to produce toothbrushes, then it is inefficient to make more infrastructure unless it will reduce use of resources and labor in the future, and maybe have social benefits.

Therefore if a parecon country can get goods with less investment of labor and resources from the more developed country, then it should do so. Nobody gets hurt in either country. Also, if the parecon country can get resources to build a more efficient factory or get better job training from the advanced country, it should do so. And so on.

If however, a parecon is dealing with a *less advanced* country, the parecon country is obliged to get *less* than 50% of the efficiency gains of the trade deal. In this way the less advanced economy gets most of the benefits, but not all. The parecon country gets some efficiency gains as well, but it is morally obliged to try to benefit the less advanced economy more than itself. The parecon country does not lose anything, but it does not gain as much as it could.

Why be so nice? Hahnel proposes that to do otherwise would violate the principles of a parecon (3, p. 212-213) It seems true that violating one's ethical principles would matter to a participatory democratic society, where the fair mindedness of the population would presumably rule, as I have already discussed above.

Further, this issue relates to immigration. A principle in parecon appears to be that too much immigration is held to be "bad" for a region. Since immigration rights are an important activist topic today, it is important to clarify that advocates for a participatory society are not anti-immigration. Rather just the opposite, "freedom of association" is a fundamental right in a parecon or parpolity, and such a society could not work without it. It seems hard to have a participatory democracy without people being free to live where they want and associate with whom they want within the country.

If the principle of "freedom of association" is extended, it would imply that the international border of a participatory society would be open both ways, anyone must be free to enter, and anyone must be free to leave. Having an open border might of course lead to the problem of too many people coming into the country.

Might this motivate the parecon country to restrict immigration? If there is no internal pressure for a participatory society not to put restrictions on immigration, and the external pressures can presumably be ignored, then restrictions might very well happen. At this point, I invoke the principle (above) that the majority of citizens in a participatory society are fair minded. What would a fair minded person do? One would think that having open borders (as much as possible) is the fair thing to do. You must allow refugees into the country, it is simply the fair thing to do. It is beneficial to allow skilled workers to immigrate as is done in many "first world" countries. What about people wanting to enter the country who might not have special skills? The fair thing seems to be to let them in as well. Presumably a constitution for a participatory society would have freedom of association written into it. Thus the court system of the participatory society would uphold the constitution and keep the border open, unless the situation is very dire. Further, the parecon nation can deal with immigration issues by improving the lot of other nations it trades with. If you make life better for people in other countries, then they have less reason to immigrate to your country.

Getting back to the reason why a parecon nation would be generous (allowing them more efficiency gains) to less developed countries, the parecon nation is also motivated to be fair in economic dealings due to the above principle of freedom of association. Since the border would be presumably open, the parecon country would want to raise the standard of living in other countries, otherwise be faced with overpopulation. As well, there is motivation to be friendly to other nations and form alliances, or else be attacked or sanctioned. These reasons seem enough to motivate the participatory society to trade in a way that gives the majority of efficiency gains to another country.

It might also be possible to send workers from the parecon country to less developed, non-parecon nations, and bring workers from non-parecon countries to the parecon country, as a sort of cultural exchange (if other countries are willing). This would also be beneficial in promoting goodwill amongst nations, and beneficial to the participatory society to understand other cultures and engender goodwill from them. This raises an issue that might need discussion, "What right does a participatory society have to force workers to move?" Of course, if there is no work for their particular skill set for someone in a particular region, then it seems like they should either get retraining or move. It seems very unfair to force someone to work somewhere, though. Therefore if this cultural exchange work program is done, it might have to be voluntary.

Another point is that it may be difficult for a parecon to incorporate a trade deal with another country into its participatory planning procedure. The deal would have to be negotiated prior to the participatory planning procedure, with conditions in the deal stipulating that the parecon nation does not know exactly how much of a particular good it will want, or how much it can export until after the planning procedure is done. Other countries will have to wait for exact figures, with just estimates in the meantime. There might be other ways to do this as well. There would also be difficulty in estimating the social opportunity cost of goods from other nations. Much less data will be available to determine the social opportunity cost. Also, workers in the other country would not be working in a balanced job complex, and would not be remunerated for effort and sacrifice. Rough estimates of the social opportunity cost would have to be made. Further, a parecon country would likely try to price products like organic food grown in a cooperative at low cost (and therefore order more of that good) and price automobiles produced in factory conditions very high (and order little or none of these things from the other country). This would be an encouragement to the other nation to develop in more equitable ways, and might be considered "exporting revolution," to be discussed below.

Currency Exchange

Other points to consider are that a parecon would not use money in the traditional sense, it would have no traditional capital to give another country for its goods. Credits in a parecon are for bookkeeping the effort and sacrifice of its workers. There are no banks.

There appear to be some options available to the participatory society, though. Presumably, the parecon nation could export goods to other countries and get foreign currency for them. It could then use its stores of currency to pay for things it wants to import.

However, this might not allow the Participatory Society to get the cash it needs. It might want to buy many goods from other countries (food, wood, metals, etc.), and if you can't pay for them, you can't get them. Presumably there are limits on any country in this day and age, you cannot produce everything internally, nor do you want to. Thus you need a loan. To pay back a loan, you need money that other nations would accept.

Another country might not accept parecon "credits." Credits, under the parecon philosophy, are a record of the effort and sacrifice a capitalist country or corporation gave to a parecon country, to be redeemed by that entity only for goods the parecon nation produces. Presumably a capitalist entity would want currency that can be exchanged on an international market so they can acquire other currency to buy things the parecon nation does not offer. Remember, parecon currency is not transferrable to someone else. Thus parecon credits might not be acceptable to other entities, and trading with a capitalist entity might be impossible. A solution might be to have two currencies. This solution was suggested to me by Robin Hahnel in a personal communication. One currency is internal, credits to give workers that disappear, the other is a regular currency used for international trade. Other countries and corporations and people could then redeem the other currency to get things from the parecon nation. Somehow, this would have to be incorporated into the yearly planning procedure, even if some entity wants to redeem its credits right away. Would a parecon nation issue bonds to encourage foreign investment? Would it give out loans and charge interest? I'm not an economist and don't know how this might work in detail. In my opinion it deserves a detailed answer. It is probably doable, however.

One might worry about the effects of having an external trading currency and an external bank system etc. Might it undermine the principles of parecon? One can imagine a hostile entity trying to devalue the currency. Might the IMF or World Bank try to force a parecon nation to get loans and pay them back? Could trading itself (where you negotiate the best price and enter into a sort of hostile arrangement) be contrary to parecon principles and undermine the country? Presumably this danger exists and, again, I believe this issue needs serious thought. I have not seen it dealt with in any parecon literature. On the flip side, a participatory nation will presumably face military and ideological challenges from foreign powers as well. Economic hostility is just more hostility, and a participatory society must do what it can to protect itself, perhaps trying to keep trading to a minimum, and relying on its internal resources as much as possible. In the end, just because you have an external currency that mimics normal capitalist currency should not introduce mechanical difficulties so extreme as make to a participatory society impossible.

DEFENSE OF A PARTICIPATORY SOCIETY

Existence of an Army

One may question whether a participatory society would have an army, whether it would make weapons, etc. There does not seem to be any reason to have an army beyond some sort of police force if all nations are parecons and have a parpolity. However, if the example of Cuba is anything to go by, a parecon nation would most likely be ruthlessly attacked by an entity like the United States. If not militarily, then surely economically. The political situation could easily become one where the participatory nation would have to arm itself or face easy takeover by another nation. If this is not the case, then there is no need for a standing army. If the participatory nation does face takeover, what choice is there besides arming itself for defense? This assumes that it is worth lives to keep the society participatory and free. This question would have to be democratically determined by the participatory nation.

It must be noted that there are other things it can do to defend itself besides arming itself. It can form alliances with more socialist type countries (if possible). However, it would not seem fair to the allied country to expect it to do all the fighting if the alliance is attacked. The participatory country can also trade with countries by applying the above 50% rule, and will engender goodwill by doing so.

Further, giving aid and support during crises will also help, particularly if aid and support is given to the population of nations who are likely to attack the participatory nation. The participatory society would also have motivation to strengthen and be an active and obedient member of an organization like the UN. The very existence of an army might be a troubling institution for a participatory society to deal with. Soldiers must be trained to kill, other countries see a force that is trained to kill them. The socializing effects of an army seem negative. For instance, today some soldiers see being a warrior as part of being a true "man." It is this very thing that a participatory society is designed to get away from. We want to make a peaceful society. Perhaps soldiers in a participatory society will see themselves as reluctant defenders. Hopefully, the army would have a primary role as an emergency response team or a manual labor team, and a secondary role as a killing force.

Draft?

Assuming that the participatory society will arm itself for defense, who will do the fighting? An interesting answer comes from Noam Chomsky:

*"One preliminary question is whether it is a democratically determined community decision that an army is necessary. Sometimes the answer is pretty clearly Yes: in World War II, for example. There were some people who refused conscription, dedicated pacifists mostly: courageous and honorable, but doesn't bear on the issue.• Suppose that assumption holds. Then conscription is not a violation of basic human rights any more than parceling out other unpleasant work equitably is. Say garbage collection. In a decent society it shouldn't be "volunteer" in the sense that it's undertaken only by people who are driven to it by need. Rather, it should be equitably distributed — which one can call "conscription" if one likes. These are basic issues discussed in all thinking about decent participatory societies, within the PARECON discussions, for example."*6

Here Chomsky is replying to a query on the Znet sustainers forum regarding conscription. He makes a good case for the idea that military service in a participatory society should be mandatory on the grounds that it is hard and very dangerous work, and thus it should be shared, like rote work is shared in a parecon. I think his point is well made, and leads us to conclude that in the event of a war, a participatory society might have to use a draft to defend itself, or perhaps make military service mandatory for all citizens when they are young, as is done in some countries. I find this a surprising conclusion, but cannot see any way around it.

Would a Participatory Society invade Another Country?

Why do countries invade one another? Traditionally, elites in one country see a chance to expand their power, or become richer by invading another country. Also there could be strong racism between the two countries, or one country might wish to terrorize another country to keep it from asserting its rights, etc. What motivation might a participatory society have to invade another country, if the participatory society does not have an elite?

The only scenario I can think of where a participatory society would have motivation to invade another country for its own benefit is if a large majority of the society voted to subjugate the other country to make the participatory society better off as a whole. Since this would need a large majority, it seems unlikely that a large percentage of any population might vote to be that cruel, again invoking the principle that the majority of the population is fair minded. However, one should that remember that early societies regularly practiced slavery on a large scale, so it is definitely not impossible. It seems particularly unlikely without a media and propaganda system to egg them on (assuming a functioning "unbiased" media). Given how the majority of people today react to the thought of war and oppression, even as their own governments carry out this oppression, it also seems unlikely. However the possibility remains. A measure against this would also be in the court system of the participatory society, where the high court would have the ability to review and block any vote to do this, just as it would block a majority decision to oppress a minority within its own borders.

It is of course possible to concoct a scenario where it would be ethical to send troops to another country. The example of the genocide in Rwanda in particular speaks to this. If it is possible to stop a horrible calamity by sending in troops, then it seems the participatory society would be morally obligated to do so. There might be a provision in the constitution where if the courts and a high majority of a population agree that something must be done, and there is good intelligence on what exactly the situation is (like Rwanda), than it is imaginable that the decision could be made to send in troops. The troops would have to be withdrawn at the earliest opportunity. Hopefully writing this stipulation into the constitution would be enough to make it enforced.

It might also be wise to stipulate that any high level council that directs the defense of the participatory society when it is invaded would have to resign once the war is over. War causes negative effects like establishing permanent hierarchies. It might even be necessary to allow a high level council to stay on longer than normal if elections are impossible. Again, measures would have to be taken to get anyone out of power once a war is over.

Hierarchy in the Military

Presumably it is possible to have a balanced job complex in an army or navy. Generals and captains can clean toilets with the best of them. However, it may be very difficult to deal with military hierarchy and have a proper democracy. Military leaders need to be few for reasons of secrecy and expertise, and people must follow orders because there may be little time to explain them. It is of course possible to rotate the captaincy of a ship between four or five people, and it is possible to explain strategy to all people in the army and vote on it. One can even rotate for expertise, when the ship is in combat, only two out of three captains (for example) might be qualified to give orders, otherwise other people can captain the ship when the ship is not in combat.

The Spanish revolution provides examples where officers partied with the troops and troops voted on whether they would take a hill. According to people who fought this way, it worked. One can go beyond this and rotate the position of officer amongst those qualified. Those not fit for command can do other empowering tasks such as planning strategy or programming war games, or even have an empowering job outside the military.

Even with all this to try, when it comes to fighting you want the best (nastiest?) people to be in charge and you need to follow orders. Otherwise people die and you lose. There is no getting around this. One can only hope that invasions into a participatory society can be beaten off quickly, so that the predictable negative effects of permanent hierarchy and loss of self management can be fixed.

DECIDING FOREIGN POLICY IN A PARTICIPATORY SOCIETY

High Level Councils

As described above, laws would be made by various level councils in a participatory society. It seems natural that the highest level council could represent the population in international events and decide on foreign policy. There could also be a separate high level council chosen in some manner from lower level councils for this purpose as well (if there is too much of a work load). In any case, this council would take general guidance from the population on foreign policy issues and deliberate the details of foreign policy.

For instance if the lower councils send a message that it is time for increased trade with willing countries, then this council would hammer out the details (which countries, what things to trade, consult with facilitation boards for estimates on indicative pricing on non-parecon countries, etc.). The council would then inform its ambassadors with instructions on what to negotiate for and what parameters to negotiate under (bottom line for deals and so forth).

Ambassadors

There does not seem to be any reason why a participatory society would not have an ambassador(s) in other countries and an embassy. Since the job must be balanced, it would necessary to have a team of ambassadors and negotiators, whose other jobs would be cleaning the embassy, sorting mail and maybe taking dictation. If there is not enough rote work for the team to do at the embassy, they would go back home to do it for a few months of the year. Ambassadors would be mandated to only make statements and negotiate settlements as guided by the high level council they are answerable to.

EXPORTING REVOLUTION

How wise is it to interfere in the lives of people in other countries? Should a participatory society do what it can to export revolution, and try to convince other countries to follow its lead?

Suppose some country becomes a participatory society successfully, then a little while later, a resistance group from another country contacts the participatory society asking for military aid to overthrow their own government. What to do? Would a participatory society want to support and get involved in a bloody revolution in some other country? What if it fails and the participatory society gets attacked? What if it is successful, but only at great cost of life, and the results of the revolution turn out to be not successful? This also bears on the issue of encouraging certain forms of work life in other countries. A parecon country would naturally encourage cooperatives that do not pollute the environment in another country and self managed workplaces, and try to buy from them. Is it right to interfere in this way? I would say yes in this case. In any case, there are certainly no easy answers, and the right thing to do would depend on each unique case. This presumes that the majority of the population wants to do the right thing, which should hold up, as reiterated above. A general "hands off" policy (in military matters) might be wisest, simply due to the unpredictable nature of such an endeavor, even with the best of intentions.

TOURISM?

What if people from another country wanted to take a vacation in a participatory society? Of course, there is no reason to deny this, however they will have to exchange their foreign currency for parecon credits. This foreign currency can be put towards buying goods from other countries and giving it to parecon citizens that wish to travel abroad. Why give parecon credits to someone who has not worked for the society? It is a bookkeeping system, after all. Notice though that the parecon nation benefits from these currencies, as it can use them. Since there is this benefit, it seems fair to allow the tourists credits.

There is no issue regarding tourism between two participatory societies. Since the two countries would likely order things from each other during the participatory planning process, work would be done for the benefit of each, regardless where it was done. Thus credits from one country would be redeemable in another participatory country.

ESPIONAGE?

Would a participatory society spy on other countries? Would it keep secrets from its own population? Would it spy on its own population? Would care if other countries spied on it? Let us try to address these questions in turn. First, note that espionage is not against international law, though it is against the law of any nation who is being spied on. Whether espionage should be against international law is another question.

Is there any motivation for a participatory society to spy on other non-participatory countries? It would seem there is. Perhaps another country is planning an attack on the participatory country. My guess is that knowledge of the time and location and means used in this attack would be pretty useful information. Or perhaps the participatory society would like to know how to construct a really useful piece of technology, like a drug or a computer program, developed in a capitalist country, whose method of manufacture is a secret. Would a participatory society respect copyright laws and patents? A reason to respect them would be to engender goodwill towards capitalist nations. If a parecon nation manufactures and sells a drug at 1/100 of the cost of the corporation that owns the patent, they are going to be upset, and there might be repercussions. If the repercussions are severe, then you don't want to do this, unless the costs are worth it. Beyond negative relations with other countries, I see no reason for a participatory society to care one whit for copyright laws or patents. Knowledge and the ability to produce what you want would be seen as something for the greater good. Respecting the right of an inventor to profits is not in the parecon philosophy.

Thus it stands to reason that there is motivation to spy on other countries. Is it worth the lives of agents to get these secrets? there would be volunteers willing to risk their lives to technology or get vital intelligence on an aggressive enemy. Should they be allowed to go? Would spying be worth the risk of upsetting other countries, and fostering mistrust from other nations? Perhaps this would be best left up to a general vote by the polity, which is a funny thing to do, as you are openly announcing that you intend to spy on other countries. If allowed, then the appropriate branch of the foreign affairs council would train and send spies into other countries, and use the information gathered appropriately.

Would a participatory society care if it was being spied on? Presumably it would not care if someone was trying to steal a formula for a beneficial drug. Let them have it. However, not everything is beneficial. We don't want a foreign power to have a formula for toxic gas that researchers in a participatory society have found, either accidentally or deliberately. Therefore there would be secrets to protect in a participatory society. If a participatory society decides to have an army for defense, they should have fairly modern weapons, otherwise they pose no credible deterrent. Thus either a participatory society will have to keep up to date on cutting edge weapons by espionage, or failing that, put research and development into developing means to kill people, as distasteful as that sounds. Indeed, the socializing effects of having a military makes one wonder if it is really worth it. If research and development is going into making weapons, then do we want countries willing to attack us to know how to make them too? Presumably not, but then again it might not matter, if everyone has similar weapons technology, then attacking the participatory society would still be costly. However, maybe you don't want your enemies to know the exact capabilities of your weapons. Thus whether or not you allow people to spy on you is debatable, but might actually be allowed.

Since it is assumed that a participatory society would not have weapons of mass destruction, the method of manufacture for these weapons would be best forgotten, and knowledge of how to manufacture should be kept a secret (or destroyed?).

Finally, would a participatory society spy on its own population? There might be motivations for this if there were, for example, people committed to capitalism that for some reason conspire to commit acts of terrorism. Certainly knowledge of this sort of plot would be desirable. Of course this must be balanced by the need to not harass and monitor the countries own citizens, as this has a very negative social effect. Investigating ones own population (before any crime is committed) is routinely carried out in countries today, and is part of the work of intelligence agencies and police. One would assume that citizens of a participatory nation would have little tolerance for being investigated by their own officials, thus it seems reasonable that gathering intelligence on its own citizens would be quite limited in a participatory nation.

UNITED NATIONS?

Would a participatory society follow international law, and heed the rulings of a world court? Would it heed the rulings of the World Trade Organization, would it accept loans from the IMF and/or World Bank? What sort of member of the United Nations would it be? How would it prefer that the United Nations be organized?

There are a lot of questions. In general, one would assume that a participatory nation would want to respect the decrees of the UN, as long as it believes the structure of the UN is sound. It is important to respect the idea of an international arbiter and thus support it by obeying it, as the general idea could lead to peace around the world. Of course the democratic potential of the UN is far below the level of a participatory society. Particular problems today include the permanent members of the security council whom have veto power. Positive measures can be blocked by a powerful state with veto power. Other problems include the toothlessness of the UN, as it cannot enforce any decree that a military power like the US chooses to ignore. If the institution is compromised, why obey its decrees? I suppose that it depends on how compromised the UN is. If it becomes a totally worthless organization, why bother supporting it? However it should be supported as long as it is somewhat functional, as I would think this is an important global principle a participatory society would want to support. Participatory societies can also form their own international organizations, with much more democratic structures if need be. One can imagine a participatory UN, where delegates from participatory societies are sent to the international body, where they deliberate on international rules and arbitrate disputes, or decree whom can attack whom and so on. Would it be logical to give such a body its own military? It might make sense that participatory nations would transfer all their military might to a proper international organization, only to be used if the member nations all agree. Then there would be no standing army in any participatory society, only on the neutral soil of the participatory UN. Whether or not this is a good idea needs discussion. It could lead to a situation where whomever is in charge of the collective army and weapons attacks and takes over the nations that donated their army.

As far as the IMF and World Bank are concerned, it is doubtful that a participatory society would have anything to do with them, as the loans given by these organizations tied to structural changes in the receiving country, benefitting the rich and not the poor. Even in a severe economic crises, it would probably be foolish for a participatory society to accept a loan from these institutions. Accepting such a loan might even make it impossible to continue as a participatory society.

SPLITTING UP OF A COUNTRY?

Shalom2 has already provided some ideas regarding the secession of a participatory society. A summary of his position as follows: Secession is not desirable, as it means you have failed to live together, but must be allowed, otherwise you encourage the tyranny of the majority. However, secession should not be allowed if it gives more resources to one fragment of the original nation. A part of a country with vast oil reserves should not be allowed to separate from the other nation unless they would both have equal access to this wealth. Also a secession should not be allowed if it leads to some minority being oppressed by a majority. Democratic rights must also be protected in some fashion.

Shalom goes further. He argues that politically distinct subunits in a participatory society might want join another council than the one they are in. This allows for another check on the tyranny of the majority. The drawback is that less diversity is fostered. In the end, secession must be dealt with on a case by case basis. I personally find all this quite reasonable, and have no other issues to raise.

RESPECTING THE LAWS OF OTHER COUNTRIES?

To what extent would a participatory society respect the laws of other nations?

I suppose the short answer is "To the extent they are reasonable." I would imagine that a participatory society would not have a death penalty, and would protect people who would face a death penalty if deported from the participatory nation. Further, if a Participatory Society believes in rehabilitation rather than punishment, it is unclear to what extent it would allow any "criminal" to be deported to the nation where the crime was committed. To make this more clear, consider what might happen if we do away entirely the concept of punishment for a crime. What if someone committed a murder (say a wife kills her husband after he is abusive to her) and after being examined by a series of psychologists it is determined that there is very close to 0% chance this person would ever murder again. What point is there in locking them up? Seemingly none, the murderer is no danger to anyone. Thus a participatory society might have a different conception of justice than other nations.

Not respecting the laws of other nations leads to conflict, of course. However, countries today do not allow supposed criminals they capture to be deported if they think they will be tortured. At least that is the stated policy of countries like Canada. I don't see any particular problems beyond the international strife a participatory nation would face in any event.

7

POLITICAL CORRECTNESS

INTRODUCTION

As Russell Kirk wrote, one of conservatism's most important insights is that all ideologies are wrong. Ideology takes an intellectual system, a product of one or more philosophers, and says, "This system must be true." Inevitably, reality ends up contradicting the system, usually on a growing number of points. But the ideology, by its nature, cannot adjust to reality; to do so would be to abandon the system.

Therefore, reality must be suppressed. If the ideology has power, it uses its power to undertake this suppression. It forbids writing or speaking certain facts. Its goal is to prevent not only expression of thoughts that contradict what "must be true," but thinking such thoughts. In the end, the result is inevitably the concentration camp, the gulag and the grave.

While some Americans have believed in ideologies, America itself never had an official, state ideology – up until now. But what happens today to Americans who suggest that there are differences among ethnic groups, or that the traditional social roles of men and women reflect their different natures, or that homosexuality is morally wrong? If they are public figures, they must grovel in the dirt in endless, canting apologies. If they are university students, they face star chamber courts and possible expulsion. If they are employees of private corporations, they may face loss of their jobs. What was their crime? Contradicting America's new state ideology of "Political Correctness." But what exactly is "Political Correctness?" Marxists have used the term for at least 80 years, as a broad synonym for "the General Line of the Party." It could be said that Political Correctness is the General Line of the Establishment in America today; certainly, no one who dares contradict it can be a member of that Establishment. But that still does not tell us what it really is.

This short book, which Free Congress has decided to make available free over its website, seeks to answer that question. It does so in the only way any ideology can be understood, by looking at its historical origins, its method of analysis and several key components, including its place in higher education and its ties with the Feminist movement. Finally, it offers an annotated bibliography for those who wish to pursue the subject in greater depth.

Perhaps the most important question facing Americans today is, "Do we really want America to be an ideological state?" Because conservatives know where all ideologies lead, our answer, resoundingly, is "NO!" But if we expect to prevail and restore our country to full freedom of thought and expression, we need to know our enemy. We need to understand what Political Correctness really is. As you will soon see, if we can expose the true origins and nature of Political Correctness, we will have taken a giant step to its overthrow.

WHAT IS "POLITICAL CORRECTNESS"?

Most Americans look back on the 1950s as a good time. Our homes were safe, to the point where many people did not bother to lock their doors. Public schools were generally excellent, and their problems were things like talking in class and running in the halls. Most men treated women like ladies, and most ladies devoted their time and effort to making good homes, rearing their children well and helping their communities through volunteer work. Children grew up in two–parent households, and the mother was there to meet the child when he came home from school. Entertainment was something the whole family could enjoy.

What Happened?

If a man from America of the 1950s were suddenly introduced into America in the 2000s, he would hardly recognize it as the same country. He would be in immediate danger of getting mugged, carjacked or worse, because he would not have learned to live in constant fear. He would not know that he shouldn't go into certain parts of the city, that his car must not only be locked but equipped with an alarm, that he dare not go to sleep at night without locking the windows and bolting the doors – and setting the electronic security system.

If he brought his family with him, he and his wife would probably cheerfully pack their children off to the nearest public school. When the children came home in the afternoon and told them they had to go through a metal detector to get in the building, had been given some funny white powder by another kid and learned that homosexuality is normal and good, the parents would be uncomprehending.

In the office, the man might light up a cigarette, drop a reference to the "little lady," and say he was happy to see the firm employing some Negroes in important positions. Any of those acts would earn a swift reprimand, and together they might get him fired.

When she went into the city to shop, the wife would put on a nice suit, hat, and possibly gloves. She would not understand why people stared, and mocked. And when the whole family sat down after dinner and turned on the television, they would not understand how pornography from some sleazy, blank-fronted "Adults Only" kiosk had gotten on their set.

Were they able, our 1950s family would head back to the 1950s as fast as they could, with a gripping horror story to tell. Their story would be of a nation that had decayed and degenerated at a fantastic pace, moving in less than a half a century from the greatest country on earth to a Third World nation, overrun by crime, noise, drugs and dirt. The fall of Rome was graceful by comparison.

Why did it Happen?

Over the last forty years, America has been conquered by the same force that earlier took over Russia, China, Germany and Italy. That force is ideology. Here, as elsewhere, ideology has inflicted enormous damage on the traditional culture it came to dominate, fracturing it everywhere and sweeping much of it away. In its place came fear, and ruin. Russia will take a generation or more to recover from Communism, if it ever can.

The ideology that has taken over America goes most commonly by the name of "Political Correctness." Some people see it as a joke. It is not. It is deadly serious. It seeks to alter virtually all the rules, formal and informal, that govern relations among people and institutions. It wants to change behavior, thought, even the words we use. To a significant extent, it already has. Whoever or whatever controls language also controls thought. Who dares to speak of "ladies" now?

Just what is "Political Correctness?" "Political Correctness" is in fact cultural Marxism – Marxism translated from economic into cultural terms. The effort to translate Marxism from economics into culture did not begin with the student rebellion of the 1960s. It goes back at least to the 1920s and the writings of the Italian Communist Antonio Gramsci. In 1923, in Germany, a group of Marxists founded an institute devoted to making the translation, the Institute of Social Research (later known as the Frankfurt School). One of its founders, George Lukacs, stated its purpose as answering the question, "Who shall save us from Western Civilization?" The Frankfurt School gained profound influence in American universities after many of its leading lights fled to the United States in the 1930s to escape National Socialism in Germany.

The Frankfurt School blended Marx with Freud, and later influences (some Fascist as well as Marxist) added linguistics to create "Critical Theory" and "deconstruction." These in turn greatly influenced education theory, and through institutions of higher education gave birth to what we now call "Political Correctness." The lineage is clear, and it is traceable right back to Karl Marx.

The parallels between cultural Marxism and classical, economic Marxism are evident. Cultural Marxism, or Political Correctness, shares with classical Marxism the vision of a "classless society" i.e., a society not merely of equal opportunity, but equal condition. Since that vision contradicts human nature – because people are different, they end up unequal, regardless of the starting point – society will not accord with it unless forced. So, under both variants of Marxism, it is forced. This is the first major parallel between classical and cultural Marxism: *both are totalitarian ideologies*. The totalitarian nature of Political Correctness can be seen on campuses where "PC" has taken over the college: freedom of speech, of the press, and even of thought are all eliminated. The second major parallel is that both cultural Marxism and classical, economic Marxism have *single-factor explanations of history*. Classical Marxism argues that all of history was determined by ownership of the means of production. Cultural Marxism says that history is wholly explained by which groups – defined by sex, race and sexual normality or abnormality – have power over which other groups.

The third parallel is that both varieties of Marxism *declare certain groups virtuous and others evil a priori*, that is, without regard for the actual behavior of individuals. Classical Marxism defines workers and peasants as virtuous and the bourgeoisie (the middle class) and other owners of capital as evil. Political Correctness defines blacks, Hispanics, Feminist women, homosexuals and some additional minority groups as virtuous and white men as evil. (Political Correctness does not recognize the existence of non-Feminist women and defines blacks who reject Political Correctness as whites).

The fourth parallel is in means: *expropriation*. Economic Marxists, where they obtained power, expropriated the property of the bourgeoisie and handed it to the state, as the "representative" of the workers and the peasants. Cultural Marxists, when they gain power (including through our own government), lay penalties on white men and others who disagree with them and give privileges to the groups they favor. Affirmative action is an example.

Finally, both varieties of Marxists employ a method of analysis *designed to show the correctness of their ideology in every situation*. For classical Marxists, the analysis is economic. For cultural Marxists, the analysis is linguistic: deconstruction. Deconstruction "proves" that any "text," past or present, illustrates the oppression of blacks, women, homosexuals, etc. by reading that meaning into words of the text (regardless of their actual meaning). Both methods are, of course, phony analyses that twist the evidence to fit preordained conclusions, but they lend a "scientific" air to the ideology. These parallels are neither remarkable nor coincidental. They exist because Political Correctness is directly derived from classical Marxism, and is in fact merely a variant of Marxism. Through most of the history of Marxism, cultural Marxists were "read out" of the movement by classical, economic Marxists. Today, with economic Marxism dead, cultural Marxism has filled its shoes. The medium has changed, but the message is the same: a society of radical egalitarianism enforced by the power of the state.

Political Correctness now looms over American society like a colossus. It has taken over both political parties – recent

Republican conventions were choreographed according to its dictates, while cultural conservatives were shown the door – and is enforced by many laws and government regulations. It almost totally controls the most powerful element in our culture, the entertainment industry. It dominates both public and higher education: many a college campus is a small, ivy-covered North Korea. It has even captured the clergy in many Christian churches. Anyone in the Establishment who departs from its dictates swiftly ceases to be a member of the Establishment. The remainder of this short book will explore the subject of Political Correctness further: its history, its method of analysis (deconstruction), and the means by which it has attained its influence, especially through education.

But one more question must be addressed at the outset, the most vital question: how can Americans combat Political Correctness and retake their society from the cultural Marxists?

To that end, it is not sufficient to criticize Political Correctness. It tolerates a certain amount of criticism, even gentle mocking. It does so through no genuine tolerance for other points of view, but in order to disarm its opponents, to let itself seem less menacing than it is. The cultural Marxists do not yet have total power, and they are too wise to appear totalitarian until their victory is assured.

Rather, those who would defeat cultural Marxism must defy it. They must use words it forbids, and refuse to use the words it mandates; remember, sex is better than gender. They must shout from the housetops the realities it seeks to suppress, such as the facts that violent crime is disproportionately committed by blacks and that most cases of AIDS are voluntary, i.e., acquired from immoral sexual acts. They must refuse to turn their children over to public schools. Above all, those who would defy Political Correctness must behave according to the old rules of our culture, not the new rules the cultural Marxists lay down. Ladies should be wives and homemakers, not cops or soldiers, and men should still hold doors open for ladies. Children should not be born out of wedlock. Open homosexuals should be shunned. Jurors should not accept race as an excuse for murder. Defiance spreads. When other Americans see one person defy Political Correctness and survive – and you still can, for now – they are emboldened. They are tempted to defy it, too, and some will. The ripples from a single act of defiance, of one instance of walking up to the clay idol and breaking off its nose, can range far. There is nothing the

Politically Correct fear more than open defiance, and for good reason; it is their chief vulnerability. That should lead cultural conservatives to defy cultural Marxism at every turn.

While the hour is late, the battle is not decided. Very few Americans realize that Political Correctness is in fact Marxism in a different set of clothes. As that realization spreads, defiance will spread with it. At present, Political Correctness prospers by disguising itself. Through defiance, and through education on our own part (which should be part of every act of defiance), we can strip away its camouflage and reveal the Marxism beneath the window-dressing of "sensitivity," "tolerance" and "multiculturalism." Who dares, wins.

THE HISTORICAL ROOTS

America is today dominated by an alien system of beliefs, attitudes and values that we have come to know as "Political Correctness." Political Correctness seeks to impose a uniformity of thought and behavior on all Americans and is therefore totalitarian in nature. Its roots lie in a version of Marxism which seeks a radical inversion of the traditional culture in order to create a social revolution.

Social revolution has a long history, conceivably going as far back as Plato's *Republic*. But it was the French Revolution of 1789 that inspired Karl Marx to develop his theories in the nineteenth century. In the twentieth century, the success of the Bolshevik Revolution of 1917 in Russia set off a wave of optimistic expectation among the Marxist forces in Europe and America that the new proletarian world of equality was finally coming into being. Russia, as the first communist nation in the world, would lead the revolutionary forces to victory.

The Marxist revolutionary forces in Europe leaped at this opportunity. Following the end of World War I, there was a Communist "Spartacist uprising in Berlin, Germany lead by Rosa Luxemburg; the creation of a "Soviet" in Bavaria led by Kurt Eisner; and a Hungarian communist republic established by Bela Kun in 1919. At the time, there was great concern that all of Europe might fall under the banner of Bolshevism. This sense of impeding doom was given vivid life by Trotsky's Red Army invasion of Poland in 1919. However, the Red Army was defeated by Polish forces at the battle of the Vistula in 1920. The Spartacist, Bavarian Soviet and Bela Kun governments all failed to gain widespread support from the workers and after a brief time they were all overthrown. These events created a quandary for the Marxist revolutionaries in Europe. Under Marxist economic theory, the oppressed workers were supposed to be the beneficiaries of a social revolution that would place them on top of the power structure. When these revolutionary opportunities presented themselves, however, the workers did not respond. The Marxist revolutionaries did not blame their theory for these failures. They blamed the workers.

One group of Marxist intellectuals resolved their quandary by an analysis that focused on society's cultural "superstructure" rather than on the economic substructures as Marx did. The Italian Marxist Antonio Gramsci and Hungarian Marxist Georg Lukacs contributed the most to this new cultural Marxism.

Antonio Gramsci worked for the Communist International during 1923-24 in Moscow and Vienna. He was later imprisoned in one of Mussolini's jails where he wrote his famous "Prison Notebooks." Among Marxists, Gramsci is noted for his theory of cultural hegemony as the means to class dominance. In his view, a new "Communist man" had to be created before any political revolution was possible. This led to a focus on the efforts of intellectuals in the fields of education and culture. Gramsci envisioned a long march through the society's institutions, including the government, the judiciary, the military, the schools and the media. He also concluded that so long as the workers had a Christian soul, they would not respond to revolutionary appeals. Georg Lukacs was the son a wealthy Hungarian banker. Lukacs began his political life as an agent of the Communist International. His book *History and Class Consciousness* gained him recognition as the leading Marxist theorist since Karl Marx. Lukacs believed that for a new Marxist culture to emerge, the existing culture must be destroyed. He said, "I saw the revolutionary destruction of society as the one and only solution to the cultural contradictions of the epoch," and, "Such a worldwide overturning of values cannot take place without the annihilation of the old values and the creation of new ones by the revolutionaries."

When he became Deputy Commissar for Culture in the Bolshevik Bela Kun regime in Hungary in 1919, Lukacs launched what became known as "Cultural Terrorism." As part of this terrorism he instituted a radical sex education program in Hungarian schools. Hungarian children were instructed in free love, sexual intercourse, the archaic nature of middle-class family codes, the out-datedness of monogamy, and the irrelevance of religion, which deprives man of all pleasures. Women, too, were called to rebel against the sexual mores of the time. Lukacs's campaign of "Cultural Terrorism" was a precursor to what Political Correctness would later bring to American schools. In 1923, Lukacs and other Marxist intellectuals associated with the Communist Party of Germany founded the Institute of Social Research at Frankfurt University in Frankfurt, Germany. The Institute, which became known as the Frankfurt School, was modeled after the Marx-Engels Institute in Moscow. In 1933, when Nazis came to power in Germany, the members of the Frankfurt School fled. Most came to the United States.

The members of the Frankfurt School conducted numerous studies on the beliefs, attitudes and values they believed lay behind the rise of National Socialism in Germany. The Frankfurt School's studies combined Marxist analysis with Freudian psychoanalysis to form the basis of what became known as "Critical Theory." Critical Theory was essentially destructive criticism of the main elements of Western culture, including Christianity, capitalism, authority, the family, patriarchy, hierarchy, morality, tradition, sexual restraint, loyalty, patriotism, nationalism, heredity, ethnocentrism, convention and conservatism. These criticisms were reflected in such works of the Frankfurt School as Erich Fromm's *Escape from Freedom* and *The Dogma of Christ*, Wilhelm's Reich's *The Mass Psychology of Fascism* and Theodor Adorno's *The Authoritarian Personality*. *The Authoritarian Personality*, published in 1950, substantially influenced American psychologists and social scientists. The book was premised on one basic idea, that the presence in a society of Christianity, capitalism and the patriarchal-authoritarian family created a character prone to racial prejudice and German fascism. *The Authoritarian Personality* became a handbook for a national campaign against any kind of prejudice or discrimination on the theory that if these evils were not eradicated, another Holocaust might occur on the American continent. This campaign, in turn, provided a basis for Political Correctness.

Critical Theory incorporated sub-theories which themselves were intended to chip away at specific elements of the existing culture, including "matriarchal theory," "androgyny theory," "personality theory," "authority theory," "family theory," "sexuality theory," "racial theory," "legal theory" and "literary theory." Put into practice, these theories were to be used to overthrow the prevailing social order and usher in social revolution based on cultural Marxism.

To achieve this, the Critical Theorists of the Frankfurt School recognized that traditional beliefs and the existing social structure would have to be destroyed and then replaced. The patriarchal social structure would be replaced with matriarchy; the belief that men and women are different and properly have different roles would be replaced with androgyny; and the belief that heterosexuality is normal would be replaced with the belief that homosexuality is "normal."

As a grand scheme intended to deny the intrinsic worth of white, heterosexual males, the Critical Theorists of the Frankfurt School opened the door to the racial and sexual antagonisms of the Trotskyites. Leon Trotsky believed that oppressed blacks could be the vanguard of a communist revolution in North America. He denounced white workers who were prejudiced against blacks and instructed them to unite with the blacks in revolution. Trotsky's ideas were adopted by many of the student leaders of the 1960s counterculture movement, who attempted to elevate the black revolutionaries to positions of leadership in their movement.

The student revolutionaries were also strongly influenced by the ideas of Herbert Marcuse, another member of the Frankfurt School. Marcuse preached the "Great Refusal," a rejection of all basic Western concepts, sexual liberation and the merits of feminist and black revolutions. His primary thesis was that university students, ghetto blacks, the alienated, the asocial, and the Third World could take the place of the proletariat in the Communist revolution.

In his book, *An Essay on Liberation*, Marcuse proclaimed his goals of a radical transvaluation of values; the relaxation of taboos, cultural subversion; Critical Theory; and a linguistic rebellion that would amount to a methodical reversal of meaning. As for racial conflict, Marcuse wrote that white men are guilty and that blacks are the most natural force of rebellion.

Marcuse may be the most important member of the Frankfurt School in terms of the origins of Political Correctness, because he was the critical link to the counterculture of the 1960s. His objective was clear: "One can rightfully speak of a cultural revolution, since the protest is directed toward the whole cultural establishment, including morality of existing society..." His means was liberating the powerful, primeval force of sex from its civilized restraints, a message preached in his book, *Eros and Civilization*, published in 1955. Marcuse became one of the main gurus of the 1960s adolescent sexual rebellion; he himself coined the expression, "make love, not war." With that role, the chain of Marxist influence via the Frankfurt School was completed: from Lukacs's service as Deputy Commissar for Culture in the Bolshevik Hungarian government in 1919 to American students burning the flag and taking over college administration buildings in the 1960s. Today, many of these same colleges are bastions of Political Correctness, and the former student radicals have become the faculties.

One of the most important contributors to Political Correctness was Betty Friedan. Through her book *The Feminine Mystique*, Friedan became the mother of the modern feminist movement in America. Friedan was not a member of the Frankfurt School, but she was strongly influenced by it. Her work offers a useful case study of the Marxist roots of Political Correctness. Friedan devoted almost a full chapter of *The Feminine Mystique* to Abraham Maslow's theory of self-actualization. Maslow was a social psychologist who in his early years did research on female dominance and sexuality. Maslow was a friend of Herbert Marcuse at Bandeis University and had met Erich Fromm in 1936. He was strongly impressed by Fromm's Frankfurt School ideology. He wrote an article, "The Authoritarian Character Structure," published in 1944, that reflected the personality theory of Critical Theory. Maslow was also impressed with the work of Wilhelm Reich, who was another Frankfurt School originator of personality theory.

The significance of the historical roots of Political Correctness cannot be fully appreciated unless Betty Friedan's revolution in sex roles is viewed for what it really was – a manifestation of the social revolutionary process begun by Karl Marx. Friedan's reliance on Abraham Maslow's reflection of Frankfurt School ideology is simply one indicator. Other indicators include the correspondence of Friedan's revolution in sex roles with Georg Lukacs' annihilation of old values and the creation of new ones, and with Herbert Marcuse's transvaluation of values. But the idea of transforming a patriarchy into a matriarchy – which is what a sex-role inversion is designed to do – can be connected directed to Friedrich Engels book *The Origin of the Family, Private Property, and the Sate.* First published in 1884, this book popularized the now-accepted feminist belief that deep-rooted discrimination against the oppressed female sex was a function of patriarchy. The belief that matriarchy was the solution to patriarchy flows from Marx's comments in *The German Ideology,* published in 1845. In this work Marx advanced the idea that wives and children were the first property of the patriarchal male. The Frankfurt School's matriarchal theory (and its near-relation, androgyny theory) both originated from these sources.

When addressing the general public, advocates of Political Correctness – or cultural Marxism, to give it its true name – present their beliefs attractively. It's all just a matter of being "sensitive" to other people, they say. They use words such as "tolerance" and "diversity," asking, "Why can't we all just get along?"

The reality is different. Political Correctness is not at all about "being nice," unless one thinks gulags are nice places. Political Correctness is Marxism, with all that implies: loss of freedom of expression, thought control, inversion of the traditional social order and, ultimately, a totalitarian state. If anything, the cultural Marxism created by the Frankfurt School is more horrifying than the old, economic Marxism that ruined Russia. At least the economic Marxists did not exalt sexual perversion and attempt to create a matriarchy, as the Frankfurt School and its descendants have done.

This short essay has sought to show one critical linkage, that between classical Marxism and the ingredients of the "cultural revolution" that broke out in America in the 1960s. The appendices to this paper offer a "wiring diagram" which may make the trail easier to follow, along with a more detailed look at some of the main actors. Of course, the action does not stop in the '60s; the workings of Frankfurt School are yet very much with us, especially in the field of education. That topic, and other present-day effects of Frankfurt School thinking, will be the subjects of future chapters in this book.

Profiles

Georg Lukacs

- He began his political life as a Kremlin agent of the Communist International.
- His *History and Class-Consciousness* gained him recognition as the leading Marxist theorist since Karl Marx.
- In 1919 he became the Deputy Commissar for Culture in the Bolshevik Bela Kun Regime in Hungary. He instigated what become known as the "Cultural Terrorism."
- The Cultural Terrorism was a precursor of what was to happen in American schools.
- He launched an "explosive" sex education program. Special lectures were organized in Hungarian schools and literature was printed and distributed to instruct children about free love, the nature of sexual intercourse, the archaic nature of the bourgeois family codes, the outdatedness of monogamy and the irrelevance of religion, which deprives man of all pleasure. Children urged thus to reject and deride paternal authority and the authority of the Church, and to ignore precepts of morality, were easily and spontaneously turned into delinquents with whom only the police could cope. This call to rebellion addressed to Hungarian children was matched by a call to rebellion addressed to Hungarian women.
- In rejecting the idea that Bolshevism spelled the destruction of civilization and culture, Lukacs stated: "Such a worldwide overturning of values cannot take place without the annihilation of the old values and the creation of new ones by the revolutionaries."
- Lukacs' state of mind was expressed in his own words:
  - "All the social forces I had hated since my youth, and which I aimed in spirit to annihilate, now came together to unleash the First Global War."
  - "I saw the revolutionary destruction of society as the one and only solution to the cultural contradictions of the epoch."
  - "The question is, Who will free us from the yoke of Western Civilization?"

- o "Any political movement capable of bringing Bolshevism to the West would have to be 'Demonic'."
- o "The abandonment of the soul's uniqueness solves the problem of 'unleashing' the diabolic forces lurking in all the violence which are needed to create a revolution."

- Lukacs' state of mind was typical of those who represented the forces of Revolutionary Marxism.
- At a secret meeting in Germany in 1923, Lukacs proposed the concept of inducing "Cultural Pessimism" in order to increase the state of hopelessness and alienation in the people of the West as a necessary prerequisite for revolution.
- This meeting led to the founding of the Institute for Social Research at Frankfurt University in Germany in 1923 – an organization of Marxist and Communistoriented psychologists, sociologists and other intellectuals that came to be known as the Frankfurt School, which devoted itself to implementing Georg Lukacs's program.

Antonio Gramsci

- He was an Italian Marxist on an intellectual par with Georg Lukacs who arrived by analysis at the same conclusions as Lukacs and the Frankfurt School regarding the critical importance of intellectuals in fomenting revolution in the West.
- He had traveled to the Soviet Union after the Bolshevik Revolution of 1917 and made some accurate observations that caused him to conclude that a Bolshevikstyle uprising could not be brought about by Western workers due to the nature of their Christian souls.
- Antonio Gramsci became the leader of the Italian Communist Party, which earned him a place in one of Mussolini's jails in the 1930s, where he wrote *Prison Notebooks* and other documents.
- These works became available in English to Americans.
- His advice to the intellectuals was to begin a long march through the educational and cultural institutions of the

nation in order to create a new Soviet man before there could be a successful political revolution.

- This reflected his observations in the Soviet Union that its leaders could not create such a new Soviet man after the Bolshevik Revolution.
- This blueprint for mind and character change made Gramsci a hero of Revolutionary Marxism in American education and paved the way for creation of the New American Child in the schools by the education cartel.
- The essential nature of Antonio Gramsci's revolutionary strategy is reflected in Charles A. Reich's *The Greening of America*: "There is a revolution coming. It will not be like revolutions in the past. It will originate with the individual and the culture, and it will change the political structure as its final act. It will not require violence to succeed, and it cannot be successfully resisted by violence. This is revolution of the New Generation."

Wilhelm Reich

- In his 1933 book entitled *The Mass Psychology of Fascism*, he explained that the Frankfurt School departed from the Marxist sociology that set "Bourgeois" against "Proletariat." Instead, the battle would be between "reactionary" and "revolutionary" characters.
- He also wrote a book entitled *The Sexual Revolution*, which was a precursor of what was to come in the 1960s.
- His "sex-economic" sociology was an effort to harmonize Freud's psychology with Marx's economic theory.
- Reich's theory was expressed in his words: "The authoritarian family is the authoritarian state in miniature. Man's authoritarian character structure is basically produced by the embedding of sexual inhibitions and fear in the living substance of sexual impulses. Familial imperialism is ideologically reproduced in national imperialism..the authoritarian family..is a factor where reactionary ideology and reactionary structures are produced."
- Wilhelm Reich's theory, when coupled with Georg Lukacs' sex education in Hungary, can be seen as the source for

the American education cartel's insistence on sex education from kindergarten onwards and its complete negation of the paternal family, external authority, and the traditional character structure.

- Reich's theory encompassed other assertions that seem to have permeated American education:
    - o The organized religious mysticism of Christianity was an element of the authoritarian family that led to Fascism.
    - o The patriarchal power in and outside of man was to be dethroned.
    - o Revolutionary sexual politics would mean the complete collapse of authoritarian ideology.
    - o Birth control was revolutionary ideology.
    - o Man was fundamentally a sexual animal.
- Reich's *The Mass Psychology of Fascism* was in its ninth printing as of 1991, and is available in most college bookstores.

Erich Fromm

- Like Wilhelm Reich, Fromm was a social psychologist of the Frankfurt School who came to America in the 1930s.
- His book *Escape from Freedom,* published in 1941, is an ideological companion to Wilhelm Reich's *The Mass Psychology of Fascism.*
- Fromm asserted that early capitalism created a social order that bred a sadomasochistic and authoritarian character of which Martin Luther and Adolph Hitler were prime examples.
- He asserted that the same capitalistic social order resulted in Calvin's Theory of Predestination, which reflected the principle of the basic inequality of men that was revived in Nazi ideology.
- He asserted the authoritarian character experiences only domination or submission and "differences, whether sex or race, to him are necessarily of superiority or inferiority."
- He asserted that "Positive Freedom" implies the principle that there is no higher power than the unique individual

self; that man is the center and purpose of life; that the growth and realization of man's individuality is an end that can never be subordinated to purposes which are supposed to have a greater dignity.

- Fromm made the real meaning of this "Positive Freedom" clear in another of his many books – *The Dogma of Christ*.. wherein he describes a revolutionary character such as himself as: the man who has emancipated himself from the ties of blood and soil, from his mother and father, and from special loyalties to state, race, party or religion.
- Fromm makes his revolutionary intent very clear in *The Dogma of Christ*... "We might define revolution in a psychological sense, saying that a revolution is a political movement led by people with revolutionary characters, and attracting people with revolutionary characters."

Herbert Marcuse

- Like Wilhelm Reich and Erich Fromm, Herbert Marcuse was an intellectual of the Frankfurt School who came to America in the 1930s.
- He has often been described as a Marxist philosopher, but he was in fact a fullblooded social revolutionary who contemplated the disintegration of American society just as Karl Marx and Georg Lukacs contemplated the disintegration of German society: "One can rightfully speak of a cultural revolution, since the protest is directed toward the whole cultural establishment, including the morality of existing society..there is one thing we can say with complete assurance: the traditional idea of revolution and the traditional strategy of revolution has ended. These ideas are old-fashioned..What we must undertake is a type of diffuse and dispersed disintegration of the system."
- Marcuse published *Eros and Civilization* in 1955, which became the founding document of the 1960s counterculture and brought the Frankfurt School into the colleges and universities of America.
- He asserted that the only way to escape the one-dimensionality of modern industrial society was to liberate the erotic side of man, the sensuous instinct, in rebellion against "technological rationality."

- This erotic liberation was to take the form of the "Great Refusal," a total rejection of the capitalist monster and its entire works, including technological reason and ritual-authoritarian language.
- He provided the obtuse intellectual justifications for adolescent sexual rebellion, and the slogan "Make Love, Not War."
- His theory included the belief that the Women's Liberation Movement was to be the most important component of the opposition, and potentially the most radical.
- His revolutionary efforts would blossom into a full-scale war by revolutionary Marxism against the European white male in the schools and colleges.

Theodor Adorno

- He was another Marxist revolutionary and member of the Frankfurt School who came to America in the 1930s.
- Along with others, Adorno authored *The Authoritarian Personality*, which was published in 1950.
- Adorno's book was inspired by the same kind of theoretical assertions revealed in the works of Wilhelm Reich, Erich Fromm and Herbert Marcuse based on analytical studies of German society that were begun in 1923.
- The basic theme was the same. There was such a thing as an authoritarian character that was the opposite of the desired revolutionary character. This authoritarian character was a product of capitalism, Christianity, conservatism, the patriarchal family and sexual repression. In Germany, this combination induced prejudice, anti-Semitism and fascism according to Frankfurt School theory.
- It so happened that most Americans were products of capitalism, Christianity, conservatism, the patriarchal family and sexual repression in their youth. So Theodor Adorno and other members of the Frankfurt School had a golden opportunity to execute Georg Lukacs's and Antonio Gramsci's program for creating social revolution in America instead of Germany.
- They would posit the existence of authoritarian personalities among Americans with tendencies toward

prejudice, and then exploit this to force the "scientifically planned re-education" of Americans with the excuse that it was being done in order to eradicate prejudice.

- This scientifically-planned re-education would become the master plan for the transformation of America's system of fundamental values into their opposite revolutionary values in American education so that school children would become replicas of the Frankfurt School revolutionary characters and thus create the New American Child.
- This can be confirmed by noting that *The Authoritarian Personality* is the key source of the affective domain of Benjamin Bloom's *Taxonomy of Educational Objectives* of 1964, which guided the education cartel thereafter.

CORRECTNESS IN HIGHER EDUCATION

On a growing number of university campuses the freedom to articulate and discuss ideas – a principle that has been the cornerstone of higher education since the time of Socrates – is eroding at an alarming rate. Consider just one increasing trend: hundreds (sometimes thousands) of copies of conservative student newspapers have been either stolen or publicly burned by student radicals. In many cases these acts have taken place with the tacit support of faculty and administrators. The perpetrators are rarely disciplined.

While it would be easy to dismiss such demonstrations of intolerance as student pranks, these incidents are the surface manifestations of a more pervasive and insidious trend – a trend that has as its goal the destruction of the liberal arts tradition that has helped create and sustain Western civilization.

Though some pundits have claimed that the prevalence of the ideological intolerance known as Political Correctness has been exaggerated, the opposite is closer to the truth. Political Correctness has become so deeply ingrained in American higher education that many campuses are now dominated by an atmosphere of uncertainty and apprehension. An increasing number of dedicated students and faculty members now live in fear that their intellectual pursuit of truth will offend the Grand Inquisitors of Political Correctness. The techniques of Political Correctness are now well known: attacks on the curriculum in the name of "multiculturalism," the imposition of restrictive and vaguelyworded "speech codes" and mandatory "sensitivity training" courses for freshman that are little more than systematic efforts at ideological indoctrination. But the influence of Political Correctness has spread in other disturbing ways. Consider a few recent incidents from the university battlefield.

- At Amherst College in Massachusetts, a homosexual student group covered the university's sidewalks with graffiti, including the slogan "Queer by Divine Right," which was scrawled in front of the campus chapel on Good Friday. When the *Amherst Spectator*, a conservative student newspaper, criticized these chalkings as promoting "hatred and division," student protestors publicly burned copies of the paper.
- When the *Cornell Review*, another conservative student newspaper, published a parody of the course descriptions from Cornell's heavily-politicized Africana Department, campus militants blocked traffic at the center of the campus for several hours and burned stolen copies of the *Review* in a metal trash can. The militants went on to demand that the university provide "racial sensitivity" classes for incoming freshman, a campus speech code and more money for segregated minority programs such as a blacks-only dormitory.
- Students who participate in ROTC programs have told friends and family that they are afraid to show up for class wearing their uniforms because their grades have been arbitrarily marked down by faculty members who are hostile to the military.
- In the wake of a rash of sexual harassment charges that have been filed by extreme feminists against their alleged enemies, some professors have begun to take out insurance policies to protect themselves from the crushing financial burden of malicious and frivolous lawsuits.
- A faculty questionnaire at the University of Massachusetts asks professors what "contribution to multi-culturalism" they have made. The questionnaire is then used in making decisions about tenure and promotion. It is worth remembering that for every dramatic and well-publicized

example of Political Correctness, there are innumerable instances where its influence is more subtle, but just as real.

The Origins of Political Correctness in Higher Education

While the ideology of Political Correctness is hardly restricted to our campuses, there is no doubt it originated there. The intellectual roots of this phenomenon stretch back over centuries. Ultimately, the origins of PC can be traced to the rise of modern ideology and its quest for power. In contrast to the classical and Judeo-Christian traditions, which stressed man's need to understand the moral order and conform himself to it, modern ideologies have sought to dominate and control the world. In the twentieth century these ideologies finally gained political power in Communist states. But in the West, ideology has not been able to make such a direct assault on our traditions of ordered liberty. Rather, radical intellectuals have sought to undermine the foundations of knowledge itself, concentrating their efforts on the transformation of the university.

The turning point in the academy came in the 1960s, when militant students launched a guerilla attack on the traditions of Western culture and the liberal arts. Seeing that they could not gain lasting power through demonstrations alone, many of these militants opted to remain "in the system," going on to become professors themselves. This generation of "tenured radicals" (to use Roger Kimball's phrase) has now become the establishment in the vast majority of our institutions of higher learning. As university presidents, deans, and department chairmen, they have set about hiring other ideologues in their own image and have instigated the repressive policies we know as Political Correctness. These politicized academics will be extremely difficult to dislodge from their current positions of power.

Ideology vs. Liberal Education

The stakes in this war of ideas are high, for they include the very concept of freedom itself. Americans have always understood the intimate and vital connection between liberal education and political liberty. That is why Political Correctness is nothing less than a death blow aimed at the heart of our republic. In his seminal book, *The Idea of a University*, Cardinal John Henry Newman defined the "liberal arts" as a pursuit of knowledge for its own sake. By way of contrast, he defined the "servile arts" as those modes of study that serve only specific, immediate ends. The liberal arts are liberating, Newman argued, because they enable men to discover the underlying principles that guide us toward wisdom and virtue. Were he alive today, Newman would view Political Correctness as "servile" because its purpose is to advance a political agenda to a position of national power. Militant professors in increasing numbers are shamelessly turning their podiums into pulpits, abandoning the search for objective truth and setting about the task of indoctrinating their students.

The Devastated Curriculum

The proponents of Political Correctness have concentrated their efforts on the core of a liberal education, the curriculum. Their efforts will radically alter what new generations of Americans will learn. In this battle the handmaiden of Political Correctness has been the "multicultural" movement. A number of critics have rightly pointed out that multiculturalism is more than an argument for courses that concentrate on groups that at one time were disadvantaged or oppressed. Rather, multiculturalism involves the systematic restructuring of the curriculum so as to hinder students from learning about the Western tradition. Since the ulterior motive behind Political Correctness is an attempt to restructure American society along egalitarian lines, it is imperative for its proponents to instill in the minds of students a thoroughgoing cultural relativism.

Perhaps the most disturbing aspect of the Politically Correct assault on the curriculum is that it has occurred at many of America's elite universities. Take, for example, the case of Stanford University, an institution that has long played a leadership role in American higher education. Stanford eliminated its long-standing Western civilization requirement in 1988 and replaced it with a multicultural program known as "Cultures, Ideas, and Values." Under this new program freshmen at Stanford can just as easily study Marxist revolutionaries in Central America as they can Plato, Shakespeare or Newton.

Stanford has also led the movement away from serious study of history. Students at Stanford, like students at all but one of the other top 50 universities in the United States, are not required to take a single course in history. Instead, they are offered a choice of courses under the heading of "American Cultures." According to one recent graduate of Stanford, it is impossible to fulfill the "American Cultures" requirement by studying Protestantism, Irish Americans, or the American West, while courses that do fulfill the requirement include "Film and Literature: US-Mexico Border Representations" and "Contemporary Ethnic Drama." Stanford students must also take courses in "World Cultures" and "Gender Studies" that include "Chicana Expressive Culture" and "Misogyny and Feminism in the Renaissance." Because elite institutions such as Stanford set an example for the rest of American higher education, other universities eagerly adopt these devastating assaults on the curriculum. This "trickle-down" effect will have a long-lasting impact on the way future generations of Americans will be educated.

Intolerance and the Assault on Freedom

The two pillars that have traditionally sustained the liberal arts are academic freedom and freedom of speech. Without the freedom to pursue the truth and to write and speak freely, authentic scholarship is impossible. But both of these fundamental freedoms have been routinely abrogated by the establishment of speech codes, "sensitivity" classes, and a general atmosphere of fear and intimidation on campus.

For example, younger professors who have not received tenure must not only be careful of what they say, but of what they publish. Ideological university administrators in the 1990s have created an environment dominated by suspicion that is far more intense than anything spawned by anti-Communist Senator Joseph McCarthy in the 1950s. The most tragic victims of this age of Political Correctness are the students. The traditional goal of a liberal arts education – acculturation, whereby students absorb the inherited wisdom of the past – has been set aside. Increasingly, a university education today seems to involve rote learning of political opinions. When all is said and done, Political Correctness substitutes smug feelings of righteousness for the traditional habits of critical thinking. One distinguished scholar recently lamented that "higher education is increasingly about acquiring attitudes and opinions that one puts on like a uniform." Because the academy is a relatively isolated world, it can allow politicized administrators to turn the campus into a laboratory for experiments in social transformation. When critics of Political Correctness have compared the atmosphere on campus to that of a totalitarian state, liberal pundits have been quick to denounce them as hysterical. Few of these pundits have any first-hand experience of daily life on campus.

The Movement for Academic Reform

Despite the institutional power of the campus radicals, forces are at work seeking to spur authentic academic reform. The academic reform movement relies on the principles of accountability, communication and a commitment to authentic scholarship. One force of academic reform is a growing demand among parents for greater accountability from colleges and universities. At a time when studies show that students are paying more and learning less than ever before, parents in increasing numbers are becoming discriminating consumers.

Another force is independent student newspapers whose journalists publicize the antics of Political Correctness on campus. In the past, campus radicals thrived in the enclosed world of the university, but their actions are no longer going undetected. The advent of conservative student newspapers on dozens of campuses has forced campus militants into the open where they are most vulnerable to the scrutiny of an exasperated public.

Two years ago, those who fund the Collegiate Network asked the Intercollegiate Studies Institute to take over the administration of their program to support and enhance responsible student journalism. The Collegiate Network contributes seed money, practical help and intellectual guidance to the 60 conservative student newspapers which provide alternative forums of discussion at many of the nations most elite (and closedminded) universities.

These alternatives papers have identified abuses at all levels of academic life and engaged in investigative journalism that has been remarkably fair and accurate. Perhaps the most well-known "scoop" came from Yale University's alternative paper, *Light & Truth*, a publication supported by the Collegiate Network. The editors of *Light & Truth* discovered that the $20 million gift of alumnus Lee Bass was not being used for its intended purpose of supporting an integrated course in Western civilization. Their report broke open the scandal, which ended when Yale returned Mr. Bass's money. The subsequent furor cost Yale a great deal more than Mr. Bass's $20 million – both in monetary terms and in the loss of confidence of many Yale donors that the current administration can be trusted.

Not all the scandals uncovered by alternative campus papers are of this magnitude, but there are innumerable abuses that can be exposed by investigative student journalism. The law school at the University of North Carolina, Chapel Hill, banned representatives of the U.S. military from setting up recruiting tables there, despite receiving federal tax dollars from the Defense Department. An article about this outrageous assault on freedom that ran in both the student-run *Carolina Review* and in the national student newspaper published by ISI, *CAMPUS*, raised a hue and cry on and off campus. North Carolina legislators took immediate action and passed a bill prohibiting taxpayer-supported schools from discriminating against the military when prospective employers come to the university.

At the University of Wisconsin, Madison, the *UWM Times*, a conservative student newspaper, revealed that a university administrator had been soliciting signatures for local Democrat candidates for public office, in direct violation of a state law forbidding university employees from engaging in political campaigning. The university chancellor, despite having issued a directive against such campaigning, refused to reprimand the administrator in question – perhaps because the chancellor himself violated both the state law and his own directive by signing one of the petitions while at work. The story was picked up by the *Milwaukee Journal-Sentinel* and the abuse was brought to an end. Now that alternative newspapers and organizations dedicated to academic reform are spreading the word, the larger communities that surround our institutions of higher education are getting more involved in serious academic reform. For example, the National Association of Scholars is encouraging university trustees to take a more active and vocal role in opposing the excesses of Political Correctness. Efforts of this type must be expanded and intensified.

In the long run, the most direct method of defeating the inquisitors of Political Correctness is simply to stand up to them. Individual acts of defiance often entail serious risks: students can face star-chamber proceedings that are humiliating and demoralizing while faculty can lose their bids to receive tenure. But every act of resistance causes a ripple, encouraging others to stand up to ideological intimidation. With the support of a significant number of parents, donors and alumni, these Davids may yet slay the Goliaths who tower over them.

The Fire of True-Learning

Perhaps the strongest force for true academic reform is that which seeks to defeat the ideological depredations of Political Correctness by winning the war of ideas. The best students have a questioning intelligence that cannot be satisfied with political slogans. When such students have access to serious scholarship they respond with enthusiasm. Even today acculturation still takes place under the mentorship of outstanding scholars at various institutions around the country. Moreover, some colleges and universities continue to swim against the ideological tides of our time.

The Intercollegiate Studies Institute (ISI), in conjunction with the Templeton Foundation, has identified the best professors, departments, colleges and textbooks in American higher education today. This program, the Templeton Honor Rolls for Education in a Free Society, celebrates excellence and serves as a guide for parents and students contemplating the daunting choice of which college or university to attend. By singling out the best in higher education, the Templeton Honor Rolls also encourage donors to reward universities that preserve the traditions of the free society. Prospective college students, their parents and donors can also benefit from a comprehensive guide to 100 of the top institutions of higher learning in America published by the ISI. The guide contains substantial, essay-length treatments of all 100 institutions, including 80 elite schools that were selected on the basis of competitive admissions standards and 20 schools that ISI particularly recommends for their commitment to a liberal arts education. The ISI college guide warns students about the ideological dangers on the campuses and steers them in the direction of the best professors and departments. As best-selling author William J. Bennett wrote of this project, "All too often, Americans treat colleges and universities with a deference that prevents them from asking hard questions and demanding real results. But if there is ever to be genuine, long-lasting education reform, parents and students will have to become shrewder and better-informed consumers of education. The ISI guide is a powerful tool in this effort."

One of Edmund Burke's most famous sayings is that "the only thing necessary for the triumph of evil is for good men to do nothing." For generations, Americans have treated higher education with respect and awe – a token of their faith in the liberating power of the liberal arts. But in the face of Political Correctness, it is time for the American public to temper its respect with a critical sensibility and to undertake a more direct effort to call academia to account. It is time for good men and women to demand that American higher education live up to its best traditions and eschew the tyranny of Political Correctness.

DECONSTRUCTION AND LITERATURE

Literature is, if not the most important cultural indicator, at least a significant benchmark of a society's level of civilization. Our nature and environment combine to form each individual mind, which in turn expresses itself in words. Literature, as the words society collectively holds up as exemplary, is then a starting point of sorts – a window into the culture.

Today's literary field is therefore worth examining for the insights it provides into our current cultural milieu. The contemporary American literary field is awash in "isms:" Marxism, Freudianism, feminism, and so on. Most of these are the academic cousins of what is called in the common culture "Political Correctness." Literary theorists take their particular brand of criticism and apply it to literature in an effort to find self-affirmation in a "discovered" meaning of the text. For a feminist critic, for example, no longer does Andrew Marvel's "Upon Appleton House" have the beauty of the grounds as its theme; it speaks instead of the evils of a patriarchal line of inheritance. These "cultural critics," so named because they critique literature based on the point of view of a particular culture, arose in the 1960s, but their schools of criticism only truly began to pick up steam with the arrival of the school of deconstruction in the 1970s.

The works of the father of deconstruction, Jacques Derrida, began to be translated from the French by American professor

Gayatri Spivak in the mid-1970s, a time when the U.S. literary scene was ripe for its influence. The economic Marxists were alive and well on American campuses, and the cultural critics were still being fed by the radicalism of the times. Feminists, "queer theorists" and "literature-by-people of color" critics had gained a foothold in the earlier decade, but they had in their meager arsenals only a vague feeling of repression. What they lacked was philosophical backing – the courage prompted by having their own *logos*. The arrival of deconstruction from France provided that philosophy.

At that time, that generation of academics was doing what all academics do, telling the previous generation that it had it all wrong. In this case the rebellion was against the New Critics – so-called even now, decades after their prime. The New Critics specialized in finding the meaning of texts without regard to background information such as authorial intent, a process that had "the text is everything" as its guiding principle.

The new generation of critics set out to turn that principle on its head. Instead of "the text is everything," the new generation claimed that "everything is text" and turned to analyzing anything and everything in relation to the literary work. If a poet wrote a poem that included a female character, the critics would look into the poet's relationship with his mother, his wife, his sister and so on in an effort to offer up an interpretation of the work. This could have (and often did have) the positive effect of using biographic information to gain new understanding of the work; however, these new interpretations were not attempts to discern the true meaning of the work (as the New Critics had done) or even to discover the author's intended meaning (as traditional readings attempted). This new generation of critics instead became prime practitioners of what is known in literary circles as "cultural criticism." They strained to view literature from the "woman's point of view" or the "gay point of view" or the "radical minority point of view." Their attempts were not to find meaning – they were influenced too greatly by relativists for that – but to find sexism, racism or "homophobia" in the works of male, European or heterosexual authors.

Derridean deconstruction became a tool for these cultural critics. Simply stated, deconstruction is a school of thought that posits that words have no meaning. Instead, words have "traces" of meaning. The meaning of a word is continually disappearing, leaving us with only the memory, or trace, of what that meaning once was. (Similar to Heidegger's term being, Derrida often uses the crossed-out word trace in an effort to indicate a meaning that is simultaneously present and disappearing.) A metaphor may be helpful to understand the underlying philosophy of deconstructionism. If I say the word "pen," then you think of the object there in the desk drawer. But if I throw the pen at someone, then the word "pen" begins to lose the benign meaning of a writing apparatus with ink; to use deconstructionist terms, the original understanding of the word "pen" undergoes erasure to leave only a trace. Instead the word "pen" becomes associated with a weapon, a projectile, a means of expressing (perhaps) anger. If the pen strikes someone, then the word "pen" to that person means something painful, a personal injury, impetus for striking back and so on. These meanings constantly grow and change because the human mind is always interpreting and reinterpreting. Because of this, deconstruction argues, it never fully settles on *the* stable meaning for the word "pen." Based on this linguistic argument, deconstructionists conclude that since any meanings in words are so quickly diffused, we can never really communicate at all. Words no longer have meaning.

The postmodern catch word "differance," along with terms like "erasure" and "trace," entered American scholarship through Derrrida's writings. By combining the concepts of (and the French words for) "deferment" and "difference," Derrida came up with this name for the endless deferment of meaning that takes place. Derrida claims that differance is the reason that words cannot have meanings; the mind continually understands things in different ways so that the original meaning loses its importance as the *proper* meaning - it becomes a mere trace.

Ultimately this is insufficient for today's cultural critics – they need words to mean things so that they can point to artistic works and bemoan how they illustrate or exemplify the repression of minority cultures. But other than its general philosophy, deconstruction offered something more important. It offered the techniques to "show" how all language deconstructs itself. The deconstructionists specialized in "deconstructing" literary works– although they steadfastly insist that the works deconstruct themselves and the critic only illustrates how this happens. These techniques of deconstruction usually involve isolating the surface meaning of the literary work – the "traditionalist" meaning – and attempting to show how the work itself violates that traditional meaning. For example, they will take a love poem and pick apart the language until they find something that they can interpret as unloving. Elizabeth Barrett Browning's sonnet "How Do I Love Thee? Let Me Count The Ways," ends with the words "I shall but love thee better in death." The clever deconstructionists might combine these with Browning's earlier words, "when feeling out of bounds for the edge of beauty and ideal grace," to conclude that Mrs. Browning is actually reaching for her husband's death. "Why is she looking for the *edge* of beauty?" the deconstructionist asks. "She clearly does not want to remain in or before beauty; instead, she is seeking some way around it." The deconstructionist attributes this apparent disparity to the problem with language, "differance," and quickly concludes that the poem – like all other language – has no meaning.

Once they realized the power of this school of thought, the cultural critics embraced it readily, for here they discovered a method of attack on the traditional interpretations of literary works. They used deconstruction to remove traditional meaning and replaced it with *new* meaning. That meaning was the Political Correctness that infests our society today. For example, after the traditional meaning of "How Do I Love Thee?" has been destabilized in the process described above, a feminist critic might come along and - in the absence of a stable traditional interpretation – declare that the poem is "really" concerned with how women in nineteenth-century England were conditioned to see themselves as secondary to men.

Since "everything is text" in the postmodern mantra, the cultural critics did not hesitate to apply their methods to music, movies, television and anything they encountered. They found that they could remove the meaning from all cultural phenomena and substitute the values of whichever group they preferred. For example, homosexual analysts could remove the truth from the Bible and instead interpret it as full of homophobic hate – God's truth was torn down, and a human political agenda was inserted. This example is not particularly outrageous, as Derrida's stated goal in deconstructionism was to remove the idea of what he called the "transcendental signified." Standard models of linguistics operate with respect to a signifier-signified pair. The signifier is the word, and the signified is that which the word represents. When differance enters the picture, the thing signified is deferred continually until it can be deferred no longer – that is, until it reaches into the realm of metaphysics. The final meaning reached by any word is God, as He is the ultimate meaning of traditional Western thought.2 The "transcendental signified" of which Derrida is trying to rid himself and the Western world is in fact God. Derrida labels belief in God a product of deficient Western thinking, and in true Nietzchean fashion he claims that God is a construct of language rather than the other way around.

Naturally, Derrida quickly became the darling of the American university establishment. He lectured at universities along the Eastern seaboard, and grew to love that area of America. Soon America returned that affection by granting him a position in the English department of Yale University. Yale then began to draw to other deconstructionists and postmodernists; J. Hillis Miller, Geoffrey Hartman and others. Another European, Paul DeMan, also came to America and began teaching deconstruction. DeMan's history provides yet another reason why deconstructionists sought so avidly to remove meaning from language. In pre-World War II Belgium, DeMan had worked for an explicitly pro-Nazi newspaper. DeMan's detractors note that removing the meaning from language was an excellent way to dismiss his pro-Nazi writings.

Through deconstruction the cultural critics adopted a tool that turned literature, philosophy and culture into nonsense. For instance, in his own writing, in order to remain true to his own philosophy, Derrida eschews all forms of the verb "to be." In deconstructionist terms the verb "to be" implies meaning; thus, it cannot exist. Derrida therefore goes back and crosses out all "to be" verbs, making his writing all but incomprehensible. In beginning to attack the signifier-signified construction, Derrida writes "the sign is that ill-named thing, the only one, that escapes the instituting question of philosophy: 'What is..?'" At the same time Derrida is attempting to communicate his ideas about traditional linguistic models, he is forced by his own philosophy to scratch out the very words that allow him to communicate.

If Derrida were to follow the logic of his own theories he would find that the very concept of communicating his ideas by written or spoken word should be impossible. If deconstructionist theories were even remotely accurate, all verbal communication– and by extension all other forms of communication – would be impossible. As New Critic Dr. M. H. Abrams of Cornell University states, "I hope that Derrida remembers that words do mean things next time someone warns him of an oncoming bus."

Not only does the embrace of deconstruction harm logical philosophy, it also renders the creation of literature virtually impossible. If words mean nothing, then they are nothing more than sounds. True, Lewis Carroll did create a well-known poem using nonsensical but pleasant-sounding words, but how many poems like "jabberwocky" can be created before we reach the saturation point? (Some would argue that we have already reached that point.)

As university literature departments "progress," the divide widens between those who produce literature and those who analyze and teach it. While Samuel Taylor Coleridge, T.S. Eliot and an entire cadre of great authors were well-educated men, it seems that a literary education in an American university actually *hinders* one's ability to write well. As professors of literature embrace the philosophy of deconstruction they lose the ability to write beautifully because meaning is necessary for beautiful writing. As a result, a distinction has emerged within English departments between M.F.A. (Master of Fine Arts) and Ph.D. programs – to the extent that they now have distinct faculties. America's greatest hope for good literature today lies not in the universities, but in the "amateurs" writing after their nine to five work days or while the kids are at school. The intelligentsia has forgotten its literature in its haste to promote its politics. Already there is a backlash against deconstructionism. Just as the current thriving generation of critics looked upon New Criticism as passé, so the students of today are beginning to look upon deconstruction as obsolete. Derrida still lectured up to his recent death (he spoke in Washington, D.C. as recently as 1995), but, like their forebears, today's literature students are beginning to rise up and tell their predecessors that they had it all wrong. A primary factor in this backlash is the difficulty that lies in communicating deconstructionist ideas (note that what is offered here is merely an outline, not the actual methods of deconstructing a literary work). As a result of this difficulty, today's MTV generation has stumbled upon a positive side effect of their fifteen-second attention spans: They lack the patience to wade through Derrida's nearly unintelligible syntax and decipher his terminology.

Unfortunately, that has not stopped the cultural critics from indoctrinating this new generation in feminist interpretation, Marxist philosophy and so-called "queer theory." Requirements for reading Shakespeare, Milton, Chaucer, and other dead white males are disappearing to be replaced by options to take studies in "the Roles of Women in the Renaissance" (an excuse to lament the sexism of the past) or "The Bible as Literature" (a course designed to denigrate the Bible as cleverly crafted fiction instead of God's truth).

Deconstruction has succeeded in destabilizing the traditional meanings of texts. What happens next remains to be seen, but there are indications that its influence is waning. Already we see Shakespearean plays revived in the cinema; "Much Ado About Nothing," "Hamlet," and "Romeo and Juliet" – all recently adapted for the screen – have long since been abandoned by the American academy in favor of lesser works. Jane Austen's novels, once highly touted by the intelligentsia as undiscovered works of a female author, are now derided in our universities as being too conservative because of their themes of love and marriage. The popular culture has, in a moment of taste, seen the worth of these and revived them as cinema adaptations.

But the real death knell for deconstruction will sound when the next generation of literary critics realizes that the very nature of what it does – read, think, analyze – is antithetical to deconstruction's philosophical goals. The reliable savior of the intelligentsia is the common man and his common sense. Common sense dictates that words do mean things, and as deconstruction posits otherwise it will be relegated to the margins of society. Sadly, its effects will linger on – it has given a sense of validity to cultural criticism and established a marketplace for its ideas. The deconstructionists are already abandoning their enclave at Yale as their school of thought is eclipsed by trendier, simpler and narrower ideologues. These are the feminists, Marxists and queer theorists – none of whom are leaving their tenured offices peacefully. Instead, they have begun to recruit and train new graduate students to take their places. Applications for graduate and teaching degrees are at an all time high as these campus establishment "radicals" encourage the next generation to help them enshrine their ideology permanently in the American university system.

RADICAL FEMINISM AND POLITICAL CORRECTNESS

Perhaps no aspect of Political Correctness is more prominent in American life today than feminist ideology. Is feminism, like the rest of Political Correctness, based on the cultural Marxism imported from Germany in the 1930s? While feminism's history in America certainly extends longer than sixty years, its flowering in recent decades has been interwoven with the unfolding social revolution carried forward by cultural Marxists.

Where do we see radical feminism ascendant? It is on television, where nearly every major offering has a female "power figure" and the plots and characters emphasize inferiority of the male and superiority of the female. It is in the military, where expanding opportunity for women, even in combat positions, has been accompanied by double standards and then lowered standards, as well as by a decline in enlistment of young men, while "warriors" in the services are leaving in droves. It is in government-mandated employment preferences and practices that benefit women and use "sexual harassment" charges to keep men in line. It is in colleges where women's gender studies proliferate and "affirmative action" is applied in admissions and employment. It is in other employment, public and private, where in addition to affirmative action, "sensitivity training" is given unprecedented time and attention. It is in public schools, where "self awareness" and "self-esteem" are increasingly promoted while academic learning declines. And sadly, we see that "a woman's right to choose" leads many fellow Americans, including many with stewardship of public law and culture, to believe it is "the right thing to do" to allow the most helpless to be put to death.

While it is the theme of this essay that the radical feminist movement is embraced by present day Political Correctness ideology, derived from cultural Marxism, feminism as such does have earlier roots. Feminism was conceived and birthed in America in the 1830s, in the generation experiencing the first stage of the industrial revolution. Women, who for centuries had shared the challenges of surviving in an agrarian life, were becoming part of a middle-class gentry with more time and energy to spend writing newspaper articles and novels for their "sisters." The initial stages of the feminization of American culture had started. These feminists, radical in their time, became a staple of the idealistic Transcendentalists, who included Ralph Waldo Emerson, Henry David Thoreau and many radical Unitarian ministers of the day. They were also abolitionists, bent on destroying slavery and Southern culture as well. Spurred by the rhetoric of Harriet Beecher Stowe (author of *Uncle Tom's Cabin*), Julia Ward Howe (author of the words to

"The Battle Hymn of the Republic"), and Margaret Fuller (the first radical feminist newspaper columnist), the men and women of this idealist Transcendentalist generation propelled our nation toward Civil War.

Who were these Transcendentalist idealists, and why should we be reminded of them today? They were the precursors of today's idealistic Boomer generation. While we cannot draw a continuous link between the Transcendentalists and today's Boomers, their characteristics are very similar. We may glimpse where the elite Boomers are leading us by reviewing the history of the Transcendentalists and their causes.

The Transcendentalists supported abolition of slavery, women's rights, temperance, pacifism (but not in the anti-slavery cause), and other causes which we now observe in New Age popular culture. They developed into spiritualism (talking with the dead), Eastern mysticism and phrenology (discerning personality by the shape of one's skull). They would be right at home in today's New Age milieu. Luther George Williams points out, referring to women's groups and civil rights groups that: Freed slaves secured the vote only after the 13th, 14th and 15th Amendments (ratified in 1870), but women fared worse. They did not receive the vote until the passage of the 19th Amendment in 1920. However, the substantial political victories that these groups achieved (during the Civil War period) guaranteed that they would remain allies. Today, their political organizations dominate every aspect of society, politics and education in America – including the military.2 Indeed, the present-day radical feminist assault on VMI and the Citadel has a political parallel to the Transcendentalist activism of the Civil War period. This current assault is in part a continuation of a century-old effort to destroy Southern culture. In contrast to today's radical feminists, social feminists of the 1890s and early 20th century were of a less totalitarian character.

They stood for women's suffrage but also advocated the strengthening of the family.

Today, the feminization of American culture, moving rapidly since the 1960s continues to intensify. Radical Feminists demand that women be allowed to "choose" entry to the infantry, artillery, special forces and combat engineering positions in the Army and Marine Corps. These demands follow the Feminization of combat aviation in the U.S. Navy, Air Force and Army since 1993.

The feminization of American politics was advanced in the 1996 presidential election, when parties produced "feminized" conventions featuring soft, emotional, Oprah Winfrey-type orations and sentimental film clips of the presidential candidates. Both candidates were portrayed as soft, gentle, emotion-driven creatures sufficiently in touch with their feelings that all women across America would feel "comfortable" in their care.3 With 60 million female votes at stake, both parties pandered to America's "feminine" side.

There is no doubt in the media that the "man of today" is expected to be a touchyfeely subspecies who bows to the radical feminist agenda. He is a staple of Hollywood, the television network sitcoms and movies, and the political pundits of talk shows. The feminization is becoming so noticeable that newspapers and magazines are picking up on it. For example, the *Washington Times* and *National Review* magazines combined to tell us that "behind the breezy celebration of 'guy stuff' in today's men's magazine lurks a crisis of confidence. What does it mean to be masculine in the 90s?" It is revealed that today's men's magazines (*Esquire, GQ, Men's Health, Men's Fitness, Men's Journal, Details, Maxim, Men's Perspective)*"are all geared to a new feminized man..."6 Some examples? The old masculine attitude toward personal appearance is disappearing. If memory serves, our fathers' acts of personal upkeep were mostly limited to shaving and putting on a tie. According to Lowry:

> It's hard to imagine them interested in articles on 'A Flat Belly for the Beach' (Verge), or the three new men's fragrances for the fall season (GQ), or even 'The New Fall Suit' (Esquire). But somewhere along the line men became less concerned with being strong and silent, and more worried about making themselves pretty.

Indeed the feminization of American culture is nearly completed. And the last bastion of male domination, the U.S. military, is under assault. If this "feminization" trend were driven only by radical feminists seeking to pull down a perceived male-dominated hierarchy, there would be more hope that the cycles of history would move America toward a stable accommodation between men and women. But the drive is deeper, and it will not be satisfied by any accommodation. The radical feminists have embraced and been embraced by the wider and deeper movement of cultural Marxism. For dedicated Marxists, the strategy is to attack at every point where an apparent disparity leaves a potential constituency of "oppressed" persons – in this case women, who are the largest of all constituencies. Cultural Marxists, men and women, are making the most of it, and the theory developed by the Frankfurt School provides the ideology.

The Frankfurt School theorized that the authoritarian personality is a product of the patriarchal family. This idea is in turn directly connected to Engels's *The Origins of the Family, Private Property and the State,* which promotes matriarchy. Furthermore, it was Karl Marx who wrote in *The Communist Manifesto* about the radical notion of a "community of women." He also, in 1845, wrote disparagingly in his *The German Ideology* of the idea that the family was the basic unit of society. The concept of the "authoritarian personality" is not just to be interpreted primarily as a model for the conduct of warfare against prejudice as such. It is a handbook for psychological warfare against the American male, to render him unwilling to defend traditional beliefs and values. In other words, the aim was to emasculate him. Undoubtedly the Institute for Social Research at Frankfurt University meant this, as it used the term "psychological techniques for changing personality." The "authoritarian personality," studied in the 1940s and 1950s by American followers of the Frankfurt School, prepared the way for such psychological warfare against the male gender role. The aim was promoted by Herbert Marcuse and others under the guise of "women's liberation" and under the New Left movement in the 1960s. Evidence that psychological techniques for changing personality are intended to focus in particular on the emasculation of the American male has also been provided by Abraham Maslow, founder of "third force humanist psychology" and promoter of psychotherapeutic techniques in public school classrooms. 8 He wrote that "the next step in personal evolution is a transcendence of both masculinity and femininity to general humanness."

Cultural Marxist stalwarts apparently know exactly what they want to do and how they plan to do it. They have actually already succeeded in accomplishing much of their agenda.

How did this situation come about in American universities? Gertrude Himmelfarb has observed that it slipped past traditional academics almost unobserved until it was too late. It occurred so "quietly" that when they "looked up", postmodernism was upon them with a vengeance. "They were surrounded by such a tidal wave of faddish multicultural subjects such as radical feminism, deconstructed relativism as history and other courses" which undermine the perpetuation of Western civilization.10 Indeed, this tidal wave slipped by just as Antonio Gramsci and the Frankfurt School had envisioned – a quiet revolution that could not be resisted by force. The Frankfurt School had devised the concept of designating the opponents of the Marxist cultural revolution as "authoritarian characters." According to available accounts: There was a meeting of American scholars at a conference on religious and racial prejudice in 1944. Over the next five years, a Frankfurt School team under the direction of Max Horkheimer conducted in-depth social and psychological profiles of Americans under a project entitled "Studies of Prejudice." One of the results was a book entitled "The Authoritarian Personality" by Theodor Adorno, et al, that summarized one of the largest public opinion surveys ever undertaken in the United States. It was published in 1950, and conformed to the original Critical Theory in every respect. As a document which testified to the belief system of the Frankfurt School revolutionaries it was essentially anti-God, anti-Christian, anti-family, anti-nationalist, anti-patriot, anti-conservative, antihereditarian, anti-ethnocentric, anti-masculine, anti-tradition, and anti-morality. All of these are elements in critical theory.

"Cultural Marxism," as preached by the Frankfurt School alumni in the U.S., is being implemented by the elite Boomers. This has laid the foundation for and spurred the widely popular and destructive concepts of "affirmative action," "multiculturalism" and "diversity." One can't escape these terms today. They have grown from the study of anti-Semitism and discrimination by the Institute for Social Research during the 1940s and the systematic infusion of the language of "discrimination," "civil rights," 'women's rights," and other "minority rights" into American culture. According to Raehn:

Critical Theory as applied mass psychology has led to the deconstruction of gender in the American culture. Following Critical Theory, the distinction between masculinity and femininity will disappear. The traditional roles of the mothers and fathers are to be dissolved so that patriarchy will be ended. Children are not to be raised according to their biological genders and gender roles according to their biological differences. This reflects the Frankfurt School rationale for the disintegration of the traditional family.

Thus, one of the basic tenets of Critical Theory was the necessity to break down the traditional family. The Frankfurt School scholars preached: Even a partial breakdown of parental authority in the family might tend to increase the readiness of a coming generation to accept social change.

The transformation of American culture envisioned by the cultural Marxists goes further than pursuing gender equality. Embodied in their agenda is "matriarchal theory," under which they purpose to transform American culture to be female-dominated. This is a direct throwback to Wilhelm Reich, a Frankfurt School member who considered matriarchal theory in psychoanalytic terms. In 1993, he wrote in "The Mass Psychology of Fascism" that matriarchy was the only genuine family type of "natural society."

Erich Fromm, another charter member of the Institute, was one of the most active advocates of matriarchal theory. Fromm was especially taken with the idea that all love and altruistic feelings were ultimately derived from the maternal love necessitated by the extended period of human pregnancy and postnatal care: Love thus was not dependent on sexuality, as Freud had supposed. In fact, sex was more often tied to hatred and destruction. Masculinity and femininity were not reflections of "essential" sexual differences, as the romantics had thought. They were derived instead from differences in life functions, which were in part socially determined. This dogma was a precedent for today's radical feminist pronouncements appearing in newspapers and in TV programs, including TV newscasts. For its promoters, male and female roles result from cultural indoctrination – an indoctrination carried out by the male patriarchy to the detriment of women. Indeed, cultural Marxism has, in the 1990s, melded with radical feminism in the elite Boomer generation, that throwback to the dangerous Transcendentalists of the early 19th century. A cauldron of discontent is forming in our nation, a discontent which has the potential to dismantle American civilization.

Destructive criticism of primary elements of American culture inspired the 1960s counter-culture revolution. Idealistic Boomers coming of age strove to transform the prevailing culture into its opposites, in the spirit of social revolution. Now the elite Boomers are in positions of power, and they are working to destroy the nation's historic institutions. They aim to destroy as well the heritage we call "Western Civilization." Richard Bernstein has written in his book on multiculturalism, "the Marxist revolutionary process for the past several decades in America has centered on race and sex warfare rather than class warfare" as in earlier times. This reflects a scheme more total than economics to restructure American society. As the social revolutionaries readily proclaim, their purpose is to destroy the hegemony of white males. To accomplish this, all barriers to the introduction of more women and minorities throughout the "power structure" are to be brought down by all means available. Laws and lawsuits, intimidation, and demonizing of white males as racists and sexists are pursued through the mass media and the universities. The psycho–dynamic of the revolutionary process aim for psychic disempowerment – decapitation – of those who oppose. Steve Forbes has emphasized:

> This country's founders recognized three primal values in the Declaration of Independence, and they ranked them properly: Life, liberty, and the pursuit of happiness.

Forbes observes that if the order of these fundamental human rights is switched – with happiness before liberty or liberty before life – we come to moral chaos and social anarchy.

This very condition is what Judge Robert Bork describes as "modern liberalism." He defines its characteristics as "'radical egalitarianism' (equality of outcomes rather than of opportunities) and 'radical individualism' (the drastic reduction of limit to personal gratification)." Judge Bork also identifies radical feminism as "the most destructive and fanatical" element of this modern liberalism. He further describes radical feminism as "totalitarian in spirit."

Most Americans do not realize that they, through their institutions, are being led by social revolutionaries who think in terms of the continuing destruction of the existing social order in order to create a new one. The revolutionaries are New Age Elite Boomers.18 They now control the public institutions in the United States. Their "quiet" revolution, beginning with the counter-culture revolution of their youth, is nearing completion. A key, or even a dominant element because purportedly it represents that largest political and social constituency among their potential followers, is feminism. The Marxist movement in its "quiet" cultural latter-day phase is seemingly sweeping all before it. With its sway over the media, fully in the grip of feminism, it is hard to discern the stirrings of a counter-culture. Are the elite Boomers, the New Totalitarians, the most dangerous generation in America's history? William Strauss and Neil Howe suggest so, in their book *Generations: The History of America's Future – 1584 – 2069.* 19 James Kurth writes: The United States itself has become a great power that opposes much of what was once thought of as Western Civilization, especially its cultural achievements and its social arrangements. The major American elites – those in power in politics, business, the media, and academia – now use American power, especially the "soft power" of information, communications, and popular entertainment, to displace Western Civilization not only in America but also in Europe.

Will American men, of every race, and more traditionalist women of every age and circumstances – who may well be a silent majority of their sex – rise to challenge Political Correctness? Or will American men continue in voluntary submission toward a future of peonage under a new American matriarchy? Would that be a precursor to a condition of anarchy, and an end to America's experiment with democracy? It may well be that the fate of American civilization depends on American men steadfastly resisting Politically Correct feminism. Even more, they must resourcefully oppose the wider grip of Political Correctness, the cultural Marxism for which radical feminism is only one avenue of attack.

READINGS ON THE FRANKFURT SCHOOL

This is the sixth and final chapter in the Free Congress Foundation's book on Political Correctness, or – to call it by its real name – cultural Marxism. It is a short bibliographical essay intended not as an exhaustive resource for scholars but as a guide for interested citizens who want to learn more about the ideology that is taking over America.

As readers of the earlier chapters in this book already know, to understand Political Correctness and the threat it poses it is necessary to understand its history, particularly the history of the institution most responsible for creating it, the Frankfurt School. The Frankfurt School, or the Institute for Social Research as it was formally known, was established at Frankfurt University in Germany in 1923. This fact alone is important, because it tells us that Political Correctness is not merely a leftover of the American student rebellion of the 1960s.

Another fact from that long-ago year, 1923, is equally significant: the intended name for the Frankfurt School was the Institute for Marxism. The Institute's father and funder, Felix Weil, wrote in 1971 that he "wanted the Institute to become known, and perhaps famous, due to its contributions to Marxism as a scientific discipline..."1 Beginning a tradition Political Correctness still carries on, Weil and others decided that they could operate more effectively if they concealed their Marxism; hence, on reflection, they chose the neutral-sounding name, the Institute for Social Research (Insitut für Sozialforschung). But "Weil's heartfelt wish was still to create a foundation similar to the Marx-Engels Institute in Moscow – equipped with a staff of professors and students, with libraries and archives – and one day to present it to a German Soviet Republic." In 1933, this disguised "Institute for Marxism" left Germany and reestablished itself in New York City, where in time it shifted its focus to injecting its ideology into American society. The most readable English-language history of the Frankfurt School is Martin Jay's book, The Dialectical Imagination: A History of the Frankfurt School and the Institute for Social Research, 1932 - 1950 (University of California Press, Berkeley, CA, 1973 – new edition in 1996). This book is in print in paperback and can be ordered through any bookstore. The reader should be aware that Jay's book is, in the words of another work on the Frankfurt School, a "semiofficial' history3, which is to say that it is largely uncritical. Like virtually all other English-language authors on the Institute, Jay is on the political left. Nonetheless, the book provides a solid factual introduction to the Frankfurt School, and the reader should have little trouble discerning in it the roots and origins of today's Political Correctness.

In his first chapter, "The Creation of the Institut für Sozialforschung and Its First Frankfurt Years," Jay lays bare the Institute's Marxist origins and nature, and equally its efforts to conceal both: "The original idea of calling it the Institut für Marxismus (Institute for Marxism) was abandoned as too provocative, and a more Aesopian alternative was sought (not for the last time in the Frankfurt School's history)." Of the Institute's first director, Carl Grünberg, Jay writes, "Grünberg concluded his opening address by clearly stating his personal allegiance to Marxism as a scientific methodology. Just as liberalism, state socialism, and the historical school had institutional homes elsewhere, so Marxism would be the ruling principle at the Institut."5 Jay's first chapter also introduces the Institute's critical shift that laid the basis for today's Political Correctness, a.k.a. cultural Marxism: "if it can be said that in early years of its history the Institut concerned itself primarily with an analysis of bourgeois society's socio-economic substructure, in the years after 1930 its prime interest lay in its cultural superstructure."

The second chapter, "The Genius of Critical Theory," gets at the heart of the "Critical Studies" departments that now serve as the fonts of Political Correctness on American college campuses. All of these are branches and descendants of the Critical Theory first developed in the 1930s by the Frankfurt School. The term "Critical Theory" is itself something of a play on words. One is tempted to ask, "OK, what is the theory?" The answer is, "The theory is to criticize." Jay writes, "Critical Theory, as its name implies, was expressed through a series of critiques of other thinkers and philosophical traditions..Only by confronting it in its own terms, as a gadly of other systems, can it be fully understood." The goal of Critical Theory was not truth, but praxis, or revolutionary action: bringing the current society and culture down through unremitting, destructive criticism. According to Jay, "The true object of Marxism, Horkheimer argued (Max Horkheimer succeeded Carl Grünberg as director of the Institute in July, 1930), was not the uncovering of immutable truths, but the fostering of social change." The central question facing the Institute in the early 1930s was how to apply Marxism to the culture. The title of Jay's third chapter gives the answer: "The Integration of Psychoanalysis." Here, Jay's book falls down to some extent, in that it does not offer a clear understanding of how the Institute integrated Marx and Freud. The answer appears to be that Freud's later critiques were made conditional on a capitalist, bourgeois order: a revolutionary, post-capitalist society could "liberate" man from his Freudian repression.

Here again one sees key aspects of Political Correctness emerging, including a demand for sexual "liberation" and the attack on "patriarchal" Western culture. If the precise nature of the blending of Marx and Freud is left open by Jay, his next chapter makes the blend's application clear: "The Institute's First Studies of Authority." The Institute left Germany for New York in 1933 because the Nazis came to power in Germany. Not surprisingly, one of the Institute's first tasks in New York was to oppose Nazism. It did so largely by concocting a psychological "test" for an "authoritarian personality." Supposedly, people with this authoritarian personality were likely to support Nazism. Both the concept and the methodology were doubtful at best. But the Institute's work laid down an important tool for the left, namely a notion that anyone on the right was psychologically unbalanced. And it marked a key turning for the Institute in the birth of Political Correctness in America, in that the empirical research the studies demanded was done on Americans. Ultimately, the result was Institute member Theodor Adorno's vastly influential book, The Authoritarian Personality, published in 1950.

Jay's fifth chapter, "The Institute's Analysis of Nazism," continues the theme of the "authoritarian personality." But his sixth, "Aesthetic Theory and the Critique of Mass Culture," provides an answer to the question of why most "serious" modern art and music is so awful. It is intended to be. Theodor Adorno was the Institute's lead figure on high culture – he began life as a music critic and promoter of Schönberg – and his view was that in the face of the "repressiveness" of bourgeois society, art could only be "true" if it were alienating, reflecting the alienated society around it. Jay quotes Adorno: "A successful work..is not one which resolves objective contradictions in a spurious harmony, but one which expresses the idea of harmony negatively by embodying the contradictions, pure and uncompromised, in its innermost structure."

Adorno despised the new mass culture – film, radio, and jazz– in what seems to be a case of missed opportunity: today, the entertainment industry is the single most powerful promoter of Political Correctness. Another key Frankfurt School figure, Walter Benjamin, did see the potential: "he paradoxically held out hope for the progressive potential of politicized, collectivized art."10 At some point, someone – the question of who lies beyond the boundaries of Jay's book – put Benjamin's perception together with the Frankfurt School's general view, which Jay summarizes as "the Institut came to feel that the culture industry enslaved men in far more subtle and effective ways than the crude methods of domination practiced in earlier eras."11 In the remainder of the book, Jay traces the (sort of) empirical work of the Institute in the 1940s, which was beset by the same problems as their earlier survey "research," and follows the Institute in its return to Frankfurt, Germany after World War II. But by this point, the reader will already have the picture. He will have seen how Marxism was translated from economic into cultural terms; discerned the themes of sexual liberation, feminism, "victims" and so on that make up today's Political Correctness; and found in Critical Theory the origins of the endless wailing about "racism, sexism and homophobia" that "PC" pours forth. One key piece of history is missing: "an analysis of Marcuse's influential transmission of the Frankfurt School's work to a new American audience in the 1960s,"12 as Jay puts it in his epilogue. Also, Jay curiously passes over with only the most minimal discussion the effective move of the Institute, in the persons of Horkheimer and Adorno, to Los Angeles during the war. Did the connections they built there play any role in injecting the Frankfurt School's philosophy into American film and, after the war, television? Jay does not touch upon the subject.

But for the reader new to the Frankfurt School as the source of today's Political Correctness, Jay's The Dialectical Imagination offers a solid base. The book concludes with an extensive (though not annotated) bibliography of works by and about the Frankfurt School.

As to other accessible works about the Frankfurt School, the definitive modern work in German has recently been translated into English: The Frankfurt School: Its History, Theories and Political Significance by Rolf Wiggershaus, (translated by Michael Robertson, The MIT Press, Cambridge, MA, first paperback edition 1995). This covers much of the same ground as Martin Jay's book, although it also follows the Institute from its post-war return to Germany up to Adorno's death in 1969. Wiggershaus is more detailed than Jay, and, although he too is on the left politically, he is more critical than Jay. In the book's Afterword, Wiggershaus offers a brief look (and a hostile one) at some German conservative critiques of the Frankfurt School. A picture emerges that will seem familiar to Americans entrapped in the coils of Political Correctness:

Since the publication in 1970 of his book The Poverty of Critical Theory, Rohrmoser has promulgated, in constantly varying forms, the view that Marcuse, Adorno, and Horkheimer were the terrorists' intellectual foster-parents, who were using cultural revolution to destroy the traditions of the Christian West. Academics such as Ernst Topitsch and Kurt Sontheimer, who saw themselves as educators and liberal democrats, followed in Rohrmoser's footsteps.

In 1972 Topitsch, a critical rationalist who was Professor of Philosophy in Graz, had stated that behind the slogans of "rational discussion" and "dialogue free of domination" there was being established at the universities "a distinct terrorism of political convictions such as never existed before, even under Nazi tyranny."

Additional works on the Frankfurt School include:

- The Frankfurt School by T.B. Bottomore (Tavistock, London, 1984). Another history written by a sympathizer; you are better off with Jay or Wiggershaus.
- "The New Dark Age: The Frankfurt School and 'Political Correctness'" by Michael Minnicino, in Fidelio, Vol. 1, No. 1, Winter 1992 (KMW Publishing, Washington, DC) One of the few looks at the Frankfurt School by someone not a sympathizer, this long journal article explains the role of the Institute for Social Research in creating the ideology we now know as "Political Correctness." Unfortunately, its value is reduced by some digressions that lack credibility.
- Angela Davis: An Autobiography by Angela Davis (Random House, New York 1974) Angela Davis, a leading American black radical and Communist Party member, was described by Frankfurt School member Herbert

Marcuse as "my best student." She also studied in Frankfurt under Adorno. This book shows the link between the Institute for Social Research and the New Left of the 1960s through the eyes of a key participant.

- The Young Lukacs and the Origins of Western Marxism by Andrew Arato (Seabury Press, New York, 1979). The author is, as usual, a sympathizer, but this work shows the key role Lukacs played in the thinking of the Frankfurt School and, later, the New Left.
- The Origin of Negative Dialectics: Theodor W. Adorno, Walter Benjamin and the Frankfurt Institute by Susan Buck-Morss (Free Press, New York, 1977). An important book on the relationship of the Frankfurt School and Critical Theory to the New Left.
- Introduction to Critical Theory: Horkheimer to Habermas by David Held (University of California Press, Berkeley, 1980). Yet another history by a fan of the Frankfurt School, but valuable for its discussion of the impact of Nietzsche on key Frankfurt School figures.

Beyond these secondary works lies the vast literature produced by members of the Frankfurt School itself. Some key works were written in English, and many of those written in German are available in translation. As is usually the case with Marxist works, the prose style and vocabulary are often so convoluted as to make them almost unreadable. Further, the refusal of the Frankfurt School to make its own future vision plain led many of its members to write in aphorisms, which adds yet another layer of impenetrableness.

One work, however, is of such importance that it must be recommended despite its difficulty: Eros and Civilization by Herbert Marcuse (Beacon Press, Boston, first paperback edition in 1974 and still in print). Subtitled A Philosophical Inquiry into Freud, this book holds center stage for two reasons. First, it completes the task of integrating Marx and Freud. While the Marxism is *sotto voce*, the whole framework of the book is in fact Marxist, and it is through the framework that Freud is considered. Second, Eros and Civilization and its author were the key means of transmission by which the intellectual work of the Frankfurt School was injected into the student rebellion of the 1960s. This book became the bible of the young radicals who took over America's college campuses from 1965 onward, and who are still there as faculty members. In brief, Eros and Civilization urges total rebellion against traditional Western culture – the "Great Refusal" – and promises a Candyland utopia of free sex and no work to those who join the revolution. About two-thirds of the way through the book, Marcuse offers this summary of its arguments:

Our definition of the specific historical character of the established reality principle led to a reexamination of what Freud considered to be universal validity. We questioned this validity in view of the historical possibility of the abolition of the repressive controls imposed by civilization.

The very achievements of this civilization seemed to make the performance principle obsolete, to make the repressive utilization of the instincts archaic. But the idea of a non-repressive civilization on the basis of the achievements of the performance principle encountered the argument that instinctual liberation (and consequently total liberation) would explode civilization itself, since the latter is sustained only through renunciation and work (labor) – in other words, through the repressive utilization of instinctual energy. Freed from these constraints, man would exist without work and without order; he would fall back into nature, which would destroy culture. To meet this argument, we recalled certain archetypes of imagination which, in contrast to the culture-heroes of repressive productivity, symbolized creative receptivity.

These archetypes envisioned the fulfillment of man and nature, not through domination and exploitation, but through release of inherent libidinal forces. We then set ourselves the task of "verifying" these symbols – that is to say, demonstrating their truth value as symbols of a reality beyond the performance principle. We thought that the representative content of the Orphic and Narcissistic images was the erotic reconciliation (union) of man and nature in the aesthetic attitude, where order is beauty and work is play.14 Marcuse continues after this summary to lay out the erotic content of the "reality beyond the performance principle," i.e., a new civilization where work and productivity were unimportant. "The basic experience in this (aesthetic) dimension is sensuous rather than conceptual,"15 that is, feelings are more important than logic: "The discipline of aesthetics installs the *order of sensuousness* as against the *order of reason.*"

"In German, *sensuousness* and *sensuality* are still rendered by one and the same term: *Sinnlichkeit*. It connotes instinctual (especially sexual) gratification..17 No longer used as a full-time instrument of labor, the body would be resexualized...(which) would first manifest itself in a reactivation of all erotogenic zones and, consequently, in a resurgence of pre-genital polymorphous sexuality and in a decline of genital supremacy. The body in its entirety would become an object of cathexis, a thing to be enjoyed – an instrument of pleasure. This change in the value and scope of libidinal relations would lead to a disintegration of the institutions in which the private interpersonal relations have been organized, particularly the monogamic and patriarchal family."

This in a book which Marcuse dedicated to Sophie Marcuse, his wife of fifty years! It is easy to see how this message – "If it feels good, do it" – published in 1955 resonated with the student rebels of the 1960s. Marcuse understood what most of the rest of his Frankfurt School colleagues did not: the way to destroy Western civilization – the objective set forth by George Lukacs in 1919 – was not through abstruse theory, but through sex, drugs, and rock 'n' roll. Marcuse wrote other works for the new generation that spawned the New Left – One Dimensional Man (1964), Critique of Pure Tolerance (1965), An Essay on Liberation (1969), Counterrevolution and Revolt (1972). But Eros and Civilization was and remains the key work, the one that put the match to the tinder. Other central works by members of the Frankfurt School include:

- The Authoritarian Personality by Theodor Adorno (Harper, New York, 1950). This book is the basis for everything that followed that portrayed conservatism as a psychological defect. It had enormous impact, not least on education theory.
- Dialectic of Enlightenment by Theodor Adorno and Max Horkheimer (trans. by John Cumming, Verso, London, 1979). A complex philosophical work written during World War II largely in response to Nazism (and extensively devoted to discussions of anti-Semitism), this work seeks to find a kernel of "liberating" reason in the ruins of the Enlightenment.

- Minima Moralia: Reflections from a Damaged Life by Theodor Adorno (trans. E.F.N. Jophcott, New Left Books, London, 1974). A book of aphorisms, almost entirely incomprehensible, but the effective conclusion of Adorno's work.
- Escape from Freedom by Erich Fromm (Farrar & Rinehart, New York, 1941, still in print in paperback) Fromm was the Institute's "happy face," and this book was often required reading at colleges in the 1960s. The thesis is that man's nature causes him to throw his freedom away and embrace fascism unless he "masters society and subordinates the economic machine to the purposes of human happiness," i.e., adopts socialism. At this point Fromm was in the process of breaking away from the Institute and his subsequent works cannot be considered as part of the Frankfurt School corpus.
- Eclipse of Reason (Oxford University Press, New York, 1947). Essentially a sequel to Dialectic of Enlightenment, the book is heavily the work of Adorno and other Frankfurt School personages, although only Horkheimer name appeared on it. Its contents are based on a series of lectures Horkheimer gave at Columbia University in 1944. The prose style is surprisingly readable, but the contents are odd; there is throughout a strong nostalgia, which was normally anathema to the Frankfurt School. The key chapter, "The Revolt of Nature," reflects a strange Retro anarchism: "The victory of civilization is too complete to be true. Therefore, adjustment in our times involves an element of resentment and suppressed fury."
- Critical Theory: Selected Essays by Max Horkheimer (trans. Matthew O'Connell, Seabury Press, New York, 1972). The essay, "Traditional and Critical Theory" is especially important.
- The Essential Frankfurt School Reader, ed. By Andrew Arato and Eike Gebhardt (Continuum, New York, 1982, in print in paperback) Not an introduction to the Frankfurt School, but rather a reprinting of Frankfurt School essays not available elsewhere, this book is more useful to the specialist than the novice. Nonetheless, both the editors' lengthy introductions and some of the essays are useful

(once again, the editors are solidly on the Left politically, and their style is as heavy as that of the Frankfurt School's members). This small bibliography will be enough to get an interested reader started; the full literature on and by the Frankfurt School is immense, as the bibliographies in Jay's and Wiggershaus's books attest. What has been missing from it, at least in English, is a readable book, written for the layman, that explains the Frankfurt School and its works in terms of the creation of Political Correctness. This short volume is at least a start in filling that gap.

BIBLIOGRAPHY

Ahmad, Imtiaz: *State and Foreign Policy: India's Role in South Asia*, New Delhi, Vikas, 1993.

Carl J. Friedrich: *Constitutional Government and Democracy*, Boston, Ginn, 1950.

Dikshit, D.P.: *Political History of the Chalukyas of Badami*, New Delhi, Abhinav, 1980.

English, Barbara: *The War for a Persian Lady*, Boston, Houghton Mifflin, 1971.

Hamilton, J.R.: *Alexander the Great*, Oxford, Clarendon Press, 1965.

Jack Peltason: *Federal Courts in the Political Process*, New York, Random House, 1955.

Kashyap, C.: *National Policy Studies*, New Delhi, Tata McGraw-Hill for the Lok Sabha Secretariat, 1990.

Leslie, J.: *Toward Empowerment: Women and Politics in India*, Colorado, Westview Press, 1992.

Max, Beloff: *Foreign Policy and the Democratic Process*, Baltimore, Johns Hopkins University Press, 1955.

Nevitte, Neil, and Charles H. Kennedy: *Ethnic Preference and Public Policy in Developing States*, Boulder, Lynne Rienner Publishers, 1986.

Pye, Lucian W. and Mary W.: *Asian Power and Politics: the Cultural Dimensions of Authority*, Cambridge, Mass, Belknap Press, 1985.

Robert, W.: *Public Bureaucracy and the Incentive Problem*, Washington, D.C., World Bank, 1994.

Schmidhauser, R.: *Supreme Court: Its Politics, Personalities and Procedures*, New York, Holt, 1960.

Victor G. : *Law as a Political Instrument*, New York, Random House, 1955.

INDEX

□□□